THE FUGITIVE GROUP

Louise Cowan

THE FUGITIVE GROUP

A LITERARY HISTORY

Louisiana
State University Press
Baton Rouge, La.

To Bainard

PREFACE

Infandum, regina, jubes renovare dolorem.
This line from Virgil was Allen Tate's response to an early
recounting of the story told here. And unutterably cruel it seems
to fashion out of the early lives of living men a history that by its
very nature must be painful to its subjects. My only excuse for
" renewing the griefs "—and recalling the joys—is the conviction
that the story of the Fugitive group is not a mere record of an
interesting coterie but a kind of parable demonstrating the operations of poetry (like the operations of grace) among mortal men.
And the parable seems to mean something like this: Wherever the
art of poetry is practiced humbly and perseverantly, for its own
sake, by " two or three gathered together "—if they are able to trust
and to love each other—the Muse will reveal her true nature and
her rôle in human affairs. If I have interpreted the parable accurately, then the importance of the Fugitive group apprenticeship
cannot be overestimated. And it is because of the increasing rarity

v

of this sort of association in modern letters, even on a small scale, that I have been so bold as to attempt the story of an epoch in the lives of men who have gone on to quite separate careers.

The letters and documents available for this study permitted an accuracy of chronology and a volume of content that could not have been transmitted by the memories of any number of the Fugitives; nonetheless, at times, one must realize, their very authority is misleading. Any written work, particularly by a literary man, is in a sense a creation, expressing a single aspect of an experience; and, specifically, a letter is a private communication with private references, so that its displayed effect may run counter to what is public truth. Some of Robert Penn Warren's comments on Fugitive meetings, for instance, though otherwise enlightening, throw more shade than light on the gatherings he remembers now as happy occasions. Laura Riding's brilliantly written letters have not been quoted in this study because of her belief that their use would lend a sense of wholeness to a relationship that was for her essentially partial, near the beginning of her literary career. Each of the Fugitives, like all men, would have some part of the past undone. Allen Tate feels that his behavior toward Dr. Edwin Mims reflected little honor upon himself; and, from the vantage of a long and warm friendship with John Crowe Ransom, he views with contrition the high spirits that led him into a minor public controversy—long since settled—with his friend and fellow-Fugitive. For his part, Ransom considers much of his prose writing during the period of _The Fugitive_ pretentious and not wholly submissive to its subjects. These men and the others have permitted the use of their letters only out of a deep respect for the actual and an ingrained habit of courtesy. In turn, their chronicler would here render all the Fugitives, both living and dead, the courtesy of an apology—that apology due from the possessor of a clumsy hand that, having picked up a few crumbs, rearranges them laboriously and passes them off as a loaf of bread.

This study began as a dissertation, a work to which the reader is directed for a detailed listing of the unpublished documents

pertaining to the Fugitives.[1] The files of *The Fugitive* itself and
the official Fugitive correspondence, in the possession of Donald
Davidson and held for him by the Joint University Libraries in
Nashville, furnished the framework of the account. For the early
background of the Fugitives (before they became the Fugitives, of
course), I consulted the Vanderbilt University Registrar's records,
the University catalogs, the volumes of the Vanderbilt *Alumnus*,
and the Vanderbilt student publications (*The Commodore*, *The
Hustler*, *The Jade*, and *The Observer*). Professor Mims's *History
of Vanderbilt University* [2] was an invaluable aid. The life and
spirit of the Fugitive movement were revealed to me chiefly through
the correspondence (1922–1928) of Davidson and Tate, the detailed and frequent letters between the two providing a rich sense
of the men and the times. Ransom's letters to Tate have also held
an inestimable wealth and, though fewer, the letters of Warren
to both Tate and Davidson have been helpful, as have the records
and correspondence of Alec B. Stevenson, official treasurer of the
group, and a few letters from various other sources. Conversations
with most of the living Fugitives as well as with their friends and
members of their families [3] have helped fill in the very intricate
chronology of sixteen poets and have given some notion of those
small and seemingly unimportant details that indicate character
and personality. The reader is referred to two excellent memoirs
of the group; one, written in 1942 by Tate,[4] I have relied upon
heavily; the other, written in 1958 by Davidson [5] and appearing

[1] "*The Fugitive*: A Critical History," Vanderbilt University, 1953.

[2] Nashville: Vanderbilt University Press, 1940.

[3] For their kindness in interviews and conversations I am grateful to Donald
Davidson, Allen Tate, Alec B. Stevenson, John Crowe Ransom, Robert Penn
Warren, Jesse Wills, Walter Clyde Curry, William Frierson, Sidney Mttron-
Hirsch, Merrill Moore, Alfred Starr, Edwin Mims, Mrs. James Frank, Mrs. Stanley
Johnson, Ellene Ransom, Isabel Howell, Mrs. Brainerd Cheney, Caroline Gordon,
Theresa Sherrer Davidson, and Mrs. Eric Bell.

[4] "*The Fugitive* 1922–1925: A Personal Recollection Twenty Years After,"
the *Princeton University Library Chronicle*, III, No. 3 (April, 1942), 75-84.

[5] "The Thankless Muse and Her Fugitive Poets," *Southern Writers in the
Modern World* (Athens: the University of Georgia Press, 1958), 1-30.

after my study was completed, I referred to a few times in the
final revisions of this work.

I am grateful to Dr. A. F. Kuhlman and to Miss Clara Mae
Brown of the Joint University Libraries for many special courtesies
during the course of my research and to the Princeton University
Library, where Tate's correspondence is housed. A research grant
given me by Texas Christian University in the summer of 1956
aided me in preparing my manuscript for publication. Randall
Stewart's kind invitation to the Fugitive Reunion in the spring
of 1956 and the generosity of Louis D. Rubin, Jr., the American
Studies Association, and the Rockefeller Foundation enabled me
to recreate more firmly in my own mind the atmosphere of a
meeting of the Fugitive group.[6]

My thanks are due Richmond Croom Beatty, Rob Roy Purdy,
Randall Stewart, Louis D. Rubin, Jr., and Jean Holloway for
reading the manuscript and making valuable suggestions. My sister,
Doris Shillingburg, helped me with revisions at a time when it
seemed that someone's eyes other than mine would have to see
the task completed. Mary Trippet gave generous time in revising,
typing, and proofreading. The extent of my husband's help is
impossible to assess, but I record here my considerable indebtedness
to him.

LOUISE COWAN

[6] For a record of the conversation at this meeting, see *Fugitives' Reunion*,
Rob Roy Purdy, ed. (Nashville: Vanderbilt University Press, 1959).

ACKNOWLEDGMENT

THE AUTHOR MAKES grateful acknowledgment of the following materials used in this book:

For unpublished letters and other documents:

Donald Davidson, Allen Tate, John Crowe Ransom, Alec B. Stevenson, Robert Penn Warren, Jesse Wills, William Yandell Elliott, Louis Untermeyer, Rinehart and Company, Inc., Publishers, on behalf of the Hervey Allen Estate, and LeRoy A. Percy, Executor, on behalf of the William Alexander Percy Estate.

For photographs:

Robert McGaw, Publicity Director, Vanderbilt University, the photograph of Kissam Hall and the portrait of Davidson; Isabell Howell, the portraits of Tate, Warren, and Moore; Donald Davidson, the MS. of "Corymba"; The Fugitive Collection, the portrait of Ransom, the Nashville *Tennessean* group picture, and the MS. of "Nuptials"; Rob Roy Purdy, the photographs of the Fugitives taken during the Fugitive Reunion.

For material reprinted from published volumes:

From *Poems about God*, by John Crowe Ransom (Copyright, 1919, by Henry Holt and Company, Inc., Copyright, 1947, by John Crowe Ransom. By permission of the publishers.)

From *Professor*, by Stanley Johnson (Copyright, 1925, by Harcourt, Brace and Company, Inc. By permission of the publishers.)

From *An Outland Piper*, by Donald Davidson (Copyright, 1924 and 1952, by Donald Davidson. By permission of the author.)

From *Southern Writers in the Modern World*, by Donald Davidson (Copyright, 1958, by the University of Georgia Press. By permission of the publishers.)

From *The Princeton University Library Chronicle* (Copyright, 1924, by Princeton University. By permission of William S. Dix, Librarian.)

From *The Fugitive* (Copyright 1922–1925, by the Fugitive Publishing Company. By permission of the group.)

A portion of this book appeared as an essay in *Shenandoah*, Summer, 1955.

CONTENTS

xi

ILLUSTRATIONS

INTRODUCTION

THE NASHVILLE POETS who published the little magazine *The Fugitive* during the early half of the 1920's have the distinction of being the inaugurators of the Southern literary renaissance. Among these writers were four who must be considered at once the most germinal and articulate literary men to come out of the South—John Crowe Ransom, Donald Davidson, Allen Tate, and Robert Penn Warren. Unlike many other Southern writers who have maintained a deliberate inarticulateness in literary theory —William Faulkner, for instance—these four have developed a literary criticism, a social philosophy, and even an ontology on which an increasing number of writers are building. Because these same men also played major roles in another, more controversial group—the Agrarians—the general literary public has tended to merge the two movements, not entirely without justification. Before the critic can admit their essential unity, however, he must

at least acknowledge their existential distinctness and recognize
their separate accomplishments.

The Fugitives were a quite tangible body of sixteen poets [1] who,
having no particular program, met frequently from 1915 to 1928
for the purpose of reading and discussing their own work. The
Agrarians were twelve scholars of various disciplines [2] who, from
about 1928 to 1935, were united by common principle rather than
contiguity and whose intercommunications were conducted, for the
most part, through letters and essays. The first group published
nineteen issues of *The Fugitive* (1922–1925), a journal devoted
almost exclusively to poetry, whereas the second compiled *I'll
Take My Stand* (1930), an anthology attacking industrialism and
its basic dogma, the belief in the perfectibility of man through
secular progress.

But though technically the groups were distinct—one being
purely literary and the other social and religious and only indirectly
literary—they had in fact an important connection in the four men
already mentioned, whose ideas generated and gave form to the
Agrarian convictions. The formulation of these ideas occurred
rather suddenly, just after the suspension of *The Fugitive* and a
while before the publication of *I'll Take My Stand*. It was during
this brief period that the implications of their own poetry became
apparent to Ransom, Davidson, Tate, and Warren. Thus the first
group experience, a creative adventure into the realm of intuitive
knowledge, gave rise to the critical and speculative activity of
the second.

In this joint creative adventure not only the four major Fugitive
poets but the others as well were important participants. The
enterprise was given solidity by the fact that persons of unlike

---

[1] John Crowe Ransom, Donald Davidson, Allen Tate, Robert Penn Warren,
Merrill Moore, Laura Riding, Jesse Wills, Alec B. Stevenson, Walter Clyde
Curry, Stanley Johnson, Sidney Mttron Hirsch, James Frank, William Yandell
Elliott, William Frierson, Ridley Wills, and Alfred Starr.

[2] John Crowe Ransom, Donald Davidson, Allen Tate, Robert Penn Warren,
Andrew Lytle, Stark Young, John Gould Fletcher, Frank Lawrence Owsley, Lyle
Lanier, H. C. Nixon, John Donald Wade, Henry Blue Kline.

minds and dissimilar gifts were committed to the composition of poems. Thus, members of the Fugitive circle came to view poetry as having a universal character and to assume that all educated men —not merely a select few—should be interested in reading and writing verse. But though the other Fugitives worked seriously at poetry and contributed to the group experience, in the end they turned aside from the commitment to letters made by Ransom, Davidson, Tate, and Warren. Merrill Moore, the most prolific (and in some ways the most naturally talented) poet among the Fugitives, continued until his recent death to write distinguished verse that was for him primarily an avocation, though certainly a seriously pursued one. But as his biographer points out, Moore's work is fundamentally at odds with the other Fugitive poetry.[3] Laura Riding, another member who has become an established poet, had little more than a nominal relationship with the group. The other members have made their lasting contribution in fields outside poetry and criticism; Sidney Hirsch, a student of the occult; James Frank, scholarly merchant; Walter Clyde Curry, the Chaucer and Milton scholar; William Yandell Elliott, the political scientist; William Frierson, an authority on French literature; Alec Stevenson, Jesse Wills, and Alfred Starr, financiers; Stanley Johnson, administrative educator and novelist; Ridley Wills, journalist and novelist. These twelve have produced numerous volumes but none in the cultural criticism and formal literary analysis which have come to be known as dominant Fugitive methods. They have held varying degrees of aversion to the reactionary implications of traditionalism; at least, none of them followed the trail into Agrarianism which, at the time, Ransom, Davidson, Tate, and Warren were blazing.

In a critical evaluation of the Fugitive movement, then, it is to the work of the four poets who were also Agrarians that one turns, since Ransom, Davidson, and Tate were, in Tate's words, the " final causes " of the movement[4] and Warren was in many

---

[3] Henry W. Wells, *Poet and Psychiatrist* (New York: Twayne Publishers, 1955), 45.

[4] Unpublished letter to Davidson, March 7, 1927.

senses its product. After the short storm provoked by Agrarianism these Fugitive-Agrarians went their individual ways in the profession of letters, each provided with various engagements in religion, philosophy, history, and literature sufficient to sustain him alone; the group activity was effectively over. But these four leaders were to show an astonishing versatility and productivity, publishing among them something over fifty volumes of poetry, criticism, history, biography, fiction, and textbooks.

Ransom's dry and exceptionally civilized poetry was already mature during the life of *The Fugitive*; since then he has distinguished himself also in criticism, editing, and aesthetics. His is recognized as one of the original styles in American and English letters, both in poetry and prose. Editor of *The Kenyon Review* since 1939 and a professor at Kenyon College after he left Vanderbilt in 1937, his influence on the contemporary literary scene has been vast. He continues to produce literary essays, following the neo-Kantian bent which has been present in all his writings and which has led him to diverge somewhat from the direction of Agrarianism.

Next to Ransom, Davidson was nearest maturity when the magazine expired, though his best poetry has come after the twenties, as has his searching historical method in the study of literature (as opposed to either the purely critical or the sociological approaches). The relation of literature to a culture is his continuing subject in most of his prose writings. In poetry, since it is the oral and lyric tradition that he explores, as distinct from the more highly favored ironic and paradoxical style within which the other poet-critics of this school have worked, his writing has never received the critical attention it deserves. Davidson has remained at Vanderbilt from the Fugitive days on and teaches at Bread Loaf School of English every summer.

Allen Tate has been by turns college professor, editor, and free-lance writer, having spent many years as a critical reviewer as he perfected his brilliant poetic style. For two years (1944–1946) he edited *The Sewanee Review*. Tate's biographies and his one carefully written novel have fallen into an ill-deserved neglect, but his critical essays continue to be reprinted and cited perhaps as often as those of any other critic in America; and his poetry is acknowledged to be among the best in modern letters. Now at the University of Minnesota, Tate is writing both criticism and poetry in which are embodied the full statement of themes he has been pursuing from the beginning of his career.

Though Robert Penn Warren's poetry was farthest of the four from maturity during the issuance of *The Fugitive* (he was the youngest of the group), he went on in the years after Agrarianism to intensive work in poetry and in fiction, as well as to an application of criticism to pedagogy. With Cleanth Brooks, Warren has published textbooks that disseminate not only to college students but to their teachers the methods of what has been called "the new criticism." With Brooks also he edited for the seven years of its existence (1935–1942) *The Southern Review*, a literary journal that has set the pattern for excellence in America.

In poetry, in fiction, and in literary criticism, these men have taken their places among the most noted writers today in English. Their greatest impact, however, has been in establishing a profession of letters, as much by their work in editing and setting policies for literary journals as by transforming the study of literature in the universities, their texts and their own teaching demonstrating the necessity of its being approached as an important study in its own right. Genuine men of letters, in that they pursue their craft on many fronts at once and in that they allow their critical ideas to interact with their creative imaginations, they are a group unmatched in American literature. And though there is no real theological, epistemological, or even aesthetic agreement among these four today (and their later careers have been consistent unfoldings of their earlier positions), they have in common an approach to literature and an assumption about the literary artist's function that gives them the force and intensity of a school.

Behind their strength and effectiveness as men of letters lies their own experience in poetry, an experience gained in subjection not to ideas and theories, but to language and form. One can easily discern on the surface of their poems various sorts of similarities. But there is a deeper kinship between them, one which generates the parallels of irony, of an earthy yet learned language, and of religious attitude; it lies in the element basic to their work and to a varying degree present in the work of the other Fugitives. It is an element that might justifiably be called unique in American literature. This element which sets apart the poetry of the Fugitive group in modern letters is its embodiment of the fundamental beliefs of the society out of which it came.

John Crowe Ransom's poetry, for instance, is not, like T. S. Eliot's, a vision of the deficiencies of his culture, nor like Hart Crane's, a celebration of its potentialities; neither is it, like Robert Frost's, a symbolic use of particularities in a local scene; it is instead a dramatization of the basic qualities of mind and heart in the people for whom Ransom has acted as spokesman. This is not to say, certainly, that Ransom has spoken for the Southern people in the way they would speak for themselves. They would not, indeed, see themselves as inhabiting a world " perilous and beautiful," in a " torture of equilibrium." They would not admit that they look upon death with the detachment as well as the sentiment exhibited in " Here Lies a Lady," " Bells for John Whiteside's Daughter," or " Dead Boy." Nor would they recognize themselves in the figures of " Captain Carpenter," " Tom, Tom, the Piper's Son," Jane Sneed, or John Black. But, as R. G. Collingwood has written, " No community altogether knows its own heart ";[5] and for the past fifty years the Southern heart has been almost a complete stranger to the Southern head. Ransom has not, therefore, presented the mass shibboleths in the mass language. On the contrary, he has based his verse on the values by which the South has lived, relating them to a whole intellectual tradition, which the section may be unconscious it has inherited, and ordering them into a tight and meticulous vision of reality. His is the poetry of an intelligent and passionate man, who, not in rebellion against the funda-

[5] *The Principles of Art* (Oxford: Clarendon Press, 1950), 336.

mental beliefs of his society, has consequently been free to address himself chiefly to the problem of form and language without incurring the danger of isolation.

Ransom may be profitably chosen to demonstrate the basic Fugitive quality because his writing does not at first appear to be the expression of a society but of a pungent and rare personality. It is obviously work with an individual flavor and character; it is obviously not "local color" writing; its subjects are not often Southern; yet it is as unmistakably an expression of Southern society as the *Divine Comedy* was of thirteenth-century Italy or *Hamlet* was of Elizabethan England.

T. S. Eliot has written that the poet cannot embody values in his work until he has experienced them communally.[6] It is just such a communal sacrament of which Mr. Eliot himself has been deprived; and it is this quality in the work of the Fugitives, however major or minor their individual achievements may turn out to be, that binds them together into a genuine school of poets. It is important that they be recognized as, in Allen Tate's words, "an intensive and historical group as opposed to the eclectic and cosmopolitan groups that flourished in the East."[7] The "unity of feeling" that pervaded the Fugitives (quite different from a unity of theory such as most schools of poetry have had since the seventeenth century) Tate ascribes to a "common historical myth."

What kind of society was it that provided the Fugitives with their dominant myth? For one thing, it was peopled by folk who had a great respect for learning; indeed, the South thought of itself as a continuation of the main stream of classical humanism. Middle Tennessee was particularly rich in preparatory schools; so it is not strange that, having been brought up in this region, most of the men who were to be the Fugitives received their preparatory education in academies that gave them early in life an uncommon

[6] "The Social Function of Poetry," in R. W. Stallman (ed.), *Critiques and Essays in Criticism* (New York: The Ronald Press Company, 1949), 108.

[7] "*The Fugitive 1922–1925*: A Personal Recollection Twenty Years After," *The Princeton University Library Chronicle*, III, No. 3 (April, 1942), 83.

acquaintance with the Latin and Greek classics and so developed
their sense of the presence and relevance of the past.

The Southern society provided for the Fugitives, too, a code of
manners and morals, with its underlying *gentilesse*—that blend of
gentility and spirit, honor and humility, sympathy and humor—that
made for gracious friendships and called forth intimate though
not introspective conversation. Without this courtesy, the long
association of men of such diverse talent could not have persevered,
nor could a practice of honest criticism have survived more than a
few meetings. But there are two more important contributions the
South made to the Fugitives, enormously happy gifts for poets. One
is a spoken language, which with its easiness upon the tongue, its
fine metaphorical flair, its Anglo-Saxon pungency, was the birth-
right of the Fugitives; they did not have to "invent" their language. The other is a sense of form, which their poetry possesses
to a high degree. It is this true allegory (a term for their method
which is preferable to the nineteenth-century term *symbolism*,
tinged as it is with Romantic transcendentalism) that has provided
the basic impetus of their poetry and their understanding of literature. The allegorical method of the Fugitives is the result of an
analogical view of the universe, which for the Southerner is a
hanger-on (as are so many other of his distinctive traits) from the
major European tradition, formed in the Middle Ages.

But, amidst the contending "New South" and "Old South"
philosophies, both gross and naïve oversimplifications, the true
Southern values could have been discerned only by poets, dedicated to their craft. In an article for *The Bookman*, in 1929 Allen
Tate described the peculiar character of the Fugitive poets by
saying that they began with "open minds":

They were willing to draw upon all the resources of poetry that
they knew, for it was obvious that their sectionalism, if it existed, and
their nationalism, if that existed, would take care of themselves. There
was no attempt to force the materials at hand into an easy significance
(the mistake of the South Carolina poets). Fugitive poetry turned out
to be profoundly sectional in that it was supported by the prejudices,

feelings, values, into which the poets were born. Because the approach of the Fugitives to their art was the normal one, and because the normal attitude has been absent in America for several generations, the history of the Fugitive group is not an unprofitable study.[8]

The study of the group can best be approached through a focus upon the magazine which was an objectification of these formative years. Without *The Fugitive,* no doubt the group would have continued to meet and converse, and no doubt the most serious poets among them would have published their poetry in other journals. But the necessity of fulfilling an obligation to the outside world, of gathering material into shape so that the group would not be put to shame, of making editorial comments and conducting literary contests—these tasks precipitated quarrels, arguments, and experiments that caused a group of talented men to interact upon each other and, finally, to share in an experience of reality which has provided one of the major insights in modern literature.

The group and the magazine, then, these are the concerns of this study. Beginning with the first appearance of the group at Vanderbilt University in the early 1900's, this account continues on through the suspension of the magazine to the publication of *Fugitives: An Anthology,* in 1928, since that volume was a landmark pointing in two directions: backward into the Fugitive years, forward to the Agrarian ones. Other volumes will be written concerning the mature work of the individual Fugitives; this attempts to record and interpret their formative years.

[8] "American Poetry since 1920," *The Bookman,* LXVIII (January, 1929), 504.

THE FUGITIVE GROUP

CHAPTER ONE

THE

DISCURSIVE STAGE:

1903–1916

The first issue of *The Fugitive* appeared in Nashville bookstores on April 12, 1922. Less than a month before, one of its founders—Sidney Hirsch—had suggested that the young men gathered around him publish their poems in a magazine; despite this apparent haste, however, the contents of the initial number were revised and finished pieces. Drawn from an accumulation of poems written over the past two years, they had been from time to time subjected to the affable criticism of a group of established friends: John Crowe Ransom, Donald Davidson, Allen Tate, Walter Clyde Curry, Stanley Johnson, Alec Stevenson, James Frank, Sidney Hirsch, William Yandell Elliott, and William Frierson.[1] For two years these men had held regular meetings at

---

[1] These last two had left Nashville in the fall of 1920 on Rhodes Scholarships and were never to take an active part in the production of *The Fugitive*, though they had participated in the group discussions and were listed in *The Fugitive* masthead as members *in absentia*.

3

which the topics of debate were exclusively literary; but long before that time the group had its origin in intermittent philosophic discussions at Hirsch's apartment. In a letter written during the summer of 1915 to Alec Stevenson, away on vacation in Canada, William Elliott gave vivid evidence of the "Olympian" conversation flourishing just off the Vanderbilt University campus that summer:

> Right now I am having what the debutantes twitter "a gorgeous time." Nat Hirsch, Stanley Johnson, Donald Davidson, John Ransom, and Sidney Hirsch were the company last night and it was Olympian. I am living in rare altitudes this summer, though I haven't gone to Monteagle yet. We get together often and I can feel myself grow.
>
> Sidney Hirsch is a wonder, Nat is a World Man. Sidney has the more imposing personality, and a head full of astounding mysticism. But he isn't as genuine as Nat, the One and Only. And good, old Johnny Ransom, the Rational, with Stanley Johnson, the Downright, and Donald Davidson, musical as his name, with yours, the Egotist, make up an odd group, but one that will be heard from.
>
> Out on the Hirsches' porch, with the cigar ends glowing occasionally, a debate always insured from the nature of the company, it is *The* Happiness. Last night it was the Unity of Being that was under discussion, Johnny maintaining a dualism at least—*Élan Vital* and Material Expression, I, admitting a logical duality, maintaining a pluralistic Individuality of Being, but a Metaphysical unity. I learned a great deal.[2]

These eager lines mark a point significant to the history of *The Fugitive*, for in them is described a meeting of men who possess that rare binding quality necessary to the formation of a group; in them as well is evidence that the men who became the Fugitive poets were interested, first of all, in philosophic inquiry. Here, accordingly, seven years before the beginning of the magazine, discussing formidably profound metaphysical problems with youthful certainty, are the persons who formed the nucleus of the Fugitives.

[2] Unpublished MS, July 23, 1915.

The Hirsch apartment was on Twentieth Avenue, only a block from the Vanderbilt campus, and the men gathered on the long second-storey balcony, except for Hirsch himself, were Vanderbilt teachers and students. As University men, they were regarded with fond admiration by a town that considered itself "the Athens of the South," though a Southern respect for privacy insured their being let alone and virtually unobserved. In their own minds these young men stood for the sound rationalism that has always been associated with the classical discipline. Never questioning the manliness and dignity of their unhampered conversation, they identified themselves effortlessly with the freedom of academic life. If the university was to prove indifferent to their joint creativity, it nonetheless provided the world in which, as poets, they could function.

They took their places in this world slowly, almost accidentally it seems, over a period of twelve years. The assemblage began in 1903 with John Crowe Ransom, who came to Vanderbilt an ingenuous freshman, looking even younger than his fifteen years. It was no ordinary university to which he came. In its peculiar mixture of the erudite and the homely, the universal and the local, Vanderbilt was to furnish to the Fugitives that contrast of conditions needed for the operation of intellectual creativity. That the four chief Fugitives later developed a pronounced Southern commitment was not due to an environment dominated by a narrow filiopietism such as they might have encountered in other Southern colleges. Nor did their later cast of mind spring from a reaction against an engulfing progressivism. Sometimes in cultural crises there are particular arenas where opposing ideas and beliefs can come together in close contact, as on a stage, the ensuing dramatic conflict revealing their true nature. Vanderbilt University during the first three decades of the twentieth century was such a focal point. Perhaps no other school, north or south, could have so provided the Fugitives with the opportunities for understanding, for rejection, and for affirmation.

When Ransom came to its classes, a mere thirty years after its founding, the intellectual resources of the university were not meager: the curriculum was restricted, it is true, but the subjects studied were the staple ones that have made up the civilized man's study throughout western civilization. Indeed, Vanderbilt was a stronghold of classical culture, unmatched south of the Mason-Dixon Line. At the time of its founding, in 1873, during the bitterest portion of the Reconstruction, the other universities of the section had been disabled, their efforts at restoration checked by dependence upon state funds. With its relatively high salaries, Vanderbilt drew from the best faculties throughout the South, counting among its members the ex-chancellors of two state universities and numerous prized scholars. These were men imbued with the concept of education as a process giving substance to Christian ideals and so destroying the barriers between North and South, America and the world, the present and the future. "The University arrays itself against all sectionalism," one of its leaders, Professor Andrew Lipscomb, ex-chancellor of the University of Georgia, had declared at the inaugural ceremonies.[3] Continuing this policy, Chancellor J. H. Kirkland, twenty years later succeeding the first chancellor, indicated his conception of the aims of the university: "We are working for . . . the good of the whole country," he announced. "No spirit of narrowness or prejudice controls us here."[4]

In the spirit of nonsectionalism Vanderbilt had been conceived, and to that broad view it remained committed, though it participated little in the egalitarian desire of the New South leaders to make the section like the rest of the nation. Its internationalism was aristocratic, based on a respect for the best that had been known and thought in the world. The men who guided it were unswervingly dedicated to a nineteenth-century liberalism calculated to produce cosmopolitan American citizens—cultivated, humane, and successful. The dichotomy that characterized the Victorian mind—made up, on the one hand, of an intellectual attachment to progress and, on the other, of a sentimental attachment to old

[3] Quoted in Edwin Mims, *History of Vanderbilt University* (Nashville: Vanderbilt University Press, 1946), 64.

[4] *Proceedings and Addresses at the Installation and Inauguration of James Hampton Kirkland, Ph. D.* (Nashville: Published by the University, 1893), 46.

virtues and old times—was nowhere more apparent than in the guiding minds behind this liberal Southern school. But the surrounding land nurtured a conservative society whose easy manners and customs endowed the school with a gentler aspect, providing its students with a homogeneous outlook and a hardy traditionalism. Thus, the bases upon which the university stood were comparative prosperity, sound intellectual achievement, and a sturdy popular approval, all undergirded by a liberal Protestantism. So supported, Chancellor Kirkland viewed his faculty with confidence and tolerance. "We demand first of all that our professors shall be Christian men and competent scholars," he proclaimed, "but further than that we have no questions to ask and no instructions to give." [5]

And it was with scholars and Christian gentlemen that the teaching staff was filled and, further, with men who were drawn from various locations outside the South. When Ransom entered the university, Chancellor Kirkland himself, with his Ph.D. from Leipzig, was Professor of Latin. Herbert Cushing Tolman, who had received the doctorate from Yale, was Professor of Greek. One of the nation's ablest scholars in Greek and Sanskrit, Tolman instilled in his students an understanding of the nobility and grandeur of Greek literature and was thus to have a profound effect on the young men who became the Fugitives. Richard Jones, Professor of English, had received his doctorate at Heidelberg; and J. H. Stevenson, an expert in Hebrew and Old Testament Exegesis, had taken his degree from Chicago. Nine other doctors of philosophy were on the faculty of the Academic Department, their cosmopolitanism manifesting that freedom from localism which the university's founders had proclaimed as an ideal.

But even so outstanding a faculty could hardly have maintained the university's standards without adequately prepared students. Fortunately, these were supplied by preparatory schools, their character determined and their custom established some time before Tennessee's public school system was at all satisfactory. The first

[5] *Ibid.*, 46.

of these, the famous Webb School, had been established in Culleoka, Tennessee, by a returning veteran, William R. ("Old Sawney") Webb, a man of firm will and strict moral principle, who was later joined by his brother, John ("Old Jack"). The aim of these two was high; as Donald Davidson has written, "They toadied to no educational fashion. Their staple diet was Greek, Latin, and mathematics, with some concessions to history and English. Out of the Spartan necessity enforced by the hard times they made a glory and a moral." [6] Numerous university training schools, patterned after the Webb model, sprang up throughout middle Tennessee as well as Kentucky, Alabama, Arkansas, and Mississippi. These academies sent their most promising students to Vanderbilt and were rewarded by receiving from the university some of its best graduates as instructors. That a co-operation on matters of curriculum and standards should grow up between the university and its satellites was inevitable, the exchange making for a brilliant and self-sustaining educational constellation.

It was to one of these preparatory institutions—the Bowen School in Nashville—that John Ransom had been sent at eleven years of age. [7] The training he received there was of germinal importance to his later development and consequently to the whole

---

[6] *The Tennessee* (New York: Rinehart and Company, 1948), II, 143.

[7] Ransom had come of a learned family: his father, Dr. John James Ransom, a native of Rutherford County, Tennessee, was a missionary in the Methodist church, a man with an established reputation in the South as linguist and theologian. In his early life he had spent nine years in Brazil, making there the first official connection for the Methodist church, had come back to Tennessee and married Miss Ella Crowe, who had been teaching at the Martin School in her native town of Pulaski, Tennessee, and after a final two-year stay in South America, had come back to Pulaski long enough for John Crowe Ransom to be born, April 30, 1888, the third of four children. After two years in Cuba, the family returned to Tennessee, where young John received his early education chiefly from his parents, since the Ransoms continued to move about from place to place, in the custom of Methodist ministers' families.

Even in his childhood, John Ransom was amiable and talkative, yet reticent about his private feelings, fitting well into a family whose attitude was a curious mixture of reserve and gregariousness. He and his father often argued about an idea until Mrs. Ransom had to caution them that the neighbors would think they were quarreling.

group of Fugitives, since to a degree he led the way for them all. Of Headmaster A. G. Bowen, who taught Latin and Greek, Ransom wrote later, " Certainly he did more for my education than any other man. . . ."[8] Professor Bowen sometimes allowed the boy to accompany him on Saturdays to Goodpasture's Bookstore, where he and other learned gentlemen discussed the classics. Thus Ransom grew accustomed early to an atmosphere of lively conversation—passionate yet objective—that can exist only in surroundings providing both leisure and the conviction that talk is not a waste of time.

At fifteen, well prepared, Ransom took Vanderbilt's rigorous entrance examinations in English, history, mathematics, Latin, and Greek, his papers in each of the first three subjects earning a first prize. His initial year's work consisted of courses in Latin, Greek, German, mathematics, and English, this latter course ending with a consideration of Southern literature, as had been the custom at Vanderbilt since the founding of the university. Professor Jones's predecessor, William Malone Baskervill, who had come to Vanderbilt from Wofford College, had in 1897 published a volume of biographical and critical studies of various " new " Southern authors, the local colorists and espousers of industrialization and technological progress—Irwin Russell, Joel Chandler Harris, Maurice Thompson, Sidney Lanier, George W. Cable, and Charles Egbert Craddock.[9] As a result of Baskervill's faith in contemporary Southern letters, the university's program of cosmopolitanism was not allowed to obscure entirely the fact that " literature " need not be limited to remote ages and places. Indeed, the school literary magazine, *The Observer*, in 1903 labelled its age one which " in some respects may be called the renaissance of American literature, particularly in the South." [10] But the renaissance was to hold off

[8] The Nashville *Banner*, November 10, 1948.

[9] *Southern Writers: Biographical and Critical Studies* (Nashville: Publishing House, M. E. Church, South, 1897). After Baskervill's death, some of his former pupils brought out a second volume (1903).

[10] " Literature and the Student," *The Observer*, XXVI, No. 1 (October, 1903), 3.

for a score of years awaiting the maturity of the boy who was that year a freshman.

Upon completion of his sophomore year in 1905, Ransom left Vanderbilt for a brief period of preparatory school teaching in Mississippi. Two years later, however, he returned to the university where he soon began taking an important part in campus literary activities. President of the Dialectic Society, he was one of the school's prize debaters. His ability in writing found outlet in the campus newspaper, in *The Observer* (of which he was editor in his senior year), and in the Calumet Club, a literary group made up of students and faculty members. The Calumet Club met informally in a suite at Kissam Hall, the men's dormitory, to discuss literature and, specifically, to study modern authors. Something of the long tradition of conversation out of which *The Fugitive* was to emerge is revealed in the spirit of this club, which was to exert strong influence at Vanderbilt during the twenties and to continue on up to the present day. Many of the Fugitive poets later credited the Calumet Club with introducing them to contemporary literature. But there was no real literary tradition at Vanderbilt before Ransom; the only writers the school had produced were David Morton, the poet, and Grantland Rice, the sports writer. Inasmuch as the reigning ideal of scholarship found its embodiment in men with a broad knowledge of several disciplines, at Vanderbilt the purely literary man did not exist. Always literature was related to life and—except for the token paid to regionalism—to the classical past; and though the later Fugitives were to rebel against this gentlemanly dilettantism as an approach to literature, they were nonetheless in many ways shaped by it.

When the second member of the Fugitive group, Donald Davidson,[11] entered Vanderbilt in 1909, Ransom had already received

[11] Of pioneer Tennessee stock (Davidson's great-great-grandfather, Andrew Davidson, was an early settler of Bedford County, one of the latest counties in Tennessee to be formed), most of Davidson's forebears had been farmers. But his father, William Bluford Davidson, was a schoolteacher. He had been born in Blue Stocking Hollow, near Richmond, Tennessee, not long after the Battle of Shiloh, and he learned his Latin and Greek at one of the little schools the

his B. A. degree and had left to teach for a year at Lewisburg before going on to Oxford as a Rhodes Scholar. As Ransom was to be the intellectual leader of the Fugitive group, so Davidson was to provide its cohesive force. His warmth and loyalty were to pass continuously amidst and about the group, binding it into an entity which, though several in mind, was singular in affection. Like Ransom, Davidson had spent his boyhood acquiring a classical foundation that would underlie all his later learning; indeed, the education he received at the Branham and Hughes Preparatory School (where he studied four years of Latin and three of Greek) was so rigorous that on first entering Vanderbilt he found his study easy by comparison. He was a bright, gentle student with dark, disconcerting eyes, not as much interested in the literature of his own language as in Latin and music.

His interest in literature quickened, however, during his freshman year. Besides all of Kipling, he read Dostoevsky, Tolstoy, some of the other Russians, and Maupassant; in fact, as he said later, he started in to read the library straight through. The Maupassant he borrowed from the well-stocked shelves of books owned by Ben and Varnell Tate, junior students from Ashland, Kentucky, whose younger brother, Allen, would enter the university

---

returning veterans founded. When he decided to be a teacher, he attended colleges at Troy, Alabama, and Winchester, Tennessee, and earned his degree from Holbrook Normal in Lebanon, Ohio. His wife (Elma Wells, of Chapel Hill, Tennessee) was a music and elocution teacher, who played the guitar and the piano, passing on her love of music to her children.

Donald Grady Davidson was born August 18, 1893, in Campbellsville, but spent most of his boyhood in nearby Lynnville, a little town about sixty-five miles south of Nashville, in the bluegrass hills of middle Tennessee. He was the oldest of five children, of whom two others have well-developed literary ability. His family, like Ransom's, moved from town to town through the pleasant rural section of middle Tennessee, as his father changed schools.

There was a good library in the Davidson home; the boy pored over Plutarch's *Lives*, Shakespeare's works, Ramsey's *Annals of Tennessee*, and the ninth edition of the *Encyclopedia Britannica*. By the time he enrolled in Branham and Hughes in 1905, he had already grown familiar with the world existing behind the printed page. His uncle, Wallace Wells, had gone to Vanderbilt after finishing at Branham and Hughes. Davidson, following in his uncle's footsteps, entered Vanderbilt in 1909.

nine years later. But Davidson's leisurely reading was interrupted: his father, a schoolteacher, found himself unable to continue his son in college. Davidson had entered Vanderbilt, as he later put it, "on a $100 loan and a little odd cash." [12] He was able to get a further loan to finish out the year, but the next four years he spent teaching in small towns, determined to save enough to complete his work at Vanderbilt.

While Davidson was away from Nashville, four students later to become part of the pre-Fugitive group entered the university: Stanley Phillips Johnson in 1911, Alec Brock Stevenson in 1912, and William Yandell Elliott and Nathaniel Hirsch in 1913. Johnson, who had attended Hume Fogg, a public high school in downtown Nashville, was not equipped with a classical background to match that of Ransom and Davidson, though he had studied three and a half years of Latin. [13] Without the prerequisite of Greek for the B. A., Johnson enrolled for work leading to the B. S. degree and concentrated on philosophy and modern languages, rather than on the classics. He was a forthright, pragmatical boy who could always give his teachers a good argument. More than any of the other Fugitives, he was in rebellion against his upbringing, mistrusting the ideas with which he had grown up, convinced that he had to prove everything for himself.

Alec Stevenson was of a very different sort from Johnson; the son of Professor J. H. Stevenson, who taught Semitic Languages at Vanderbilt, he had perhaps the best precollege education of any of the group. With parents who were both literary, he had grown up, as he himself expressed it, "in a welter of words and books." After four years' preparatory work in the Duncan School, adjoining the Vanderbilt campus, Stevenson was well equipped to become, in 1914 and 1915, the literary leader among the university undergraduates. [14] Elliott, entering from Webb School, had to his credit

[12] *Southern Writers in the Modern World* (Athens: University of Georgia Press, 1958), 9.

[13] Johnson was a Nashville boy, born November 5, 1892, the son of W. D. Johnson and Jessie Bryson Johnson.

[14] Born in Toronto, December 29, 1895, the young Stevenson came to Nash-

four years of Latin and two and a half of Greek.[15] He was from the beginning a leader, a hearty, huge-framed boy who was both studious and active. The other new student, "Nat" Hirsch, although he was never to be a member of the Fugitives, nevertheless played a rôle in the formation of the group. Like Stanley Johnson, he had attended Hume Fogg. He was to stay at Vanderbilt only two years, but it was through him that the other boys' friendship with his older brother Sidney was initiated.

Ransom returned to Vanderbilt as an instructor in 1914, having taught Latin at a preparatory school in Litchfield, Connecticut, for a year after he had received his B. A. in the Literary Humanities from Christ Church College, Oxford, in 1913. At Oxford, where he was a Rhodes Scholar for three years, he had belonged to a literary group known as the Midwives, founded by his friend Christopher Morley. Ransom's literary activities as an undergraduate at Vanderbilt had developed his keen-cutting prose style, and the associations at Oxford further committed him to the literature of his own tongue.

In his year of teaching Latin in New England, the conviction had grown upon him increasingly that his real loyalty lay with English literature because in it was embodied, he thought, a greater

---

ville with his parents within a few weeks after his birth, to grow up on the Vanderbilt campus. His early education was conducted by his mother and father. His mother (nee Evelyn Sutherland) came from a long line of teachers and writers in Canada; her father, Alexander Sutherland, was a Methodist minister who as a boy had been a printer's devil. Young Stevenson spent his summers in Canada at his grandfather's, and the doughty old Scotsman had a great influence on him. His paternal grandfather had come to Ontario from the north of Ireland, and it was in Ontario that Alec's father had started out as a circuit rider in the Methodist church. A friend of Chancellor Kirkland, he had been invited to Vanderbilt in 1893 to fill a temporary appointment, but it soon became apparent that his connection with Vanderbilt was permanent. An only child, young Stevenson spent his time until he was ten in the company of adults. Other professors at the university were frequent visitors in the Stevenson home, particularly Dr. Tolman, who had no children of his own, and who spent hours with the bright little boy who could read *Uncle Remus* in dialect at the age of five.

[15] Elliott was born in Murfreesboro, Tennessee, May 12, 1896. His parents were S. William Yandell Elliott and Annie Mary (Bullock) Elliott.

concreteness than the classical languages possessed. His preference at the time for Shakespeare and Browning tied in with his conviction that the poet should deal with experience dramatically rather than discursively. Even at twenty-five Ransom was developing what he later called his "fury against abstraction,"[16] his concern with the actuality of the human situation rather than with theoretical constructs revealing what was later to be more explicit, an "existentialist" cast to his thinking. The three years abroad, with holidays on the continent, had given him also a new appreciation of the South, which he now saw less as a unique and peculiar society than as a continuation of the major European tradition. Consequently when he was invited to join the Vanderbilt faculty by Dr. Edwin Mims, the new head of the English department, Ransom was delighted—both to return to the South and to teach his native language.

He took a room in Kissam Hall, joining a company of eight other bachelor instructors, whose rooms were a haven for students. Indeed, most of the faculty members lived on the campus, so that their relations with the students extended well beyond the classroom. The jostling encounters of daily life singled out those professors who were penetrated by a consistent philosophy, and around them students gathered, turning Vanderbilt's out-of-class hours into something of a peripatetic school. As Robert Penn Warren was later to acknowledge, Vanderbilt's surprisingly large production of creative men might be attributable to the presence on campus of a few professors of great stature—a few, but not too many—of whom the student could become for a time a disciple.[17] Had there been more such original thinkers, as there were in the Eastern universities, students likely would have turned from one to another, skimming from each the impressive surfaces but never uncovering

[16] This phrase and some of the immediately preceding information about Ransom's days at Oxford are taken from an unpublished dissertation by John Lincoln Stewart (The Fugitive-Agrarian Writers: A History and a Criticism, Ohio State University, 1947), 42-45.

[17] May 4, 1956, at a session of the Fugitive Reunion, sponsored by the American Studies Association and the Rockefeller Foundation, at Vanderbilt University.

the deep insights which the intensive delving into one man's understanding could yield. As it was, the serious student tended to borrow for a time one persuasive teacher's world view until he knew how it operated, how it ordered existence; and in the process of probing another's mind, he discovered the wellsprings of his own originality.

The teaching of Herbert Charles Sanborn was an excellent example of this training by apprenticeship. He alone made up the philosophy department; and in study under him the student had to come to terms with a completely developed *weltanschauung.* Sanborn had come to Vanderbilt in 1911 as head of the department, replacing Collins Denny, with whom Ransom had studied.[18] A pupil of Borden P. Bowne at Boston University, Sanborn had received his doctorate at Munich, after other study at Heidelberg, Berlin, Halle, and Leipzig. He was a brilliant scholar and linguist, whose finest work was in aesthetic theory. Of his teaching, Davidson has written: "One could but be awed and obedient when Dr. Sanborn strode vigorously to his desk, cloaked in all the Olympian majesty of Leipzig and Heidelberg, and, without a book or note before him, delivered a perfectly ordered lecture, freely sprinkled with quotations from the original Sanskrit, Greek, Latin, German, French, or Italian, which of course he would not insult us by translating." [19] It would be difficult to assign limits to Sanborn's influence upon the various Fugitives. A defender of the universals, a vigorous foe of scientific materialism, he gained his students' respect whether or not they agreed with him.

In 1914, the same year Ransom came back in his capacity as instructor, Donald Davidson likewise returned to the university.

---

[18] At the Fugitive Reunion (May 1–5, 1956) Ransom described amusingly his experience at Oxford with his tutor in philosophy. Collins Denny, Ransom's teacher, was a pupil of Noah K. Davis and used his former professor's books as a text in every subject he taught. When the Oxford tutor asked what Ransom had read in metaphysics, the answer came: "Noah K. Davis," an authority with whom the tutor was unacquainted. When the answer remained the same for each branch of philosophy about which Ransom was questioned, both Ransom and the tutor began to realize something of the task ahead of them.

[19] *Southern Writers in the Modern World,* 11-12.

He entered as a sophomore carrying a double load of classwork and holding a teaching position at Wallace University School, a local preparatory institution. He enrolled for Ransom's Shakespeare class; and soon, with only five years separating them in age—despite the wide gap at this point in their educations—the two young men became good friends. At first Davidson was surprised and puzzled at the Oxford man's flat voice, and, although he soon changed his mind, considered him in the beginning a rather dull teacher. Almost pedantically, it seemed, Ransom analyzed the plays in class. Along with the Shakespeare course, Davidson had a survey course under Mims, who made him feel as though he had been "hit by a cyclone," he later said. He had never realized that English literature *had* a history, and Mims's broad acquaintance with the different periods was to the younger man tremendously exciting.

Edwin Mims had returned to Vanderbilt as head of the English department two years before. A graduate of Vanderbilt, he had received his doctorate from Cornell, afterward teaching at Trinity and the University of North Carolina. His volume on Sidney Lanier [20] and an edition of Southern writers which he and a former pupil had published [21] placed him as an authority on Southern literature. Consequently it was with real enthusiasm that he continued at Vanderbilt the emphasis upon regionalism. Mims was always to be interested in sponsoring those elements in Southern writing which gave it local color and flavor and so, as he considered it, enriched American literature without tending toward a bigoted sectionalism. Despite his own work in American letters, however, it was his "Victorian Lit" course, along with excerpts from the Victorians in the survey course, that had most effect upon students. Tennyson's poems had marked a kind of conversion in his life; consequently Mims tried to share with his pupils what seemed to him "a new heaven and a new earth." [22] He was a

[20] *Sidney Lanier* (Boston: Houghton Mifflin Company, 1905).

[21] Edwin Mims and Bruce Payne, *Southern Literature for Schools* (New York: Charles Scribner's Sons, 1910).

[22] Quoted in the Durham, N. C., *Morning Herald*, March 4, 1956, Sec. IV.

popular lecturer, and most students responded, as did Davidson, to the impact of his personality and enthusiasm.

About this same time, Davidson was meeting another literary man of huge persuasiveness and charm—Sidney Mttron [23] (pronounced Me-tát-tron) Hirsch, who had achieved "something of a reputation as poet, journalist, orientalist, and linguist," according to an article in the 1913 *Current Opinion*.[24] Sidney Hirsch was the eccentric older half-brother of Nat Hirsch, who had made friends particularly with Bill Elliott, Alec Stevenson, and Stanley Johnson. When Nat invited these boys to his home, Sidney was delighted at the opportunity to converse with percipient young men. By his very makeup an eclectic, he had so prodigious a memory that he could recite a page of printed material almost perfectly after a single glance. Along with this amazing faculty went a flair for the occult and a magnetic, dominating personality, so that he always stood in need of an audience.[25] He had been sent to the Webb School, but his independent temperament made him incapable of submitting to Old Sawney's discipline. His higher education had been similar, punctuated by trips from college to college, his family finally acknowledging that so pronounced a genius must not be intended to have a formal education. He ran off to the navy for three years and afterwards travelled through the Far East, his receptive mind soaking up Oriental art and mysticism. When he returned, his family secured for him a tutor— a sculptor named Chase—who was acquainted with and had taught numerous figures prominent in art circles. Hirsch travelled abroad with Chase, enjoying the privilege of moving in a world of celebrities. He stayed for a while in New York as part of the company of such fashionable writers and artists as Percy Mackaye, Edith

[23] The name of the great Angel-Prince (in the Kabbalah) who constitutes the visible manifestation of the deity.

[24] "A Greek Pageant in Tennessee," *Current Opinion*, LV, No. 3 (September, 1913), 174.

[25] Hirsch had been born in Nashville, sometime in the 1880's, into a cultured Jewish family. His father, by a first marriage, had two children—Rose and Sidney. After the death of his wife Mr. Hirsch had married again, two more children—Nathaniel and Goldie—issuing from this second marriage.

Thomas, Lorado Taft, and Jock Whitney. In New York he had a
hand in several short dramatic skits and, after coming back to
Nashville, in 1913 wrote and produced what *Collier's Weekly*
called " the most artistic and ambitious spectacle ever given in the
South," [26] a Greek pageant entitled *The Fire Regained*. Hirsch had
become convinced that an esoteric symbolism lay behind all great
works of literature and explained the Greek dramatic poet's method
(which he attempted to employ in his pageant) as a symbolical one.
The whole community had taken part in the production, much in
the spirit of a Panhellenic festival. Some of the features of the
performance were " a chorus of five hundred, a flock of five hundred
doves, a drove of three hundred sheep and a chariot race." [27]

Sidney's brother Nat was one source through whom Johnson,
Stevenson, Elliott, and Davidson had access to this brilliant and
eccentric man. His sister Goldie Hirsch was another connection.
Davidson was taking work during the summer of 1915 at Peabody Summer School, across the street from Vanderbilt, where
Miss Hirsch was also enrolled. With Stanley Johnson, Davidson
made up a foursome with Goldie and Will Ella Tatum, who was
later to become Johnson's wife. Davidson was drawn into the magic
circle of the Hirsch household, which had become a frequent meeting place for the young intelligentsia. Hirsch was in and out of
Nashville, his sophistication impressing his protegées as no academic training could have done. His expansive, enveloping warmth
and his flattering attention to their ideas buoyed the spirits of his
young audience, who, having no personal acquaintance with the
glamorous world of which he spoke, were pleased at seeming considerable to a man of such parts.

Conversation grew so exciting and momentous that Davidson
invited Ransom to join the group. Ransom brought with him the
literary sophistication of Oxford and a more rigorous turn to the
group discussion. Where Hirsch had encouraged in the young men
an enthusiastic but somewhat undisciplined largeness of thought,

[26] Quoted in " A Greek Pageant in Tennessee," *loc. cit.*, 174.
[27] *Ibid.*, 174–75.

Ransom made his influence felt by the example he set in fine discrimination between ideas. In argument, Ransom was a formidable opponent; and in conversation he was tentative, dry, and incisive. The cool logic which he thrust into the group's talks was a spur in particular to Stanley Johnson, who had become imbued with Borden P. Bowne's philosophy of Personalism. And though Johnson's main allegiance was always to be with action, still he enjoyed wrestling with knotty problems and could stand up to Ransom in argument. Davidson remembers " how stubbornly and constantly " Johnson argued with Ransom and Elliott and " how sternly he refused to give ground." [28] This was the period of the letter from Bill Elliott to Alec Stevenson, describing the evening of " Olympian " conversation. These were, indeed, the halcyon days. Sometimes there were gay occasions when Davidson played the piano and sang, the others joining in on choruses. But most of the time there was nothing more than good conversation. Hirsch's expounding of occult mysteries was not allowed to get very far out of hand; either Ransom's empiricism or Johnson's pragmatism pulled him back into the realm of intelligibility. But frequently there was a probing into metaphysical obscurities in which distinctions became very fine indeed. By the time Stevenson returned from Canada in the fall, he found the group well established; and he quite happily joined it.

That same fall a young doctor of philosophy from Leland Stanford came to the Vanderbilt faculty; Walter Clyde Curry, like most of his colleagues, had a rural Southern background that his polished suavity was likely to belie.[29] He was a scholar dedicated more to a philosophical and historical approach to literature than to a

[28] *Southern Writers in the Modern World,* 12.

[29] Curry was born near Gray Court, South Carolina, January 6, 1887, and often took pleasure in reminding his classes that he had known the feel of clods breaking under bare feet as he plowed. His undergraduate days were spent at Wofford College in nearby Spartanburg, but he went west for his graduate work, where he wrote his doctoral dissertation on the Middle English ideal of personal beauty (*The Middle English Ideal of Personal Beauty; as found in the Metrical Romances, Chronicles, and Legends of the XIII, XIV, and XV Centuries,* Baltimore: J. H. Furst and Company, 1916).

creative one, even though he was to write some good poetry and, under the stimulus of the Fugitive group, become seriously interested in aesthetic questions. It was not long before Davidson invited him to the meetings on Twentieth Avenue, where his philological training was welcomed, particularly by Hirsch, whose interest in languages exceeded his mastery of them.

The group interest remained primarily philosophical, even though Alec Stevenson, who had a facility in verse forms that his associates lacked at this point, was writing some accomplished poetry and prodding others to do so. As editor of *The Observer* in 1915, Stevenson was adversely critical of the quality of literature produced at Vanderbilt, lamenting the lack of an advanced course in writing.[30] At the same time, literary discussion in the Calumet Club grew more intense, and arguments about the "new poetry" began to spill over into the Hirsch group. Stanley Johnson became convinced that he and his friends should be writing in the new idiom. One day he took Davidson up to his room in Wesley Hall and solemnly showed him a new book—*Spoon River Anthology*. "We should have done this," he said grimly. "He's beaten us to it."

The young men at Vanderbilt were not writing the new poetry, nonetheless. By June, 1916, the *vers libre* controversy had stimulated an article on that subject in *The Observer*;[31] but, though Johnson himself tried the new technique and a few other students experimented with it, there was no concerted effort in that direction until, a short while later, Ransom tried his hand at poetry. One day in the fall of 1916 Ransom showed Davidson the first poem he had ever written, "Sunset." His poem reflected a reading of Frost and Robinson, though it is in the new free verse. It begins:

> I know you are not cruel,
> And you would not willingly hurt anything in the world.

[30] No. 1 (September, 1915), 36. One was added in 1917 for John Ransom to teach, but since he left for the army in May of that year, the course was not well established until he returned to the university in 1919.

[31] Clopper Almon, "Vers Libre and the Spoon River Anthology," XXXVIII, No. 4, pp. 40–47.

There is kindness in your eyes,
There could not very well be more of it in eyes
Already brimful of the sky.
I thought you would some day begin to love me,
But now I doubt it badly;
It is no man-rival I am afraid of,
It is God.

The meadows are very wide and green,
And the big field of wheat is solid gold,
Or a little darker than gold.
Two people never sat like us by a fence of cedar rails
On a still evening
And looked at such fat fields.
To me it is beautiful enough,
I am stirred,
I say grand and wonderful, and grow adjectival,
But to you
It is God.[32]

There are four more stanzas in the same style. In spite of the
ineptness of its lines, something of Ransom's wry flavor comes
through in this first poem; and certainly it makes use of one of
Ransom's most frequently encountered and most successfully
handled later subjects: the physical world menaced by the terrible
simplicity of an idea, as in "Spectral Lovers" and "History of
Two Simple Lovers," later entitled "The Equilibrists."

At twenty-eight, Ransom had written much good prose, but had
not attempted verse before, whereas Davidson had written a kind
of poetry ever since he could remember. And now, when Davidson
liked "Sunset," as did Ransom's other friends to whom he showed
the poem, Ransom continued in the same vein with three more
pieces. He sent all four to *The Independent*, where they were
accepted; and, soon after, Christopher Morley reprinted some of
them in his column "The Chaffing Dish," in the Philadelphia
Evening Public Ledger.

[32] "Sunset," *Poems about God* (New York: Henry Holt and Co., 1919),
13–14.

Ransom had taken up poetry now in earnest. But Davidson was as yet unawakened to its potential seriousness. He had contributed verses to the school paper at Branham and Hughes; had composed both words and music for an operetta at Cedar Hill Institute, where he taught after his freshman year in college; and had published occasional poems in the Vanderbilt *Observer*, all without awareness of the inner nature of poetry. To him at the time, poetry was principally song, with no great burden of thought. Indeed, the close conjunction of poetry and music was always to be apparent in his work. When his keen logic was to couple with his urgent sense of history to give substance to his mature poems, they were still to have a structuralizing aural quality.

Actually, though the group conversation had not yet turned overtly to literature, the elements of their later poetry were gathering in all the members of the group. Their native heritage provided them with an earthy colloquial language full of metaphor and concreteness, with traditional rhythms, with a tendency to view life analogically and dramatically, and with a set of shared, though unspoken, cultural convictions. Their university study made available a recondite vocabulary, classical metres, and a fund of abstract ideas. The group experience in philosophy had made possible an intellectual exchange; and, far from weakening individuality, the intermingling of various personalities defined and strengthened identity. Hirsch, Ransom, Curry, Davidson, Stevenson, Johnson, and Elliott—all young men, unmarried and committed to learning— these were fashioning unconsciously the implements of poetry in their evening philosophical speculations, which were interrupted by the great disjunctions of the first world war.

CHAPTER TWO

DISRUPTION, REASSEMBLY,
AND THE
TURN TO POETRY:

1917–1921

W ITH THE BEGINNING of the European war, discussions of world affairs, of politics, and of programs for action cut into the leisurely and free talk on the Vanderbilt campus. Sentiment at the university was not dominantly pro-Ally; a grave distrust of nationalism predisposed many students and professors to remain neutral in their sympathies. In 1915 Ransom wrote an article which portrayed the conflict as involving not the powers of right and wrong, but two equally tenable philosophies. "Each, as I conceive it," he wrote, "stands on solid moral ground; and the tragedy is that two good ideals should prove so irreconcilable. This is not a new phenomenon. It happened in our own Civil War, where the North was fighting with the loftiest missionary zeal to emancipate an oppressed class, and the South was fighting for political freedom." [1] The lesson learned by Southerners from the

---

[1] "The Question of Justice," *The Yale Review*, IV (July, 1915), 684.

Civil War—that right is seldom univocal—was only fifty years old
and hence in Nashville not entirely out of mind.

It was no Southern bias, however, that caused one faculty
member to adopt an open sympathy for Germany. Professor Sanborn had received a great part of his education in that country—
had, in fact, taken his doctorate at Munich. As Mims has written
of him, "He absorbed the technique and the spirit of German
scholarship when it was in its most flourishing period. German philosophers and psychologists were, to him, the heroes of thought." [2]
It was not inconsistent, therefore, that he should defend German
principles in the war. He was allowed to express his opinion freely,
in speeches, in articles, in the classroom—until the declaration of
war by the United States, at which time Chancellor Kirkland
quietly called the forthright philosopher to his office and directed
him to be silent. Indeed, at that point, the whole university will-
ingly curtailed some of its freedom of thought and set about
reorganizing itself to help in the fight, assuming without question
that the atmosphere of gentlemanly liberality would be resumed
after the emergency.

Crowds of students and young faculty members applied for
admission to Officers' Training Camp. Ransom was among the few
chosen from Vanderbilt to go to Fort Oglethorpe, Georgia, May 12,
1917; and at the same time, Davidson, who had been teaching at
the Massey School in Pulaski, was included in the quota from
nearby Columbia. The two friends were delighted to encounter
each other at Oglethorpe, and, on Sundays, sat and talked under
the pine trees at the foot of Snodgrass Hill, with Ransom reading
the poems that afterwards made up *Poems about God,* his first
published volume.

The Hirsch circle had disintegrated. Hirsch himself and Curry
remained in Nashville, but the animating spirits were missing, with
Ransom and Davidson gone, as well as Johnson and Elliott, both of
whom had by now joined the armed forces. Alec Stevenson, who
on his graduation in 1916 had taken a position with the Philadelphia *North American,* came home after the declaration of war

[2] Mims, *History of Vanderbilt University,* 247.

with the intention of entering the navy. When his Canadian citizenship prevented his acceptance, he took up the study of chemistry to qualify himself for work in a war industry and spent the summer of 1917 on the Vanderbilt campus. As always, his home provided a gathering place for friends; along with Davidson, who came to Nashville frequently, Ransom and Elliott spent evenings and weekends with him. But these visits could not recapture the atmosphere of the meetings at Hirsch's apartment. The temper of the times had changed, and the men themselves were in no mood for disinterested rational inquiry. In September the army proved less discriminating than the navy; Stevenson was drafted and in May sent to France to attend the Officers' Training School at Saumur.

Even overseas, the friends encountered each other from time to time. Ransom had been commissioned a first lieutenant in the Fifth Field Artillery at Fort Oglethorpe and sent to France, where, after four months' service in the field, he was sent back to Saumur as an instructor. When Stevenson arrived there, William Frierson (a Vanderbilt student who was later to become a member of the Fugitive group) was one of ten other Vanderbilt men taking the Officers' Training course concurrently. As Stevenson later commented, "Fate seemed always to throw some of the Fugitives together, wherever we were." Davidson reached France a short while later, as a second lieutenant in the infantry. He and his company were moved into a quiet sector of the front in France, and, on November 2, were ordered to advance to an active frontal section. After a few days' heavy fighting, they received news of the Armistice, but were not mustered out until the following June, when the company returned to Camp Jackson, South Carolina, its place of origin.

In the period after the Armistice, when an indulgent government arranged for its heroes to sample the offerings of various European universities, Elliott and Frierson took courses at the Sorbonne, Ransom at Grenoble, and Stevenson at the University of Clermont. In the spring of 1919, just before embarking for the

United States, Stevenson ran into Ransom again in Brest. They were overjoyed at seeing each other and spent the afternoon in a small tavern, talking and reading poetry—much of it from *Poems about God*, which had just been published.

Before Ransom left Vanderbilt for the army, some of his poems had already appeared in *The Independent*, the Philadelphia *Evening Public Ledger*, and *Contemporary Verse*, a little magazine published in Philadelphia. These poems gave him the idea for his first volume: he was surprised, he wrote in the introduction, to find that they centered around the word God: "I studied the matter a little, and came to the conclusion that this was the most poetic of all terms possible; was a term always being called into requisition during the great moments of the soul, now in tones of love, and now indignantly; and was the very last word that a man might say in the presence of that ultimate mystery to which all our great experiences reduce." [3] The rest of the poems for the volume he composed consciously around this schematism, after having ruled that he would make use of only those situations in which he genuinely felt the name God could be pronounced " sincerely and spontaneously, never by that way of routine which is death to the aesthetic and religious emotions." [4] The poems were all finished before he left the States, and, by the time he wrote his introduction to the volume (May 13, 1918), he was able, as he said, to "look back upon these antebellum accomplishments with the eye of the impartial spectator, or at most with a fatherly tenderness, no more." [5] He sent the poems to Christopher Morley, who showed them to Robert Frost. Frost read them and recommended them to Henry Holt and Company for publication; early in April, 1919, the book issued from the press.

Poems about God was not extraordinarily well-received; yet for a first volume, from an unknown, its notices were not inconsequential. [6] Its most important bit of recognition came from Louis

[3] *Poems about God*, vi–vii.
[4] *Ibid.*, vii.
[5] *Ibid.*, v.
[6] Charles W. Stork, "Recent Verse," *The Yale Review*, IX (April, 1920),

Untermeyer, writing in *The Dial*, though his review missed the animating impulse behind the poetry he labelled as part of the "return to brutality." None of Ransom's reviewers perceived the essential quality of his verse, which was neither harsh and bitter, as some thought, nor, as others felt, merely realistic. Though ragged in form and many times uncertain, *Poems about God* revealed Ransom's primarily metaphysical bent: the idea that teased him into his experiment was the old Parmenidean paradox of the One and the Many; and the conclusion intended by Ransom was of the same sort as that reached in the Socratic "dialogues of search," where a specific idea is shown as incapable of being limited to a set definition or to a series of individual instances. But Ransom's allegiance, unlike Socrates', was to the fulness of individual experience rather than to the universal toward which the experience tended. His dominant attitude was an anti-abstractionism manifesting itself as a preoccupation with the uniqueness of individual experience, in which the dualism of man's condition becomes apparent. To Ransom, at this stage as always, abstract ideas were the fruit merely of man's desire for order in a disorderly universe. One of the poems in the volume—"The Swimmer"—to take an example in point, presents a view of man in a state of perilous imbalance—desiring to swim forever in the cool water of rationality, away from the heat of physical being:

> I have no home in the cruel heat
> On alien soil that blisters feet.
> This water is my native seat,
> And more than ever cool and sweet,
> So long by forfeiture escheat.
>
> .   .   .   .
>
> And what if I do not rise again,
> Never to goad a heated brain
> To hotter excesses of joy and pain?

664; Maurice Egan, *The Bookman*, L (October, 1919), 222–23; Alice Corbin Henderson, "An American Georgian," *Poetry*, XVI (April, 1920), 51; Louis Untermeyer, "The Cult of Brutality," *The Dial*, LXVI (May 31, 1920), 562.

> Why should it be against the grain
> To lie so cold and still and sane?
>
> Water-bugs play shimmer-shimmer,
> Naked body's just a glimmer,
> Watch ticks every second grimmer:
> *Come to the top, O wicked swimmer!* [7]

This first volume convinced Ransom that he could write poetry that could in some measure embody his insight into the nature of existence. The problem of expressing his perceptions accurately and fully in verse resolved into a matter of mastering technique; accordingly he set himself diligently to work.

His return to Vanderbilt in the fall of 1919 came after some deliberation on the problem of whether to resume teaching or turn to journalism in New York. During the war he had time for reading and reflection, and more and more he had found it impossible to dismiss his own attempts at writing.[8] In a letter to Charles Cason, Secretary of the Vanderbilt *Alumnus*, Ransom wrote, " The fact is I love English literature; and if I am left alone I would love to teach it in my own way, as well as always, whatever happens, to do a certain amount of scribbling fatigue of my own." [9] But, he realized, if he did return to teaching, it would have to be to a position of more responsibility than a mere instructorship.[10] Mims settled the problem by offering him an assistant professorship, and at thirty-one Ransom took up his teaching, especially the new advanced composition course, with fresh interest.

The Hirsch group, scattered by the war, reassembled somewhat slowly; but, in the end, not one man would be lost to it—except Nat Hirsch, who had left for Harvard before the war. The first stage of its reassembly came in the fall of 1919, when Ransom and Curry began coming to visit Hirsch. They found that he had

[7] *Poems about God,* 4–5.

[8] Letter, *The Vanderbilt Alumnus,* III, No. 3 (January, 1918), 77. The letter is apparently addressed to a friend, dated December 1, 1917, from " Somewhere in France."

[9] Unpublished MS., March 5, 1918.

[10] *Ibid.*

moved in with the James Franks, at 3802 Whitland Avenue, a large two-storey red-brick house in a quiet wooded section of town, a few miles west of Vanderbilt. Mr. Frank, the husband of Rose Hirsch, Sidney's sister, was a businessman in his fifties with a background of culture and refinement.[11] In reality a very learned man, he possessed a quiet modesty about his own talents, content to lavish appreciation on those he considered more gifted than himself. Thus his wife's brother Sidney—the genius, the seer—became for Frank the object of veneration. An injury that Hirsch had suffered in the Orient confined him frequently to his chaise longue; as a consequence, the four Frank servants, as well as Mr. and Mrs. Frank themselves, were at his command. But later on, when the Fugitives met at his house, they most respected and revered James Frank, the sweet and gentle man who, not seriously dedicated to poetry himself, fostered it in others.

Ransom took a room in Kissam Hall near Curry, who had remained in Nashville during the war; and the two frequently shared their knowledge in literature and philosophy. Ransom was dissatisfied with his work in *Poems about God* and had turned to experimentation with the sonnet form. He and Curry traded sonnets back and forth, and frequently the discussion of their poems extended to an evening at the Franks'. Ransom found his friends little changed. Hirsch's provoking intellect, turned now to an examination of the symbolical aspects of etymology, and Curry's genuine, though conservative, literary taste combined with Frank's

[11] A native of Marshall County, Frank was born in 1867 of a brilliant German-born Jewish father and a mother who came from a noted Southern family, the Harrises. Her grandfather and father had founded Harrisburg and received a government grant of three thousand acres. James Frank's father, who had come to this country when he was about ten, was a fine violinist; when he married, he took over the management of his wife's farm, but without much success. A serious crop failure in Frank's thirteenth year caused the family to give up farming and come to Nashville to live. As a boy Frank had gone to Howard School; and, after graduating from Peabody College, had taught a few years, finding teaching a profession for which he had great natural inclination. Nevertheless, by the time he was thirty, he felt heavily the responsibility of supporting his family and so went into the custom shirt business, at which he was quite successful.

graciousness to provide a peculiarly suitable foil for Ransom's thought. Sometimes present were William Elliott and William Frierson, both back at Vanderbilt from the Sorbonne, Elliott to teach on the English faculty and work for his M. A. degree, Frierson to complete his senior year as an English major. Though they were younger than the others, their rather conventional taste in literature—in contrast with their iconoclasm in matters of philosophy, economics, and social thought—fitted in with the congregation of older men with no jarring dissension. More hearty and dominating than ever, Elliott was to take up his Rhodes Scholarship the next fall, but during the summer he was present for group meetings, as he was to be for almost every summer during the next five years. Frierson, too, was to be awarded a Rhodes Scholarship for 1920-21, and, after receiving his B. A. from Vanderbilt in June, would spend the summer in fellowship with the group.

The second stage of the group's reunion came in the summer of 1920, when Stevenson and Davidson were again present for meetings. Stevenson had returned to Nashville early in the year, on the death of his father, Professor J. H. Stevenson. He had been living in an apartment on Washington Square, Philadelphia, which he shared with Christopher and Felix Morley. All three were writing for newspapers: Christopher for the *Evening Public Ledger*, Felix for the *Morning Ledger*, and Stevenson for the *North American*. Back in Nashville, Stevenson went to work for the *Tennessean* in February and, a few months later, changed over to the *Banner*. But it took him only a short while to see that he was not suited for the uncertain life of a newspaperman; hence in May of that same year he accepted a position in Nashville with the American National Securities Company, the investment affiliate of the American National Bank. Stevenson was glad to take up literature again with his old friends and made a pleasant and valuable member of the group, which was rapidly regaining its old status.

Davidson was back in Nashville in anticipation of a teaching appointment at Vanderbilt for the coming fall. He had been under severe financial strain after the war. Shortly before leaving for overseas, he had married Theresa Sherrer, an Ohio girl who had been teaching Latin and mathematics in Martin College, Pulaski. Their daughter was born while he was away; hence Davidson faced serious responsibilities on his discharge from the army. When he first came through Nashville hoping to find a position, his friends had not returned: Ransom was still at Grenoble, Elliott at the Sorbonne, and Stevenson in Philadelphia. Davidson went on to Ohio to join his wife and baby and there tried unsuccessfully to find a place with one of the newspapers or with the city schools. Finally, however, a Nashville teachers' agency placed him at Kentucky Wesleyan; but once he had arrived there, despite the beauty of the surrounding country, Davidson was discontented. Neither the faculty nor the students provided the stimulation he had come to associate with a college. Consequently, when Mims offered him the opportunity of teaching freshman English and studying for his M. A. degree, he eagerly accepted. For the summer he took a temporary position as reporter on the *Evening Tennessean* and so was present at the group meetings from June on.

With Davidson's re-entry, the prewar circle was back together except for Stanley Johnson, who would return in 1921. The only additions were James Frank and Bill Frierson, neither of whom greatly affected the nature of the discussions. Yet the drift of conversation that summer at the Franks' gradually changed, turning ever more surely from philosophy toward literature, particularly poetry. Not only Ransom and Curry, but Davidson, too, was eager for practice in poetic craft; while he was in the army, using his leisure hours to write verse, he had his wife send him books from time to time, and one he asked for specifically was Amy Lowell's *Tendencies in Modern American Poetry*.[12] Back in Tennessee, he had shown some of his work—mainly in free verse—to Stevenson, who told him frankly that it had little worth. Surprised by this

[12] Ironically enough, Ransom wrote home to his friend Charles Cason for *The Home Book of Verse*. At the time he was turning out his unsentimental "modern" *Poems about God*, he seems to have been still unconcerned about the work of contemporary poets. As Allen Tate has said of him, "He was modern without knowing it."

judgment, Davidson had begun to think more seriously about the art of poetry, and added his emphasis to the critical and creative turn the group endeavor was taking. With Ransom having published a volume, and with all the other evening visitors engaged in English studies and writing verses of their own, it is not surprising that the character of the meetings should have shifted. But Hirsch was not to be deflected entirely from his expansive discourses on the ideal realm, of which the events in this world are mere symbols. And when literature was the subject of conversation, he managed to direct the examination of it into etymological channels. As Davidson has described it, Hirsch would pick out a word—

. . . most likely a proper name like Odysseus or Hamlet or Parsifal, or some common word like *fool* or *fugitive*—and then, turning from dictionary to dictionary in various languages, . . . unroll a chain of veiled meanings that could be understood only through the system of etymologies to which he had the key. This, he assured us, was the wisdom of the ages—a palimpsest underlying all great poetry, all great art, all religion, in all eras, in all lands. All true poets possessed this wisdom intuitively, he told us solemnly, repeatedly.[13]

Whatever the direction taken, it was heady conversation; thus for the young men, the group meetings held a compelling sense of importance, and the comfortable home and the food served by Mrs. Frank added to the pleasure of the occasions.

Wiser now and more mature than when they left, but at ease in their haven, these men did not realize that the world as they had known it was disintegrating. Yet even in their own small university cosmos the old order was giving way to something with which they were totally unfamiliar. Utilitarianism was becoming the controlling attitude at Vanderbilt as it had become dominant, even earlier, in most other universities in the nation. When Ransom and Davidson were students, Vanderbilt had clear-cut educational aims, based on the imperturbable structure of all past knowledge and transmitted to its students as an essentially aristocratic attitude. The new philosophy of education shifted this basis, focus-

[13] *Southern Writers in the Modern World,* 12.

ing on the recipients of knowledge rather than the disciplines themselves, with a consequent democratization of attitude, so that the
aims of education were made subject to timeliness and opportunism,
and standards began their long downward plunge. In the 1900's,
Ciceronian humanism was the ideal at Vanderbilt: the purpose of
education was not to teach vocational skills but to turn out men of
good background who could bring to their daily tasks a distinction
that derived from superiority of intellect and character. In 1908-
1909, the year Ransom graduated, all who were working toward a
B. A. degree were required to study a year of Latin, a year of Greek
(these requirements presupposed four years of Latin and three of
Greek in high school), and a year each of mathematics, English,
chemistry, history, and philosophy. A major in English literature
required two years of Latin, Greek, French, German, two and a
half of Biblical literature, and one of Anglo-Saxon.

But by 1919 neither of the classical languages was required,
although English majors were advised to include both Latin and
Greek. Referring to the new curriculum changes as a "long
step in the direction of wider service and more varied educational
opportunities,"[14] the May, 1919, *Alumnus* reported an epoch-
making event in complete oblivion of its real consequences. The
modifications could hardly represent a more striking reversal of
values: "They include an increase in the industrial courses in
Chemistry," the editors wrote, "making that subject more largely
vocational than formerly; the introduction of a Department of
Commercial Science or Business Administration . . . . the abolition
of Latin and Greek as requirements for the B. A. degree and
making all subjects elective with the exception of English, Mathematics, and Chemistry in the first year."

So ended officially at Vanderbilt the assumption that an educated man must be familiar with the classics, a demise that, as
Donald Davidson later wrote, "required the combined battering
of the elective system, compulsory school laws, tremendous financial
expenditures, and high pressure salesmanship by teachers' col-

[14] IV, No. 6, 170.

leges." [15] Such a step was not sudden; it represented the culmina-
tion of several centuries' secularism. But there was no doubt about
its efficacy; imbued with the idea of immediate practicality, students
would no longer elect to take the two "dead" languages. The old
humanistic tradition, "the collective wisdom of the race, made
memorable in literature," [16] was discarded as worn out. Indeed, the
upsurge of enthusiasm and power at Vanderbilt from the middle
of the 1910's on had been directed toward progress and liberalism.
But the university was filled with a heavy proportion of students
who had received their preparatory education from the private
schools directed by headmasters not much changed from those of
the antebellum South, to whom Homer, Virgil, and Horace seemed
more legitimate ancestors than Rousseau, or Wordsworth, or Shelley. Thus, like its prototype the English Renaissance, the Tennessee Renaissance, as it has been called, sprang from the fierce
impact of modernism upon a settled society, one which in this
instance still maintained living customs and habits from the great
European synthesis formed in the Middle Ages.

Ransom, Davidson, and the others meeting in the group sessions
were unaware that their fealty lay with the traditional Southern
way of life. They would have scorned geographical limitations
set upon their thinking or upon their artistic sources. Surrounding
them in their native territory they could see only the ugliness, the
ignorance, and the insensitivity of many of the people with whom
they dealt, and they took refuge in their world of philosophy and
poetry. It would be some years later that they discerned the sources
of the harsh and jarring elements in their local scene, just as they
reached later an understanding of the proper relationship between
art and society. But at the time their topics of discussion were
medieval, Elizabethan, Italian Renaissance, Oriental, or nineteenth-
century French—anything but Southern.

By the time Stanley Johnson returned to Vanderbilt in 1921
to teach and to work on his Master's degree, he found the group

---

[15] "The English Teacher and the Lost Humanities," *The Harvard Graduates'
Magazine*, XLII, No. CLXVII (March, 1934), 177.
[16] *Ibid.*, 187.

meeting with some regularity. Johnson had taught in the University of Manila for two years following his release from the army, and while he was in the Philippines had written a novel, *Bamboo*, which Harrison Smith Publishing Company had accepted but never printed because of financial failure. Soon after he came back to Tennessee, he married Will Ella (or as she called herself by then, Willa) Tatum, his companion in the carefree days before the war. She was a sensible, intelligent young woman who aided Johnson greatly in his literary career and who, as librarian at Vanderbilt during the days of *The Fugitive*, was a source of help to the entire group.

Ransom, too, had married. Robb Reavill, a Wellesley schoolmate of Elizabeth Kirkland, the Chancellor's daughter, had been visiting in Nashville when she met Ransom, and in December, 1920, the two were married. With Elliott and Frierson away, all the members of the group, except Curry and Hirsch, were now family men of responsibility. Four of the men, moreover, were faculty members, teachers of literature in a department which, under Mims's guidance, exchanged ideas freely but decorously. Every Saturday at noon the staff-members would meet on the campus, walk to town, and eat lunch at a French restaurant named Fauçon's. There the group would discuss literature and philosophy in the manner of gentlemanly members of a profession—not a greatly different manner from that prevailing in various organizations in town—the Round Table, the Coffee House Club, and the Old Oak Club. It was this air of the comfortable gentlemen's club that might have dominated the meetings at the Frank home, had not a new entry about this time disrupted their complacency.

In November, 1921, Davidson invited Allen Tate, a brilliant student entering his senior year, to visit the next meeting of the group, which by then had been gathering regularly every other Saturday night " to read poems and discuss ' philosophy.' " [17] John Orley Allen Tate was of the generation just young enough to miss

[17] Tate, " *The Fugitive* 1922–1925: A Personal Recollection Twenty Years After," *loc. cit.*, 75.

the war but old enough to sense the disillusionment in its wake.[18] He was native to Kentucky, where his family had lived for several generations; but his mother considered Virginia their true home and took him every summer to Fairfax County, where one of his earliest recollections was a visit to the stone foundations and ruined chimneys of "Pleasant Hill," the family "place" that had been burnt in July, 1861, by General Blenker's New York "Dutch" Brigade in the Union advance to First Manassas. Tate's education

[18] Born in Winchester, Clark County, Kentucky, on November 19, 1899, the youngest of the three sons of John Orley Tate and Eleanor Custis Varnell Tate, he was soon recognized by his family as a different sort of child from his two brothers. His father, a lumberman, had been brought up in Jefferson County on the farm of his grandfather, John Robert Allen. A native of Sumner County, Tennessee, Allen had migrated to Kentucky as a young man; the paternal grandfather, James Johnston Tate, a schoolmaster "with a Bible in one hand and a Latin grammar in the other," had come out from South Carolina about 1840. His mother had spent most of her girlhood in Washington, and part of it in St. Louis and southern Illinois, where an antislavery branch of her mother's family had come from Virginia in the 1840's; but the family was of Fairfax County, Virginia, the land Tate has since portrayed in his novel *The Fathers* (New York: G. P. Putnam's Sons, 1938). The boy's early education, like that of most of the Fugitives, was received at home. There were many books around him, among them popular histories and the standard Scott and Dickens, but for the rest the indiscriminate choice of a mother who read a novel a day for years, with no particular literary taste. There were some books from the library of his great-grandfather, Major Benjamin Lewis Bogan (1795–1870), who had edited the Alexandria (Virginia) *Gazette* for a while in the 1850's; one of these, the two-volume 1800 edition of *Lyrical Ballads*, with corrections of Wordsworth's grammar in his great-grandfather's hand, Tate was to prize in later life. In 1906, when he was six years old, Tate came with his mother and two brothers, Ben and Varnell, to Nashville, where the older boys entered Vanderbilt. In the normal course, the older brothers would have gone to Centre College in Kentucky or the University of Virginia, and Allen would have followed. But largely through the influence of their mother's cousin, William Pinkerton Ott, a young mathematics instructor at Vanderbilt, they were persuaded to make the choice upon which the future of their little brother, at any rate, was to depend. Two years later, Tate was placed in the third grade in the Tarbox School, Nashville—his first school; the next year, in Louisville, at the Cross School, a private "classical academy," he learned his first Latin declensions and conjugations, and read some of Cornelius Nepos' *Lives*, when he was ten. His haphazard education added up all told to only twelve years, including the four at Vanderbilt. His brothers had been out of Vanderbilt several years when Allen was ready for high school in 1914. After a year at the Ashland High School his prepara-

had been gained in a patchwork of public and private schools, the
Georgetown Preparatory School in Washington being the one immediately preceding Vanderbilt. He was well prepared in languages, but for his mathematics was forced to hire a tutor—the
later well-known medieval scholar, Dorothy Bethurum—who successfully "crammed" him for the entrance examination. When he
entered college, he was not greatly interested in literature, although
he had written a few verses. Except for his Greek course, taught
by Professor Tolman, Tate's first year at Vanderbilt produced
meager fruit. He found mathematics intolerable and dropped
chemistry; and neither his English nor his Latin courses were
engrossing enough to make up for what the others cost in boredom.
But Tolman's nobility of character and genuine erudition impressed him, and his breadth of vision permanently interested
Tate in the study of the classics.

During his sophomore year Tate's interest in his college work
grew more lively. He took two English courses—one under Mims,
the other under Curry. Though Tate somewhat scorned Mims, he
respected Curry, who, recognizing a brilliant student, lent him
books, talked to him about literature, and made his bachelor
quarters at Kissam available to him. But it was not so much his
English courses that started Tate on the path toward real learning
as a philosophy course under the man whom he was to consider
the most powerful teacher he ever had. It was "Cocky" Sanborn's
encyclopedic learning and particular interest in aesthetics that
awakened Tate to the natural bent of his own mind. Tate took
all of Sanborn's courses from then on.

In his junior year Tate was invited to join the Calumet Club

tory education was irregular, comprising only three years, with a part of a
year at the high school in Evansville, Indiana, where his father's business
brought the family for a brief period; then in 1917 his mother entered him in
the Georgetown University Preparatory School, from which he entered Vanderbilt
the next year. Tate's maternal grandfather had graduated in law from Georgetown University in 1852; in fact, a near cousin of this grandfather, the Reverend
Francis Neale, S. J., had been the second president of the University, succeeding
the founder, John Carroll; and Tate's mother and her sisters had been sent to
the adjoining Convent of the Visitation in the 1870's and 1880's.

(of which he became president in 1921), where he enjoyed the company of Ransom, Curry, Davidson, Stevenson, and other less specifically literary members. The Calumet Club was then sponsoring a humor magazine, and in its pages Tate published a poem modeled on Villon, "A Ballade of the Lugubrious Wench," [19] which contained some small portent of its author's later poetic ability. It was after this time that Davidson, chatting with Tate on the steps of College Hall, invited him to come to a meeting of the discussion group. Tate later entertainingly recorded this first visit in his personal recollection of *The Fugitive*. The atmosphere was not primarily literary, he recalled, but philosophic and linguistic:

> We had two hosts, Mr. James Frank, a cultivated businessman of Nashville, and his brother-in-law, Dr. Sidney Mttron Hirsch, a man of vast if somewhat perverse erudition; and it was plain that I had been invited to hear him talk. He was a mystic and I think a Rosicrucian, a great deal of whose doctrine skittered elusively among imaginary etymologies. At that time I was not very consciously a poet. I was studying Greek and Sanskrit, and if I had behaved myself I should no doubt have gone the next year to the American School at Athens. But I had not studied Hebrew, and I never knew what Dr. Hirsch's middle name, Mttron, meant; I understood that it might be an archangel. He was a large man, an invalid who never moved from his *chaise longue*, and he always presided at our meetings. On this first evening he asked me what I knew about the Trojan horse. My answer must have seemed to him ignorant, for he brushed it aside and went on to explain that *woode* in Middle English meant "mad," and that the Trojan horse being the wooden horse must be the mad horse; and that since madness is divine, the Trojan horse is the esoteric and symbolic horse. Shining pince-nez stood up on his handsome nose, and curled Assyrian hair topped a massive brow.[20]

Tate did not recall how many men were present that evening, but he remembered that all that winter five or six men were in "constant attendance" at Hirsch's chaise longue. His characterizations

---

[19] [O. A. T.] *Jade*, III, No. 1 (November 12, 1921), 17.
[20] "*The Fugitive* 1922-1925," *loc. cit.*, 76.

of them are significant: there were Stanley Johnson, " a man who would stand no nonsense from anybody and who wrote some good verse "; Alec Stevenson, who " after the first year of . . . [the] meetings wrote less and less; but he wrote some beautiful things that should have long ago gone into a book "; Walter Clyde Curry, who was a " sympathetic friend and a sonneteer who could write good lines but he was not committed to poetry "; the Starr brothers, Milton and Alfred; [21] and of course Davidson and Ransom:

Uppermost in my mind are Donald Davidson and John Crowe Ransom, who for me, at that early age, meant just about everything. Don was writing what I suppose were his first poems; they were about lovers and dragons, and there was one about a tiger-woman that I thought was remarkable; but Don's own liking for this sort of thing declined at about the time mine did; and in the summer of 1922 he began to write poems that I think are still among his best. John Ransom always appeared at the Fugitive meetings with a poem (some of us didn't), and when his turn came he read it in a dry tone of understatement. I can only describe his manner in those days as irony which was both brisk and bland. Before we began to think of a magazine John had written a poem which foreshadowed the style for which he has become famous; it was " Necrological," still one of his best poems; I marvelled at it because it seemed to me that overnight he had left behind him the style of his first book and, without confusion, had mastered a new style. We all knew that John was far better than we were, and although he never asserted his leadership we looked to him for advice. [22]

It is perhaps not odd that Tate should have caused a change in the company. Bolder than the others, younger, more dedicated to " modernism," his incisive mind provided from the beginning an unsettling influence to which Ransom and Davidson were quick to react. The exchange of energy between these three men was enor-

[21] Milton Starr, a mathematician, did not remain in Nashville and so was never a member of the Fugitives. Alfred Starr, who was to become a local movie magnate, was listed as a member in the final issue of the magazine. Neither man was a regular attendant at meetings.
[22] " *The Fugitive* 1922–1925," *loc. cit.*, 77–78.

mous, setting up an interior movement within the group, the direction of which was unnoticed by some of the members, resented by some, and immensely exciting to others. And it was at this turning point that the ones "committed to poetry," to use Tate's phrase, began to work with a new sense of power and importance.

This new sense of direction that began to reveal itself in the men meeting at the Franks' could perhaps be viewed as part of the revolt against nineteenth-century standards that was occurring among serious poets everywhere, although to describe the Fugitive movement as primarily revolt is to misunderstand the nature of the milieu out of which it came. Growing out of friendship and homogeneity of background, this poetic renaissance had its own inner core of motive and depended far less upon a program of attack than did the literary movements of Northern, Eastern, and Midwestern contemporaries. But there was of course an element of revolt in the thought of these poets, and, although they were to find as they went along that it would turn against liberalism, scientific naturalism, and the Romantic anti-intellectual aesthetic, in the beginning they recognized only a distaste for the spuriousness of many of the emotions by which they were surrounded. They were unable any longer to mouth the large ideals that were to the Victorians the stuff of poetry.

It was only through breaking with "Southern literature," as it was then piously conceived, that they could find the way to what they realized years later was the genuine Southern tradition. In its literary practice the South was still split by the two apparently antithetical attitudes which had been defined during the period from 1870 to 1900: Old South versus New South. Defeat had routed Southern authors in two directions, along two paths of escape—one into the golden age of the past, " the sweetest, purest, most beautiful civilization " America had produced, according to Thomas Nelson Page; the other into the industrially prosperous Utopia of the future, away from what Walter Hines Page described as the " ghosts " that were strangling the South. Yet, though by the period following the World War the two philosophies still had their separate adherents, they were more and more functioning as one, since both were based on an uncritical devotion to the South and on a fundamental misunderstanding of the nature of literature. The romantic diction, the use of local color, the essential sentimentality inherent in the liberal conception of man—these all combined in the beginning of the 1920's to produce a sickly stream possessing only the hollowness of an inherited pose to designate it as literature at all. The charge made by the incorrigible H. L. Mencken did not seem far wrong: "Down there," he wrote, "a poet is now almost as rare as an oboe-player, a dry-point etcher or a metaphysician." [23]

Mencken could not know, of course, that at the time he made his statement there was meeting in the South a group of poets who were to change the whole course of Southern—and indeed American—literature. But it was with no consciousness of a program that these men came together for their enjoyable evenings. Assembling on Whitland Avenue, in the spacious brick home, the members had taken on by now the affability of people who meet with relish and mutual confidence. There, with the Franks' comfortable living room and dining room thrown open and a log fire crackling, the poems were read without apology and were given honest, detailed criticism. Carbon copies of individual pieces were customarily furnished by the authors, so that the audience might mark special points during the reading. Usually, after all the poems were read, a more general topic of discussion emerged naturally from the specific criticisms; and this long debate on an aesthetic question would last well into the next morning.

Mrs. Frank never joined in the conversation; she was self-effacing, leaving the men to themselves except for talking with them affectionately before the meeting and putting out food for them—usually hot chocolate, cake, and fruit, but sometimes more elaborate concoctions such as steaming hot dishes of creole eggs, cold meats, little sandwiches, butter cookies, and various relishes. And sometimes she sat on the back stairs, hearing the voices raised in argument, knowing that the men gathered below were of no

[23] *Prejudices*, Second Series (New York: Alfred A. Knopf, 1920), 136.

ordinary breed, and savoring those precious moments when her husband was supremely happy in the kind of company he deserved.

The knowledge that a meeting was coming up goaded most of the friends into writing a poem for the occasion. It was not felt to be quite sporting to come without one; so unless the Muse failed entirely to give heed, each member of the circle appeared every other Saturday around nine in the evening with his carbon copies in his hand. Hirsch came in to his chaise, from where he presided, and the meeting began always with some formality.

Though deference was paid to Hirsch, Ransom was the real leader of the discussions. He was in his element in these meetings —charming, poised, sure of himself, scrupulously courteous. He sat with a semi-smile on his lips most of the time, maintaining always a gentlemanliness that could not be shattered. He was detached in his thinking, and his effect in an argument was always toward sound logic. "You're in the wrong compartment," he would say to an opponent who seemed to him wrongheaded. As Davidson has recalled him, ". . . always he was, as he politely declared at many a Fugitive meeting, 'literal-minded'—a term he used just before rending to bits with calm, analytical pincers some too airy fancy one of us had bounced into in a mere fit of rhyme." [24] But he never condescended; he welcomed honest criticism. Under such austere guidance, about the fire those winter nights of 1921, each member discovered for himself a world that seemed more real and more exciting than any he had heretofore inhabited. The language of this new world was poetry; and each member knew that before he could declare himself by means of it, he must practice, criticize, and revise.

[24] *Southern Writers in the Modern World*, 8.

CHAPTER THREE

THE BIRTH OF

THE FUGITIVE:

SPRING, 1922

THE MAGAZINE which was to its founders
a sudden and daring venture appears in retrospect as a near inevita-
bility; in the twenties, when eight flourishing young poets came
together, the issue of the combination was likely to be a "little
magazine." Particularly in the South was the third decade of the
twentieth century the time for a literary burgeoning, there having
appeared in one year—1921—three important new journals in different parts of the South: *The Double Dealer* in New Orleans,
The Reviewer in Richmond, and *The Lyric* in Norfolk.

The Nashville poets knew their own work was as seriously
executed as most of the current poetry being printed in America;
but they might not have begun their own publication without
Sidney Hirsch's urging. Hirsch was acquainted with a number of
recognized writers, one of whom, Witter Bynner, in Nashville to
speak at the Centennial Club, had come to a meeting at the Franks'.
Impressed with the poetry he heard there, Bynner predicted that

an audience could be found for a publication by the group, which was made up now of Ransom, Davidson, Tate, Johnson, Stevenson, Curry, Frank, and Hirsch.

Some time in March, 1922, Hirsch broached the idea of a magazine. The other members were heartily in favor of the project, and half-seriously Alec Stevenson suggested as title *The Fugitive*, after a poem of Hirsch's which had been read and discussed at an earlier meeting. They knew that the name would invite ridicule, as Allen Tate later wrote; but since they could not hope to escape teasing, they settled down cheerfully to answer the frequently encountered question concerning the reason for their flight. According to Tate, Hirsch's "most erudite irony was turned upon these jests. For a Fugitive was quite simply a Poet: the Wanderer, or even the Wandering Jew, the Outcast, the man who carries the secret wisdom around the world." [1]

It has been tempting to critics of Fugitive poetry to regard this title with great seriousness and, to many, it convicts these poets of "escapism." But such an interpretation underestimates the supporting framework of Southern manners and sociability, into which, as persons, the Fugitives fitted not uncomfortably. If, as writers, they saw themselves fleeing from anything, it was from sentimentality, which in the South was encountered in literature more than in life. In the preface to the first issue, Ransom wrote, "THE FUGITIVE flees from nothing faster than from the high-caste Brahmins of the Old South." [2] And, a year after the first publication, Davidson enlarged upon this interpretation: "If there is a significance in the title of the magazine," he wrote to Corra A. Harris, of the Charlotte *Daily Observer*, "it lies perhaps in the sentiment of the editors (on this point I am sure we all agree) to flee from the extremes of conventionalism, whether old or new. They hope to keep in touch with and to utilize in their work the best qualities of modern poetry, without at the same time casting aside as unworthy all that is established as good in the past." [3]

[1] "*The Fugitive* 1922–1925," *loc. cit.*, 79.
[2] Foreword, *The Fugitive*, I, No. 1 [April, 1922], 1.
[3] Unpublished MS., March 10, 1923.

To the group, the idea of attempting a magazine seemed, Tate wrote, "a project of the utmost temerity, if not of folly." [4] But the Hirsch circle was not over-modest; the members had developed a method of criticism that strengthened their confidence, and each respected his own ability. They were never to function actually as a unit; their thinking was too strongly individual for real group action; yet by 1922 they had decided on a few points to which they all gave assent. Primarily poetry must not be sentimental; it must not be obvious; [5] and it must be intellectual as well as emotional, the product of what Ransom was later to call "not the act of a child . . . but the act of an adult mind." [6] Other than in this tacit understanding, the criticism at Fugitive meetings was always essentially unsystematic, the members pronouncing with conviction upon each other's work and with just as much conviction ignoring or heeding the pronouncements.

For the magazine, the poets decided to use pseudonyms, "less for concealment," Tate wrote later, "than for the ' romance ' . . . ." [7] Humor and a wry self-judgment were responsible for most of the choices of names. "Roger Prim," for instance, reveals Ransom's basic awareness of his own formal and reticent temperament, as Davidson's "Robin Gallivant" evidences a lyric flair. "Henry Feathertop," Tate's name, was chosen from Hawthorne's story "Feathertop," in *Mosses from an Old Manse*, as a gesture, one can surmise, of both love and mockery toward himself. [8] The significance of neither Curry's "Marpha" nor Frank's "Philora" is immediately apparent, though perhaps Frank's pen name was intended to suggest its owner's philological tendencies; and Sidney

[4] "*The Fugitive* 1922–1925," *loc. cit.*, 79.

[5] As Stevenson wrote in a letter to Tate (August 27, 1933), quoting Ransom at a Fugitive meeting, ". . . it is the Fugitive habit never to name the Thing, to paint all the picture except the central figure."

[6] *The World's Body* (New York and London: Charles Scribner's Sons, 1938), viii.

[7] "*The Fugitive* 1922–1925," *loc. cit.*, 80.

[8] The Feathertop of the story, a straw man given by witchcraft life but no wits, saw himself for the "wretched, ragged, empty thing" he was, a perception which led to his destruction. But as his witch mother asked, "Why should my poor puppet be the only one to know himself and perish for it? "

Hirsch's "L. Oafer," superficially a pun on Hirsch's lack of vocation, probably possessed a far more profound and obscure meaning
known only to its originator. Stanley Johnson in his "Jonathan
David" fused the names of a famous pair of friends, perhaps as an
indication of his forthright conviction that he was his own best
friend. Stevenson's "Drimlonigher" is the name of a county in
north Ireland, the birthplace of his father; and his second pseudonym, adopted for the second issue, was "King Badger," based on
his middle name (Brock), which in Celtic means *badger*. This
romantic and playful gesture of the Fugitives has no real importance in itself; it is, however, indicative of their love for word-play
and for speculation concerning the derivation and archaic use of
words. Much of the Fugitive poetry is full of the peculiar, little-
known diction of amateur linguists; indeed, the curious and eager
attention which they gave to the historical aspect of meaning,
imbedded in the patterns of words, is responsible for one part of
the distinct flavor of their poetry.

The poems comprising the first *Fugitive* were selected by vote; [9]

[9] Davidson has preserved the record of that first important ballot-casting on
the back of a letter written to him by Chancellor Kirkland in reply to Davidson's
application for a university apartment. Kirkland stated that rentals were not
considered solely on the basis of order of application. (March 10, 1922).
Davidson did not get the apartment, a fact which Tate says should have told
him he was a poet ("*The Fugitive* 1922–1925," *loc. cit.*, 80). The pencilled
figures on the back of the letter record the number of votes each poem received
and, as a practical matter, the number of lines in each poem:

L'Egoist	8		44	Ransom
Sermons	8		18	Johnson
I Have Not Lived	7		14	Curry
The Dragon Book	7		32	Davidson
The Demon Brother	7		46	Davidson
To a Wise Man	7		14	Stevenson
Following the Tiger	6		60	Davidson
Imprisonment	6		14	Stevenson
House of Beauty	6		14	Stevenson
Tribute to Int D	5		55	Tate
To a Lady on her B	5		55	Ransom
Night Voices	5		50	Ransom
Intellectual's Funeral	5		15	Johnson
Burial at Sea	4			

and, because the money for the enterprise was coming out of their own pockets, the young poets took their manuscripts to the most inexpensive printer they could find, a Negro who operated a small press in an upstairs shop.

Allen Tate, the only undergraduate connected with the magazine, was assigned the chief task of enlisting support for it, but all the members were drafted into service. Each was expected to round up as many likely prospects as he could muster, the aim being to obtain both subscriptions and publicity. For instance, as soon as the first issue was printed, Alec Stevenson renewed his friendship with Felix Morley, then at Oxford, by sending a copy of the new journal and a letter requesting a dollar for a year's subscription. He explained the motives of the new enterprise: " Our sole purposes are to demonstrate that all the good poetry is not being published by the arrogant and high-priced magazines, and that poetry is not written solely in California, Indiana, and the effete New York." [10]

Tate tried unsuccessfully to sell Chancellor Kirkland a subscription; as a matter of fact, the Chancellor never became a subscriber to the magazine, even after it had attracted a good deal of national attention. Of the university's attitude Tate later wrote,

> While the Fugitive poets were read in the editorial offices of the Nouvelle Revue Francaise in Paris, they were gently ridiculed in the suburbs of Nashville; while they were well-known at the Universities of Oxford and Cambridge, they were a petty nuisance on the campus of Vanderbilt . . . . this intellectual movement never received the slightest official recognition or encouragement from the administration.[11]

According to Tate, Mims also discouraged the venture, inviting the poets to lunch and trying to dissuade them from publishing:

> His general view was, I believe, that if we were good we could be published in the Eastern journals. His emphasis as a teacher was on the

---

[10] Unpublished MS., April 14, 1922.
[11] Letter to Editor, *The Alumnus,* XXVI, No. 5 (March, 1941), 15.

New England writers of the past century, and there was not much said about Southern letters since Sidney Lanier. The necessity to import culture was the doctrine I heard in Dr. Mims' classes, and it is the doctrine preached in his *The Advancing South*, a book published several years after the Fugitive movement had begun.[12]

Quite naturally Mims, as head of the English department, would encounter some resentment among the younger men if he attempted to advise caution; and just as naturally he could not be expected to crusade for something of which he could not wholly approve— the experimental aspect of Fugitive verse. He did praise the group frequently in public addresses, and he himself subscribed to the magazine and elicited other subscriptions from friends; but the most important contribution Mims made to the Fugitives was to value creative writing as highly as scholarship in his own department, so that some of the Fugitives were provided with the means whereby to live and the inestimable privilege of teaching literature in their own way.

Thus, in spite of their lack of sponsorship—perhaps even rather glad at not possessing the encumbrance of commitments—Ransom, Davidson, and the others went ahead cheerfully with their plans for the first issue. When the initial number appeared, it announced no program; the only explanatory words accompanying it were in Ransom's ironic tone:

Foreword

Official exception having been taken by the sovereign people to the mint julep, a literary phase known rather euphemistically as Southern Literature has expired, like any other stream whose source is stopped up. The demise was not untimely: among other advantages THE FUGITIVE is enabled to come to birth in Nashville, Tennessee, under a star not entirely unsympathetic. THE FUGITIVE flees from nothing faster than from the high-caste Brahmins of the Old South. Without raising the question of whether the blood in the veins of its editors runs red, they at any rate are not advertising it as blue; indeed, as to pedigree, they cheerfully invite the most unfavorable inference from the circumstances of their anonymity.

[12] *Ibid.*

THE FUGITIVE is of very limited circulation, and is supported by subscriptions at the rate of one dollar per subscriber. It will appear at intervals of one month or more, till three to five numbers have been issued. Beyond that point the editors, aware of the common mortality, do not venture to publish any hopes they may entertain for the infant as to a further tenure of this precarious existence.

This epigrammatic manifesto accomplished the not unremarkable feat in the South during the early part of the twentieth century of proclaiming the freedom of its editors from partisanship. In fact, so free from apparent policy was this first issue that its readers must have been slightly puzzled at the intentions of a group of poets who went to the trouble and expense of publishing a magazine with no program.

And yet, the first poem in the issue, Ransom's "Ego," is a kind of apologia for the whole Fugitive temperament, as well as for Ransom's own complex sensibility. Beginning

> You have heard something muttered in my scorn:
> "A little learning addleth this man's wit,
> He crieth on our dogmas Counterfeit!
> And no man's bubble 'scapeth his sharp thorn,"

the poem refers specifically to the local misunderstanding that had arisen from the publication of *Poems about God*; but in a larger sense it concerns the whole aura of misunderstanding and distrust with which a poet finds himself surrounded, perhaps at any time but particularly in the South in the 1920's. Another element manifests itself, however, later in the poem: Ransom was apparently aware that even with his poet friends he was subject to some misconstruction. From the sixth stanza on, accordingly, the poem is addressed to them:

> Friends! come acquit me of the stain of pride:
> Much has been spoken solemnly together
> And you have heard my heart; so answer whether
> I am so proud a Fool, and godless beside.
>
> Sages and friends, too often have you seen us

> Deep in the midnight conclave as we used;
> For my part reverently were you perused;
> No rank or primacy being hatched between us;
>
> For my part much beholden to you all,
> Giving a little and receiving more;
> Learning had stuffed this head with but lean lore
> Betwixt the front bone and the occipital;
>
> Anatomy, that doled these dubious features,
> Had housed within me, close to my breast-bone,
> My Demon, always clamoring Up, Begone,
> Pursue your gods faster than most of creatures;
>
> So I take not the vomit where they do,
> Comporting downwards to the general breed;
> I have run further, matching your heat and speed,
> And tracked the Wary Fugitive with you;
>
> And if an alien, miserably at feud
> With those my generation I have reason
> To think to salve the fester of my treason:
> A seven of friends exceeds much multitude.

Though this piece lacks the dramatic framework that Ransom later used to give aesthetic distance to his work (the speaker here is undoubtedly Ransom, addressing the other Fugitives), it exhibits the wry, pedantic, and sharply metaphorical flavor to be found in his poems throughout the course of *The Fugitive*. His other poems in the issue are less successful, though in "To a Lady Celebrating her Birthday" there is expressed some of the tender irony with which Ransom came later to view the poetic object, particularly in the passage:

> Bring only tokens fixed and sure:
> Bring kind affections, merited deep and strong,
> And though poor hearts never have lasted long,
> Swear splendidly to how they shall perdure
> As true as now, as pure.

Davidson's poems, although not so critical in attitude nor so interesting in texture as Ransom's, display more metrical compe-

tence. "A Demon Brother," later to be called "An Outland Piper,"
shows a lyric symbolism not unlike Yeats's:

> Old Man, what are you looking for?
> Why do you tremble so, at the window peering in?
> —A brother of mine! That's what I'm looking for!
> Someone I sought and lost of noble kin.

Davidson's other poems in the issue are of less sturdy stuff; but
all of them, his earliest serious poems, reveal what was to become
later his dominant theme: the individual's profound sense of loss in
the modern world. His poetic method was to change radically,
and his own understanding of the nature of the bereavement was
to deepen; nevertheless, for all their romantic imagery, these early
poems are not poems of "escape" but of a search for a rightful
heritage.

Of Tate's two poems, one—"Sinbad"—is an unfinished Brown-
ingesque dramatic monologue; the other—"To Intellectual Detachment"—is more unusual in its language and metaphor:

> This is the man who classified the bits
> Of his friends' hells into a pigeonhole—
> He hung each disparate anguish on the spits
> Parboiled and roasted in his own withering soul.
>
> God give him peace! He gave none other peace.
> His conversation glided on the brain
> Like a razor honing the promise of one's decease—
> Smooth like cold steel, yet feeling without pain;
>
> And as his art, disjected from his mind,
> Was utterly a tool, so it possessed him;
> A passionate devil, informed in humankind,
> It turned on him—he's dead. Shall we detest him?

This last stanza exhibits, as Tate later commented, the influence
of E. A. Robinson; but some of the lines earlier in the poem show
the ability, unusual in a young poet, to construct conceits that are
intense yet worked out with keen analysis.

One of the most consistently maintained poems in the issue

is Johnson's "An Intellectual's Funeral." Its lines are vigorous and strong:

> On such a day we put him in a box
> And carried him to that last house, the grave;
> All round the people walked upon the streets
> Without once thinking that he had gone.
> Their hard heels clacked upon the pavement stones.
>
> A voiceless change had muted all his thoughts
> To a deep significance we could not know;
> And yet we knew that he knew all at last.
> We heard with grave wonder the falling clods,
> And with grave wonder met the loud day.
>
> The night would come and day, but we had died.
> With new green sod the melancholy gate
> Was closed and locked, and we went pitiful.
> Our clacking heels upon the pavement stones
> Did knock and knock for Death to let us in.

In many ways this is a remarkable poem; for one thing, it is the best of Johnson's ever to appear in the magazine. More noteworthy is the fact that its diction manifests a seasoned colloquialism which to later readers must inevitably suggest the influence of John Ransom. Johnson's other two poems in the issue, however, are greatly inferior to "An Intellectual's Funeral."

The three sonnets Stevenson contributed to the first issue are smoothly competent and polished. Some echoes of George Meredith sound through a few lines of "Imprisonment" with impressive force:

> The lightning feet of years appalled her heart,
> Swift days that left a restless love uncrowned;
> She sighed, and smiled at me with piteous art,
> Wishing for ending, death, or sleep as sound.

Curry's poetry, too, uses the sonnet form as cultivated gentlemen always have—in an elegant but not wholly serious expression of themselves. And yet his "I Have Not Lived" is distinguished by a diction seasoned with a tentative wry irony, as evidenced in the beginning lines:

> Though half my years besiege the aged sun,
> I have not lived. My robust preparation
> Lags tardily behind fit consummation,
> Droops sweatily in courses just begun.

Actually, Hirsch's "The Little Boy Pilgrim" is the one unpromising poem in the journal. In its romantic lyricism it is untouched by the caustic action of thought, assigning to the poet the rôle of the simple, innocent child:

> I am the little boy pilgrim,
> I wander the wold and the sea,
> And far past the reach of the star rim
> I mingle my mad minstrelsy.

This account of the naïve wisdom of the child-mystic continues for seven stanzas, concluding:

> And all that I saw in the heavens,
> And all that I see here between,—
> There's nothing so funny for laughing
> As the sense that is common and queen.

Though of course immature if judged by the standards set later by members of the group, this first issue of *The Fugitive* possessed a good share of intrinsic merit. None of its individual verses, perhaps, were up to the quality of the really good poems to be found sporadically in some of the established journals, such as *The Dial, The Little Review, Poetry,* or even *The Double Dealer;* but its totality was better than that of most other literary magazines in America. It lacked the saccharine notes often encountered in *Poetry* and the wilfully neurotic tone of *The Little Review* or *Secession.* In short, it was an obviously serious effort made by men of intellect and talent.

The Nashville papers were willing enough at first to play up the journal. The *Tennessean* adopted a sprightly tone: "Literary

Nashville has a new sport—chasing 'The Fugitive.'" [13] But beyond making a few arch comments about the "unpretentious little volume" and referring to its literary merit as a "sensation," this news article made no attempt to review the magazine. A more serious review in the Sunday *Tennessean* (written by a Vanderbilt alumna) praised especially Davidson's work. The reviewer singled out Ransom also for commendation, and in the process revealed something of the local reaction to Ransom's published volume of poetry: "Roger Prim is easily recognizable, incongruous as his nom de plume may seem with some of the more rabid 'Poems about God.'" [14]

On the same day the *Banner* also devoted considerable space to a review of the new journal. The anonymous reviewer was guarded in his commendation:

> The poetical work contained in "The Fugitive" is not in general, one would judge, the product of the amateur hand, and more than one of the selections contained therein bears such marks that the identity of the writer seems bound to be a rather open secret. If any general criticism of an adverse nature were to be attempted, in fact, it would probably be to the general effect that the little volume was somewhat smothered in the technicalities of verse writing with a subsequent loss of spontaneity. [15]

The Fugitive should be received sympathetically for two reasons, he felt: first, its poetry possessed "real merit," and second, the volume might fill "a very much-needed want in the literary life of the community."

These first local notices give hints of the ambivalent attitude which Nashville literary people were to adopt toward the work of the Fugitives. "The Athens of the South" could well afford to furnish the soil for one poetic shoot of the Southern literary flourishing; consequently local pride dictated a welcome to the Muse. But townspeople did not expect her to be garbed in such

[13] April 13, 1922, afternoon edition.
[14] April 16, 1922.
[15] April 16, 1922.

peculiar robes or to speak in a tone of such forbidding intellectuality. They were uncomfortable, therefore, and hid their uncertainty in facetiousness.

The appearance of *The Fugitive* caused great excitement in some circles on the university campus. Those who were writing poetry themselves were aware of the magazine as a possible outlet for their own pieces if they had no other interest in it. The college newspaper, *The Hustler,* feared that the magazine was "beyond the grasp of the average Philistine of the campus," but it nevertheless commended "the spirit of the enterprise." [16] But it was the Vanderbilt humor magazine, *The Jade,* listing O. A. Tate as one of its editors, that gave *The Fugitive* the only serious attention it received on campus. In a lengthy editorial devoted to *The Fugitive,* the *Jade* editors applauded the courage and talent behind the journal. After explaining that the new publication represented an attempt to discard the post-bellum Southern attitudes, *The Jade* column concluded: "The Jade can do no more than heartily welcome this new spirit in the South. It is, in our opinion, the spirit that the South has always really had, but sentiment and ignorance have obscured it for so long a time that this small group of serious thinkers is virtually staging a modern renaissance." [17]

Another *Jade* editor, Merrill Moore, four years younger than Tate, was greatly impressed with the Fugitive display of talent. He encountered Tate on the campus soon after the issue was out and thrust into his hands a poem called "To a Fetish," wondering if it would entitle him to membership in the group. Tate thought the poem "wonderful" and took it straight to Davidson. [18] It appeared in the second issue of the magazine, one of the best poems that Moore ever produced. From that time on, he attended Fugitive meetings and enlivened them in his own highly individual fashion.

Moore was brilliant, erratic, vague, and absent-minded; as Alec Stevenson has said, "He could listen in on the stream of his own

[16] Undated clipping.

[17] III, No. 4 (April 13, 1922). Tate does not remember who wrote this "very perceptive" review; at any rate, he did not.

[18] "*The Fugitive* 1922–1925," *loc. cit.,* 78.

consciousness." Davidson has recorded his recollections of Moore as he was during the early days of *The Fugitive*:

When I first came to know Merrill Moore, he was an odd, gangling youngster well along in his 'teens, uncertain of his arms and legs, a little hollow-chested and spindling, with a sparse reddish beard just sprouting on his chin to match the shock of red hair on his head. He materialized as he has a way of doing—in English classes at Vanderbilt University without anybody's realizing at first that his quiet presence meant anything unusual. But in no time at all he arrived, in the manner of his genius that we afterwards found to be as natural to him as getting up in the morning, at the local center of things—at least at what was to some poets at Nashville a center exciting and sufficient enough for the time being. The "Fugitives" were then just beginning their poetical enterprise, and somebody—it was either John Crowe Ransom or Allen Tate—discovered that Merrill Moore wrote poetry and brought him out to a meeting. His verses from the very first had the distinction that is peculiarly his; he was his own mythologist, and was capable of expanding the tiniest figment of name or fancy into an exciting lyric form, which in those days might be free or traditional verse with equal catholicity. Merrill Moore's apprenticeship was brief indeed; he became a member of the circle at a time early enough to select for himself a pseudonym according to the Fugitive fashion of those days.[19]

The pen name he selected fitted him aptly. As Tate pointed out, "Dendric" is the Greek root for *tree*, with the suffix added to make the meaning *tree-like*. "But if Merrill was like a tree," Tate remarked, "the tree was a dense fern of the primordial tropics." [20] Actually, Moore's name was probably related to his premedical study of cell structure, the tree-like formations of nervecells, *dendrites*, more than likely being involved in his choice.

Davidson wrote further of Moore's enormous capacity for getting things done: he attended Fugitive meetings, helped edit the magazine, finished his degree, taught at Watkins Institute (a Nashville night school for adults) kept up his social life, and managed

---

[19] Unpublished MS.
[20] "*The Fugitive* 1922–1925," *loc. cit.*, 80.

somehow to have spare time for small talk—all the while writing a prodigious amount of poetry. In fact, editorial committees learned to depend on Moore's verses " as a sort of goodly staple that one looks to be always on hand plenteously as salt and bread and water at a meal. Whatever gaps others left, through the failure of inspiration or lack of confidence, Merrill Moore could be counted on to fill generously out of his great abundance." [21] The strange thing about Moore as poet was his curiously offhand attitude toward his verse: unlike most of the other Fugitives—particularly Ransom, Davidson, and Tate—he gave no thought to fame or to the questions of the origins and nature of poetry. " It was enough for him," Davidson recorded, " to print his poems in *The Fugitive,* to which he gave a passionate devotion."

Moore had entered Vanderbilt in the fall of 1920, after having graduated from Montgomery Bell Academy in Nashville.[22] In college, when he became interested in writing, it was the portrayal of personality in verse that attracted him. Of his own method he later wrote: " I found that sometimes when I got a sonnet past the first three or four lines it would pick up some sort of momentum of its own and might then go on writing itself, impelled by associations and guided partly by rhyme. Some poems even got out of control and proceeded to write themselves after the first line." [23]

[21] Davidson, MS.

[22] Born September 11, 1903, in Columbia, Tennessee, the son of John Trotwood Moore and the former Mary Brown Daniel, Austin Merrill Moore had a surprisingly traditional heritage for a boy so unconventional. His father, a local writer of the old school, had chosen *Trotwood* as a pen name (from *David Copperfield*) and finally added it to his official signature. A native of Marion, Alabama, he had come to Maury County, Tennessee, in 1885, where on his farm near Columbia he raised blooded stock and wrote articles for the local paper and for the Chicago *Horse Review.* He was a lover of fine horses and of the old Southern chivalric trappings, and he turned to the writing of fiction out of a desire to portray the middle Tennessee country which he knew and admired. In 1897 he published *Songs and Stories from Tennessee* (Chicago: J. C. Bauer, 1897) and in 1901 his first novel, *A Summer Hymnal* (Philadelphia: H. T. Coates and Co., 1901). Several more novels followed; but from 1919 on, after his move to Nashville and appointment as director for the state libraries and archives, he turned his efforts largely to Tennessee history.

[23] " Note to the Reader," *Clinical Sonnets* (New York: Twayne Publishers, 1950), 5.

Because of this peculiar method and its accompanying phenomenon —a prolific output—Moore was made a rule to himself at Fugitive meetings: whereas the others had meticulously followed the custom of bringing carbon copies of their poems for criticism, Moore was released from what would have been the impossible task of providing copies of fifty or sixty poems. And in the matter of criticism Moore was also accorded individual treatment:

When Merrill's turn came to read, we simply leaned back in our chairs and relaxed for a poetical debauch. Such hard, detailed criticism as the Fugitives were in the habit of handing around to each other was impossible in Merrill's case. If you attacked one poem, he retorted by reading another one. From page to page of manuscript he would go, reading casually and with no declamatory effect in his low-pitched, husky voice, occasionally interspersing a murmured comment, " Maybe this one is better," or " This is a series I wrote while waiting for a car in the Transfer Station,"—always as if poetry were not something to shout over and be pompous about, but to take naturally as intimate conversation among friends.[24]

But for all his offhandedness, Moore was serious about his poetry; and for all the goodnatured tolerance of the other Fugitives, they were sometimes harshly critical of his hastily written lines. Once, for a while, he was barred from the magazine, in the hope that this punishment would force him to revise his work. But finally there was nothing for his colleagues to do but accept him as he was, in view of what they all recognized—the amazing fecundity of his poetic talent.

Life for the various Fugitives during this period was busy and diverting. Ransom found pleasure with his numerous unliterary friends in bridge and golf and at parties where guests played hilarious and undignified parlor games. Alec Stevenson was occupied with his friends and business acquaintances, and the Johnsons and Davidsons went out together in a rickety old car which Johnson had acquired. Tate took part in the campus social affairs as an unpredictable and slightly shocking leader. And Merrill Moore

[24] Davidson, MS.

was always turning up in the house of any of his friends, making himself completely at home, helping himself to whatever there was on hand in the kitchen, always eating. Stevenson remembers Moore's coming to his house one time with a banana in one hand and a gold Buddha in the other, ostensibly to talk. But Stevenson soon found out that the boy was hungry, and food proved more sustaining at the time than a discussion of Oriental mysticism. Of the group Curry alone lived in any sense a cloistered life. Although he was intimate with the other Fugitives, reading and criticizing their work, lending them books, talking with them in his room, he took no part in their " social " lives. A rather reserved bachelor, he was putting in long hours on his now famous Chaucer study, *Chaucer and the Medieval Sciences*, which was to be completed and published four years later.[25]

But *The Fugitive* was for most of the members their most enticing occupation. The second issue was assembled in great enthusiasm, with most of the group contributing considerable time and effort to the job. Reactions to the first issue had been gratifying, they thought; hence in the current number the editors expressed their thanks to friends who had purchased all of the earlier copies, placing the magazine "financially on a firm footing" and leading the editors to "speculate hopefully about a policy of perpetuity." These words occur at the end of "Caveat Emptor," Ransom's unsigned prefatory comment which begins:

> The editors of THE FUGITIVE are amateurs of poetry living in Nashville, Tennessee, who for some time have been an intimate group holding very long and frequent meetings devoted both to practice and to criticism. The group mind is evidently neither radical nor reactionary, but quite catholic, and perhaps excessively earnest, in literary dogma. The writers sign their work with assumed names for the present, with special reference to the local public, on the theory that the literary issue must not be beclouded with personalities.

The contents were largely made up of poems the group had on hand before the first number; consequently they were not its

[25] New York and London: Oxford University Press, 1926.

strongest offerings.[26] Moore's poem adds to the quality of the contents; but the lines of both Frank's "Fugitive Unbound" and Hirsch's "The Horses of Hell" are unfortunately limp and ineffectual. Davidson's musical lyrics are less evocative than the ones in the April number, and Tate had not yet achieved anything memorable in the way of style. One poem of Ransom's, however, distinguished the issue: "Necrological," which had been written earlier, but which, as Tate later commented, is the brilliant proclamation of a new style.[27]

The poem is a dramatization of the vast disparity between the moral and physical realms. In it a Carmelite friar who has "said his paternosters duly" comes out of his monastery to find the field around him "white like asphodel" with the bodies of dead warriors. The monk possesses himself of a blade, taken from "the belly of a lugubrious wight":

> He fingered it well, and it was cunningly made;
> But strange apparatus was it for a Carmelite.

The last stanza concludes:

> Then he sat upon a hill and hung his head,
> Riddling, riddling, and lost in a vast surmise,
> And so still that he likened himself unto those dead
> Whom the kites of heaven solicited with sweet cries.

The obvious lack of concern on the part of the natural world gives pause to the friar, committed as he is to a belief in a personal God who supposedly marks the sparrow's fall. He ends by sensing his kinship with these dead, who are subject to the hazards of an uncaring order. In the last line is implied the terrible difference between a spiritual heaven, in which only loving-kindness can be

---

[26] Stevenson's "Now this is Parting" and "More Than the Praise of Gods"; Tate's "Call on, Deep Voice"; and Curry's "Grieve Not" had all been considered for the first publication. Many of the other poems had been written earlier. Ransom's "Destitution Raiseth Her Voice" had been called originally "In Time of Industrial Depression," and his "The Sure Heart" had been, in the voting during March, "As We Two Walked at Dawn."

[27] "*The Fugitive* 1922–1925," *loc. cit.,* 77.

considered sweet, and a physical heaven, inhabited by vultures to whom the ultimate violation of man is sweet indeed. Ransom's ironic tone, his dramatic method, his dualistic theme, his quaintly archaic web of language are utilized fully here. Lacking to the poem are only the tenderness and the absolute mastery of phrase achieved in Ransom's later verse.

A review of the issue in the *Banner* indicates the growth of an attitude which Nashville at large—and Vanderbilt itself—would display increasingly toward *The Fugitive*.[28] Signed by " Queen Bee," the article adopted an amusedly patronizing tone: " The chief element of improvement [in the second issue] seems to be an added amount of intelligibility, the first poem [*sic*] having been wrapped in the mists of poetical technic or something until it was not easy for the ordinary mortal to be very certain what they were all about." After pointing out that the young authors took themselves and their task exceedingly seriously, the disguised reviewer stated her serious opinion at some length: The poems show the weaknesses of men who have spent their lives in academic circles. This attitude is distinctly " new " Southern, representing an anti-intellectualism which, after the war, was becoming quite pronounced, even in a city that had prided itself heretofore on its culture. The concluding paragraph of the review was devoted to a prediction that *The Fugitive* would never be " either popular or influential until it adopts a more intelligent brand of subjects for its poetical effusions and a more humanely understandable manner of dealing with them." A Dallas paper voiced the same opinion in a review of the issue, reprinting Tate's " A Scholar to His Lady," Hirsch's " The Horses of Hell," and Johnson's " Bethel." Though this review was seriously conceived and commendatory in tone, it nevertheless was in accord with the Nashville reviewer in finding the poems too greatly tainted by thought.[29]

In England, William Elliott was boisterously sponsoring the new project. At a lecture on modern American verse, delivered by

[28] " June Fugitive Comes from Press," July 15, 1922.
[29] The Dallas *News*, September 10, 1922.

John Gould Fletcher to a literary club at Oxford, Elliott was openly and vocally shocked at the omission of Ransom from the list of distinguished American poets. Writing of the incident fifteen years later, Fletcher said, " I had repaired the omission, not only by reading Ransom, but by becoming a subscriber and a contributor to the original *Fugitive* magazine." [30] Elliott continued his publicity campaign with other literary men at Oxford, as did Bill Frierson, and wrote the group volunteering to obtain contributors and subscribers for the magazine in England.

By the end of the school year, the Fugitives were convinced of the seriousness of their involvement in the new project. In its two issues the magazine had succeeded well enough to afford a definite impetus to Ransom, Davidson, Tate, and Johnson, each of whom spent the following summer considering at length the problems of the profession of letters. Ransom and Johnson stayed in Nashville, teaching and studying; Davidson was in and out of Nashville, though spending most of his time on the Cumberland Bluffs near Lebanon, where he was counsellor at Camp Kawasawa. Tate had found it necessary to leave school in May, just before he would have graduated. He had shown some sign of a lung complication and was sent to Valle Crucis, North Carolina, for a rest. All the others remained in Nashville and attended Fugitive sessions. Even Curry came to the meetings, though he was busy with plans for his fall trip to England, where he was to examine documents in the Bodleian Library. Frierson and Elliott, back from Oxford, were glad to be included in the group, bringing with them fresh enthusiasm for the project and dissenting voices for the poetry.

[30] *Life Is My Song* (New York: Farrar and Rinehart, 1937), 339.

CHAPTER FOUR

THE LINES DRAWN
WITHIN THE GROUP:

SUMMER AND FALL, 1922

IN THEIR ISOLATION during the summer, Tate and Davidson were forced to turn in upon their own resources; each read assiduously and worked at his writing with a new concern. They were the only Fugitives who were solitary in this promising summer so soon after their literary debut; and their correspondence, at first casual, deepened into an increasingly important channel of expression for both. In the North Carolina mountains, Tate was missing the " daily literary gossip" in Nashville,[1] finding himself not one to merge with the spirit of nature; and, in the hills near Nashville, Davidson was trying to write a photoplay in an attempt to ease his always bothersome financial pressure. Though he spent long hours working on his scenario—he felt sure it would sell, since it possessed the requisite melodrama [2]—he nevertheless allowed him-

---

[1] Unpublished MS., Tate to Davidson, June 20, 1922. All the Fugitive correspondence is as yet unpublished; henceforth in this study letters will be identified by the sender, the recipient, and the date.

[2] Davidson to Tate, July 2, 1922.

self some time every day for the writing of poetry. As a matter of fact, both he and Tate found their minds turning constantly to matters of poetic technique.

One poem of Tate's, "Euthanasia," had already been published in *The Double Dealer*, and two more, "Parthenia" and "William Blake," had been accepted for the July issue. "Euthanasia" had been accompanied by the brief note: "Allen Tate writes that he is but twenty-two and lives in Nashville, Tenn., of which two facts, says Mr. Tate, the latter is perhaps the more damning. He is a poet with a new tang." [3] The "new tang" of Tate's poetry, perceptible in such lines as

> No more the white refulgent streets,
> Never the dry gutters of the mind,
> Shall he in hellish boredom walk
> Again, for death is not unkind. [4]

was apparent, at any rate, to one of the magazine's readers. Hart Crane had translated three of Laforgue's "Locutions des Pierrots" [5] for the same issue, and in looking over the magazine saw and liked "Euthanasia." He wrote its author, saying that he could see Tate had read T. S. Eliot. (As a matter of fact, Tate wrote in his recollections, he had not read Eliot; but he soon did. [6]) Crane's letter explained his feeling for the French poet he had translated. Some of his friends had felt, he said, that his enthusiasm for Laforgue would be more genuine if he knew more about the older French literature; but he had answered them: ". . . my affection for Laforgue is none the less genuine for being led to him through Pound and T. S. Eliot than it would have been through Baudelaire." [7] Tate had read Baudelaire; and he studied Crane's transla-

[3] III, No. 11 (May, 1922), 262.

[4] This poem was later reworked and published as "Elegy: Jefferson Davis." (See Appendix.)

[5] These translations were not reprinted until the appearance of Brom Weber's study of Crane (*Hart Crane*, New York: The Bodley Press, 1948).

[6] "The Fugitive 1922–1925," *loc. cit.*, 80–81.

[7] As quoted in Warren Ramsey, "Crane and Laforgue," *The Sewanee Review*, LVIII, 3 (Summer, 1950), 441–42.

tions, together with other poems that Crane sent him in manuscript, connecting what he saw in them with what he had previously learned from Baudelaire and Mallarmé.

What Crane had considered an "Eliot" tone in "Euthanasia" Tate was ready to acknowledge. In an attempt to console Davidson for the rejection of his "Amulet" by *The Double Dealer*, Tate wrote: "You know how readily they took 'Euthanasia' and 'Parthenia' and, since I left, even 'William Blake'! All these poems, with the possible exception of 'Parthenia,' are quite inferior to your 'Amulet,' but their tone is in unison with Eliot, Pound, and Company; and so they took them." [8]

Along with copies of his own poems, Crane sent Tate back numbers of *The Little Review*.[9] Out of the ferment that these new materials induced in him came such poems as "Non Omnis Moriar," "Elegy for Eugenesis," "Bored to Choresis," "Lady Fabulous," "Long Fingers," "To Oenia in Wintertime," and "The Duchess of Malfi," all making use of a new ironic mask and a new indirection, wherein a state of mind is suggested, rather than described, by the images and allusions in the lines. "Elegy for Eugenesis" illustrates Tate's new style:

> Your death, dear Lady, was quite cold
> For all the brave tears and ultimate spasm,
> So civilized were your thin hands, I marvel
> They too, like jellyfishes, came from protoplasm.
>
> O ineffable cheeks of rhododendron bloom,
> It cannot be you've withered so mortally!
> Your husband is heartbroken—he said so,
> Winking at his cocktail, talking dollars carefully.
>
> Dear Lady, it is revealed that you were twenty-six
> And died giving us an homunculus with bald head;
> May your black hair darken even the dark Styx,
> May your soul have no tears, forgetful of protoplasm.

[8] June 20, 1922.
[9] Tate passed these on to Davidson to read, and in them Davidson first read parts of *Ulysses*.

We buried you in the unremissive ground.
I went home. Somewhere I heard the clang of a hearse.
You are very far away, dear Lady—
As I light this cigarette—and under an inscrutable curse.[10]

Tate's study of Crane was close. For instance, when Davidson was having trouble rhyming the word *counter* in his poem "Dryad," but felt he could not give the word up, Tate urged him to leave the line unrhymed, referring him to Crane's "Praise for an Urn," in the June *Dial*:

You will notice that Crane uses an unrhymed stanza as the norm, and breaks it only in the one case of two stanzas in enjambement, and then he rhymes the first and third line of the first stanza in an apparently casual manner, but really for the purpose of greater rigidity, knowing that eight unrhymed lines in irregular quick tetrameter won't hold together alone. I can't use it so freely as Crane, but there is something of the kind in "Elegy"—where, in the third stanza, I break the norm by rhyming the first and third lines as a surprise, but I pull it together again by the echo-rhyme "protoplasm," on the first stanza, in the fourth line. This same general scheme was used in the last century by the French poets, notably Laforgue, and it is not lacking in English even in Samson Agonistes. And so I implore you not to ruin a good poem with a bad rhyme.[11]

Davidson gave close attention to Tate's advice. He too was stimulated by Tate's "discovery" of Eliot, Laforgue, and Crane, although he wrote that he had purchased a copy of Eliot's poems and wondered ruefully if his dollar and a quarter were well spent.[12] He was writing poems in which he attempted a new, satiric tone— "Dryad," "Ecclesiasticus" (I and II), "Priapus Younger," "Naiad," and "Corymba." Passages from these last two named indicate the direction in which he was moving:

Nothing could dull that magic whispering,
Imperious on the river's copper slant,

[10] "Elegy for Eugenesis," *The Fugitive*, I, 3 (October, 1922), 92.
[11] July 12, 1922.
[12] To Tate, June 17, 1922.

Or hide from her the vague forms flickering
In the haunted depths, darting and vigilant.

Bathers ashore were cultivating a tan,
The fat and the lean were gauded cap-a-pie.
She thought that jerseys were not Arethusean,
And a gartered limb to her was monstrosity.[13]

and

Corymba has bound no snood
Upon her yellow hair.
But better so, no doubt,
For the pale youths look elsewhere
At sleek curves and proud glitter
And flesh powdered and bare.

She has gone with a jaded youth
To a sudatorium.
The sweating there is of movement
To a cacophonic drum.
The bodies flex, the arms twine
In rhythmic delirium.[14]

But, though Tate enthusiastically applauded these poems, and though Davidson himself was excited by this burst of creative energy induced by a reading of the moderns, Davidson's use of the new techniques remained essentially external. His impulse to poetry could not be, like Tate's, fundamentally affected by the *zeitgeist*. Tate was eventually to interpret himself and his heritage in terms of the enveloping intellectual climate of the whole literary age; Davidson's poetic insight was always to function best within the intensive realm of a tradition inherited as a human being, who lives within fixed and certain boundaries. Nevertheless, the correspondence between the two men this first summer, when both were experimenting in poetic method, made a rewarding exchange between two creative minds. They exhibited a fine candor in criticizing each other's work. " Congratulations on getting ' Wil-

[13] " Naiad," *An Outland Piper* (Boston and New York: Houghton Mifflin Company, 1924), 39.
[14] " Corymba," *ibid.*, 32.

liam Blake' accepted—that is, personally and in friendly role I congratulate, not artistically," Davidson wrote, "for I still cling to my original mulish idea there."[15] And Tate was frequently quite specific in his condemnation: "I don't like the second line, fifth stanza because of the inversion," he wrote about "Ecclesiasticus I." "You know inversions for the sake of rhyme are my pet *aversions* . . . ."[16]

In fact, the widening chasm between the artistic convictions of these two was becoming apparent. Davidson, in holding out for a more traditional poetry than Tate, could not honestly praise Tate's indirection or his wilful ambiguity:

> Perhaps if you have a fault in any of the poems it is in the direction of obscurity. . . . I can criticize you more, however, for what you don't do than for what you do. There is not, I believe, enough lyrical beauty in the two larger poems. Perhaps, while you are holding these objects up to analysis and to some sarcasm, there ought also to be an element of pity (Stanley's phrase) which would naturally express itself in beauty of a regretful, poignant sort rather than in hard, chiselled language. There should be a little more warmth (Curry's phrase) . . . . I have always heard a lot of talk about objectivity in writing, but I have never been able to conceive how in the world it can exist . . . . One must have an attitude toward his object; one must pity or scorn or accept; one cannot *simply* analyze.[17]

Nor could Davidson sympathize with the kind of modernism, dispensed in *The Dial, The Little Review,* or *Secession,* which Tate was finding so heady. In returning a copy of *Secession,* Davidson wrote that he found it to be "hokum, very smart, very sophisticated, but nevertheless hokum."[18]

But he was willing to continue trying the new attitudes and techniques. Tate had praised "Ecclesiasticus," had said it was almost on his own "posted ground."[19] So Davidson tried another in

[15] To Tate, June 25, 1922.
[16] To Davidson, July 12, 1922.
[17] To Tate, July 8, 1922.
[18] To Tate, July 15, 1922.
[19] To Davidson, July 12, 1922.

the same vein, "Ecclesiasticus II," on which he commented, "To tell the truth, I think it is easier to write this kind of thing than the other that I have been dealing in more, and for that reason I am a little inclined to doubt the artistic sincerity of those who affect this style, including you and myself both!"[20] Tate replied that he felt almost as Davidson did about *Secession*, "checked only by an opposite tendency to sympathize with almost anything revolutionary, sensible or not, and at the same time to derogate conservatism of all kinds."[21] But he did not like the second "Ecclesiasticus" as well as the first. He felt that it was "controversial, polemical; hence limited, like John's [Ransom's] 'Armageddon,'" the last line of which he considered to be a veritable "sermon."

Tate was certain that the issues involved in poetry were purely aesthetic, not philosophic or moralistic. "If I write a poem to my left foot, it would certainly take precedence over some other thing to man's immortal soul—provided I am a poet," he argued. "It's the man who writes the poem and not the arbitrarily chosen theme."[22] But Davidson's reply was dogged: "I still say, that, other things being equal, if one of two poems has a bigger theme than another that poem is a greater, though maybe not a better, poem."[23] And about Tate's two "Duchess" poems, Davidson commented, "These forms are too difficult, too deliberately casual, to bring artistic pleasure except to a very small group of extremely sophisticated people . . . ."[24] He was certain, too, that "free verse" was impossible: "I could not admit an analogy between poetry and music, except in the minor matters of rhythm and tone-color. There is where the Free Verse set went wrong, with their vague talk of 'cadence.' Their idea of a musical cadence transferred into a form of language-art pleased me very much until

[20] To Tate, July 15, 1922.
[21] To Davidson, July 21, 1922.
[22] *Ibid.*
[23] To Tate, July 25, 1922.
[24] To Tate, August 13, 1922. There is no record now of a second "Duchess of Malfi" poem, nor does Tate remember ever having composed more than one on this subject. But Davidson's letters all through this period mention two.

I found out how very unsatisfactory it was—it simply could not be done with words as a medium." [25]

The basic issues upon which the whole group of Fugitives were in disagreement reveal themselves in these letters: the problem of language (may a poet use the one he comes by or must he invent his own?); of meaning (may he approach his subject directly or must he take a more circuitous route?); of theme (may he attempt an affirmative treatment on a large scale or must he merely essay to handle well a small portion of experience?). But there was a genuine current of affection and esteem running between these two men, perhaps a closer relationship than existed between any of the others. Davidson's traditionalism—of a different sort from Ransom's but operating in conjunction with it—acted as a check upon Tate so that he was never to reach the state of disjunction in his poetry of other brilliant writers with whom he was later allied. Conversely, that Davidson received sustenance from Tate he readily acknowledged. "I know you are a hard-boiled rascal on criticism," he wrote, "and I am quite sure that you are better posted on the particular subject-matter and technique that I have recently assayed than any others of our Fugitive group. Likewise, you have given me keener and more helpful criticisms than anybody that ever read my poems, and your ideas and theories have wonderfully quickened and leavened my stodgy mind. So I am greatly indebted to you. You will never find me unappreciative . . . ." [26]

For all their large differences, their view of the world was essentially similar, inherited as it was from a traditional society; indeed none of the Fugitives (except, perhaps, Merrill Moore) felt themselves forced into either of the dominant poetic methods of the day: the one, of presenting the poetic object in terms of observables with no indication of its inner nature; the other, of analyzing intricately the mental and emotional processes involved in confronting the object. Despite their seeming opposition, both

[25] To Tate, July 25, 1922.
[26] To Tate, August 23, 1922.

these strategies, in denying universals, deny the poet's ability to say anything truthful. The Fugitive poets had grown up in a world where there was no doubt of the universals. They had made their acquaintance with learning in a university which had as its ideal the coherence of knowledge into one vast scheme, the nature of which was ultimately religious. Hence they could never for long doubt the importance nor the efficacy of the individual's interpretation of his universe.

The Fugitive meetings went on through the summer; at a July conclave Bill Elliott had read a poem twelve pages long on the subject of Mount Everest; [27] and in August there was a meeting at which Elliott, Frierson, Johnson, and Moore (besides the hosts) were present, Moore having written twenty poems in one week.[28] By the latter part of August, Davidson was back in Nashville from Camp Kawasawa. A letter he wrote to Tate at this time describes in detail a meeting of the circle:

We had a great debate at the Fugitive meeting Saturday night— the old controversy of the Moderns vs. Ancients—in which our guest, a Dr. Lockhart [Lacy Lockert] of Kenyon College, Ohio, declaimed against modernism, supported mainly by Stanley, and opposed by Ransom and others. I took little part, for I am hesitant to crystallize my present vague and nebulous ideas into comments on theories of poetry, only ranging myself against the Secession bunch, the Dadaists, and the Dialists (of the extreme type). The debate lasted until past two o'clock, but left the combatants apparently unexhausted and mutually un-convinced. I read your DUCHESS poems, with an embarrassed smile, I must confess, when I came to the passages that floored me. (You had a poor reader; I really didn't read them well, and felt very repentant. You would have been disgusted with my reading.) But nevertheless, they seemed to make a good impression, on the whole. They were more talked about than CORYMBA. The general opinion, much to my surprise, seemed to favor the second of your poems as the better one of the pair—all except Sidney and myself, who favored 1. But they did

[27] Merrill Moore had written of this to Tate (Tate to Davidson, July 21, 1922).

[28] Davidson to Tate, August 4, 1922.

not render any criticisms worth while, either for you or for me on CORYMBA—except the point about the trilobite. I had not then received your letter. In fact, though we had a good meeting, the Fugitives didn't seem to get up much enthusiasm over any poem read. So you and I are in the same boat there. I fear that we are going to be looked on as the "enfants terribles," the Turrible Two, in the Fugitive club now. William Frierson gave a criticism of the poems read at the previous meeting none of which I was familiar with except Stanley's group and my own, which I had mailed in. The Fugitives seem to like ECCLESIASTICUS best among mine. Really, I believe they are a little bit surprised at me, but they were complimentary on the whole, and think I have developed, apparently.

Ransom read a two and a half page poem of an extremely philosophic nature, which sounded very good, but which I couldn't really form an opinion of, as he didn't supply carbons. Steve's "Meditation" I thought very good, and also Stanley's new venture, which ought to be a fine poem after some revision. It took well. Bill Elliott read a very short one about a tumble-bug laying the foundations of the Egyptian pyramids. It was terse and epigrammatic, and apparently excellent, though I didn't see a copy of it, either. Mr. Frank's and Sidney's were both too esoteric for me. I hear, however, that Sidney has written recently some very good stuff, none of which I have yet seen. Merrill's two poems were pretty fair, but too hastily done, I think. He needs to cultivate restraint. The rush of language carries him away. The Fugitives jumped all over one of his poems particularly. William Frierson read a sort of prose fantasy on Oxford which we all liked very much. He also read a paper on certain theories of poetry which was too much for me to absorb from an oral reading. I am going to get it and digest it, for he's a man of valuable ideas. I got too sleepy to be a good listener. Not used to being up so late. And that's about all I have to report of the Fugitive meeting. There is to be another Monday night. I hope you'll have a new poem here by then, so that I can read it.[29]

At the next meeting, to which Davidson had referred in his letter to Tate, Lacy Lockert was again the guest, and the evening ended in a lineup of the members against him. Lockert, an ad-

[29] August 23, 1922.

Donald Davidson, about 1927, at the time of the publication of *The Tall Men*.

Robert Penn Warren in 1924.

Merrill Moore in the summer of 1923. He went to Germany as a seaman and was a month late entering school in the fall.

The Fugitive group assembled for the Fugitive Reunion, Nashville, May 4, 1956. Present are, bottom row, Tate, Ransom, Davidson; second row, Starr, Stevenson, Warren; top row, Elliott, Moore, Jesse Wills, and Hirsch.

mirer of the group but dead set against modern poetry, attacked the
Fugitives for being "sloppy technicians, obscurantists, and too
modernly modern." [30] But, though the poets were united against
so romantic a view as Lockert's, this momentary common front did
little toward eliminating their disagreement among themselves. As
Davidson wrote to Tate: "You, Ransom, Bill Elliott, Moore, and
myself are certainly more or less ranged against Stanley, Stevenson,
Hirsch, and Frank. I think the division is really a good thing." [31]
Actually, however, the divergence was more complicated than
Davidson's remark indicated. Although the ones with whom he
grouped himself were advocates of a "modern" attitude toward
poetry, Tate was alone in his championing of ultramodernism.
And his proselytizing with his friends did not succeed. The postscript to Davidson's letter indicates the braking action which Ransom and Davidson exerted upon Tate's exuberance: "Went to
see Ransom Sunday. He thinks, as I do, that you are doing remarkable things, he likes about the same poems of yours that I do, and he
also advises against going to extreme lengths in modernism." [32]

At the meeting, as a matter of fact, Johnson had read "his idea
of *your* [Tate's] idea of a poem," which caused a great deal of glee.
Tate, replying, gave warning that he would be in Nashville the
first week of September and threatened the conservatives in the
group—particularly Johnson—with some of their own methods.[33]
In considerably better health, Tate was coming through Nashville
on his way to his home in Ashland. After the September meeting
specified in his letter, he would not be present at a Fugitive session
until the following spring, when he would return to Vanderbilt
to complete his degree.

The fall issue of the magazine, which Ransom had edited, was
printed and in the mails before October 1. Ridley Wills, who was
later to become a member, gave the group the names of several
likely prospects for the journal; accordingly, the members sent out

[30] Davidson to Tate, August 29, 1922.
[31] *Ibid.*
[32] *Ibid.*
[33] To Davidson, August 31, 1922.

a number of complimentary copies, in the hope that a view of the magazine itself would convince literary men of its quality.

The third issue of *The Fugitive* gave evidence of a growing awareness of itself as a publication, with responsibilities as well as a few airs to assume. The poets disclosed their real identity, the pseudonyms being discarded, according to an editoral note, "for a number of good reasons." A chief one of these can be surmised: many reviewers had presumed the work to be that of one man— John Ransom—operating under various *noms de plume*, an idea which must have been disconcerting to the other writers. Another explanatory note concerning the puzzling organization of the magazine evidently seemed in order to the editors:

> It puts in a single record the latest verses of a number of men who have for several years been in the habit of assembling to swap poetical wares and to elaborate the Ars Poetica. These poets acknowledge no trammels upon the independence of their thought, they are not overpoweringly academic, they are in tune with the times in the fact that to a large degree in their poems they are self-convicted experimentalists. They differ so widely and so cordially from each other on matters poetical that all were about equally chagrined when two notable critics, on the evidence of the two previous numbers, construed them as a single person camouflaging under many pseudonyms. The procedure of publication is simply to gather up the poems that rank the highest, by general consent of the group, and take them down to the publisher.

This editorial perhaps made the process look a bit too simple, overlooking the long hours of toil inherent in the mere mechanics of publishing a journal, not to mention the lengthy wrangles over the selection of poems. But the project was young, and spirits were high; all pitched in enthusiastically on soliciting subscriptions and performing the various other time-consuming tasks. Davidson and Stevenson did most of what are usually considered editorial chores: proofreading and makeup, correspondence, and distribution, though from the beginning the understanding was that all were editors in the matter of choice of contents of the journal and of decisions on policy.

But Ransom had so far written the two introductory editorials.

In this issue he extended his critical remarks into a review of a book by a person of some note—*On English Poetry*, by Robert Graves. The review is a defense of traditionalism, one in which Ransom merely made use of Graves's book in order to pursue an idea that seems to have been already well thought out. *On English Poetry*, Ransom believed, did not touch upon the most absorbing problem facing poets in America: that of prosody. American poets could be said to "abhor the thought of changing the considered phrase that perfectly expresses them in the interest of an irrelevance called meter." But, Ransom wondered, is meter actually irrelevant?

. . . it would seem at least likely that the determinate mathematical regularities of meter which are imposed upon the words have as much to do with the total effect of a poem as, in a sister art, the determinate geometrical regularities of outline which are imposed upon the stones have to do with the total effect of a work of architecture.

But one cannot dogmatize here. The charming personality of Graves expresses itself without embarrassment in prosodical verse. But some of the most brilliant of contemporary minds have apparently been unable to do this. To us even who have every encouragement to be traditionalists, their work at some points seems so perfected that we would not wish it to be otherwise, their phrases so final as not to admit the suggestion of change. In illustration we want nothing better to cite than the Horatian Epode of Allen Tate's which appears in these pages. We do not believe that these words could be altered without lowering the given plane of sophistication, and that would only be to destroy one beauty on the lean prospect of getting another one.

Tate's poem is indeed one of the most striking in the issue. In fact, though the summer's work had had its effect on several of the Fugitives, the most noticeable difference lay in the work of Tate, who for the first time [34] printed in *The Fugitive* poems that he was later to consider worthy of preservation in his first volume— "To Oenia in Wintertime" and "Horatian Epode to the Duchess of Malfi." These two pieces and his other three in the issue ("Battle of Murfreesboro," "Elegy for Eugenesis," and "Non

[34] If we except his translation from Sappho, "Farewell to Anactoria," which appeared in the summer issue preceding.

Omnis Moriar ") display the attitude which may with a few reservations be said to underlie Tate's later poetic method: the relating of his subject to himself, with the knowledge that the poet cannot deal with things in themselves, but must indicate always his own reaction to them. The Self, confronted by the apparent realities of the past, seeking always to come to an understanding of itself in relation to them—this is the subject of Tate's poetry, leading him to draw upon all the processes of the mind in his verse. As he wrote later to Davidson: "Poetry is to me successive instances of the whole rhythm of thought, and that includes reason, emotion, extralogical experience, or as I put it a year or so ago, the entire phantasy of sensation." [35] This method demanded for him an obscure poetry—although his aim was not toward obscurity as an end, but toward the creation of an intricate texture of imagery and allusion out of the associations which a sensitive and well-read mind provided. And, despite their obscurity, the early poems of Tate's are far from formless.

The other poems in the fall *Fugitive* are less *avante garde* than Tate's. Davidson's work reveals his current indecision about poetic expression. "Pot Macabre" and "The Amulet" are in his earlier vein of myth-making; but "A Dead Romanticist," "Censored," and "Requiescat" reflect the impact of the new experimental techniques, evidencing themselves in his poetry chiefly in the form of bitter satire. Of Ransom's poetry, "Boris of Britain," "The Vagrant," and "Fall of Leaf" mark a further departure into allegory, an extension of the method of "Necrological," in the preceding issue. Though clumsy and grotesque, they accomplish their purpose—of giving an oblique insight into life's absurdities—without involving the author as commentator. They create a universe in which people are caught between two contradictory terms of human existence, and they depict this universe in a diction that is at once ironic and tender, pedantic and colloquial. The other poems in the issue are unremarkable, with perhaps only William Elliott's two worthy of note, in that they represent his

[35] July 25, 1925.

first appearance in the magazine. He and Frierson were added to the masthead in this issue as members *in absentia*, but Frierson contributed no poems. Elliott's " Epigrams " and " Roundhead and Cavalier," both in free verse, exhibit the terseness and rather too-easy cleverness which often mark that form.

The local papers were somewhat chary in their reviews of the third issue. On October 8 the *Tennessean* ran an interview with Elliott, which Davidson felt was "as stale as old cheese." [36] The *Banner* carried nothing. On October 16 a column in the *Tennessean*, written by Mary Pepper, a Vanderbilt alumna, contained a brief review of the magazine, commending particularly Merrill Moore and finding Ransom's style evident in the works of the other writers.[37] But *The Fugitive* was receiving increasing recognition from sources outside Nashville. Alice Hunt Bartlett, writing an article on American poetry for the London *Poetry Review*,[38] spoke highly of the magazine; and *The Literary Digest*, reporting on her article, ran a picture of the Nashville magazine along with about ten other national poetry journals.[39] Another literary figure, Horace Walpole, lunching with the Vanderbilt English faculty as a guest of the Centennial Club, was impressed with the magazine; it was a fine piece of work, he said, with "no mediocre poetry in it." [40]

The Fugitives invited two cousins, Ridley and Jesse Wills, to a session on October 7, and by November invited them to join. At a meeting about November 20, Jesse read two sonnets which the members liked exceedingly. The dauntless Ridley, however, read poems that caused "considerable debate." [41] Ridley was chosen to be critic at the next meeting and indicated that he was going to tear into the group.

Ridley Wills was back in Vanderbilt to complete his degree

[36] To Tate, October 8, 1922.
[37] October 16, 1922.
[38] " What America Is Doing for Poetry," October, 1922; cited in " The Rage for Poetry," *The Literary Digest*, LXXXV (December 2, 1922), 33.
[39] *Ibid.*
[40] Davidson to Tate, December 14, 1922.
[41] Davidson to Tate, November 24, 1922.

after an absence of five years. He had left to enlist in the army in 1917, joining the Luke Lea regiment along with Bill Elliott and Bill Frierson, and after the war had done free-lance journalistic writing in New York and had published one novel, *Hoax*,[42] which the reviewers found promising. In his student days Wills had been an irrepressible journalist and prankster, he and Frierson making up an indomitable team, involved in all sorts of skirmishes and practical jokes. Just before the end of school in 1917, Wills, as one of the editors of *The Hustler*, had written a column defending a few freshmen who were about to be expelled from school for throwing water on a faculty member from an upstairs window. In his editorial Wills emphasized the difference between such boyish pranks and really serious matters, such as cheating. Apparently the authorities did not approve of his defense, and when he left school to join the army, it was with some relief on both sides. When he returned, he was as bright and flippant as ever. By virtue of having published a novel he felt a certain authority in literary affairs and accepted as his duty the task of enlivening the intellectual life on the campus.

Ridley's cousin, Jesse, was five years his junior. A native Nashvillian, Jesse Wills had come to Vanderbilt in 1918, entering the Students' Army Training Corps. He had studied four years of Latin and had done other similarly rigorous work for his preparatory education at Wallace University School; but under the new regimen at Vanderbilt, he took freshman courses in Spanish, economics, and "War Issues," as well as the more traditional ones of English, history, mathematics, and French. English was one of young Wills's best subjects; he first took up writing verse, however, for a purely practical reason. During the fall of 1920, when Ransom announced that he would accept poems as substitutes for themes in his English 13 class, Wills turned in three sonnets. Ransom was impressed enough to see to it that Wills kept writing poetry; and during the next two years Wills found a few more literary opportunities, chiefly through the Calumet Club, where he made friends

---

[42] New York: George H. Doran and Company, 1922.

with Davidson and Tate. After his graduation, however, he resisted the urging of Mims and other English department members, deciding not to pursue graduate study in literature but to take up his responsibilities in his father's firm, the National Life and Accident Insurance Company. Thus, by the time he had become a member of the Fugitive circle, attending the late, long-drawn-out meetings, he was already a young businessman, his neat, quiet appearance belying his poetic capability.

Plans for a December Visitors' Issue of the magazine began taking shape soon after the fall term was underway. The group was fortunate in being offered poetry by three fairly well-known literary figures: William Alexander Percy, Robert Graves, and Witter Bynner. Percy was interested in the group chiefly because of his concern for Southern literature; the Fugitives, he wrote, had helped put the South " on the map, as far as poetry is concerned." [43] Bynner had been an early friend and admirer of the group. Graves contributed chiefly because of his interest in Ransom. At the Fugitive meeting November 4, the December editorship fell to Stevenson, his committee to be Johnson and Moore. Ridley Wills proposed Ransom for permanent editor, but his suggestion was vetoed.[44]

Many of the members were in favor of delegating one of the group as editor, in order that the business of answering correspondence, mailing out subscription copies, and turning in the material to the printer might be done more efficiently. The issue had been late the last two times it had appeared, and editorial matters were allowed to drag along indefinitely. Poems sent in were kept a long time—some of them disgracefully so—before being returned.[45] However, when they were sent back to their authors, they were usually

[43] To Tate, October 11, 1922.

[44] Ransom to Tate, November 5, 1922.

[45] One man who had sent in a poem and a stamped, addressed envelope in May, 1922, wrote to the editors twice after having received no word from them for months. Finally, almost a year later, he sent the poem to *American Legion Weekly*, where it was accepted. He became worried then (needlessly) that *The Fugitive* might consider that it had a right to the poem.

accompanied by a letter of seriously considered criticism, most often
written by Davidson or Tate.

But since much of the labor fell upon Davidson, who had to
slight his own affairs to work for *The Fugitive*, some of the members—Tate and Johnson particularly—favored making him editor.
But others, chiefly Ransom, opposed the move; so the matter was
allowed to rock along, a topic of dissidence at each meeting, but
one never threshed out. All during the fall of 1922 the question
was argued. On November 16 Davidson wrote Tate—now working
for his brother's firm, the United Collieries in Ashland and Cincinnati—that the topic was to be taken up at the next Fugitive
meeting: "We are going to make a move for better organization
Saturday night. Wish you were here." But nothing, apparently,
resulted from the discussion, for by December 4 Davidson was still
concerned with the same matter: "This organization question is
almost ready to come to a head now. *Something* has got to be done,
and something will be done. I think the membership are in a better
mood now for considering the question than they were last month
and before. Perhaps we will wait until Curry arrives to work out
a plan; I don't know, though. I have long been in favor of pushing
things to a conclusion." [46] The members decided, however, that
henceforward a single person should edit each issue, just as
Stevenson was in charge of the forthcoming December number.
The brethren looked forward to this next issue with a good deal
of excitement, since within its covers they were for the first time
playing host to other literary men.

Tate found himself ill at ease in the world of commerce and,
with his brother, before long realized that he was not cut out to
be a businessman. He planned a trip to New York, and Ransom
wrote him a letter of introduction to Christopher Morley. To
Tate, Ransom commented: "I think you are doing the inevitable
thing in having a fling at New York, though I am skeptical about
any good man's making his way there by literature pure and unde-
filed." [47] He feared that Tate might forget about *The Fugitive* if he

[46] Davidson to Tate, December 4, 1922.
[47] November 5 [1922].

became embroiled in the literary world of New York; and the group's loss of him would be calamitous, Ransom felt, since Tate was essential to "the scheme."

But Tate was not likely to forget *The Fugitive*. His trip to New York fell through, and he was forced to remain for a while in Cincinnati, from which location he sent in a poem and an editorial for the approaching issue of the magazine. Both caused a considerable stir. Tate sent the two pieces to Davidson, asking him to read them at the next meeting. The poem, "Nuptials," a vignette of life spent in despair in a commercialized society, Davidson considered "real poetry," he wrote Tate. It possessed "the proper balance—between the modern and the traditional—the medium in which you are destined to do your best work." [48] Perhaps, he felt, there might be still in it a little too much "of the Eliot tinge," and he did wonder if one did not owe it to himself "to pick more elevated material . . . ."

Davidson showed the poem to Stevenson, who, writing to Tate before the meetings, praised it highly, even though it did give him "an immediate impulse to go and bathe." [49] His praise delighted Tate, as he wrote, "to the point of aphasia" and inspired him to take eighteen out of the next twenty-four hours for the composition of another poem ("These Deathy Leaves," which he described as being "as pure as Mrs. Hemans"). After declaring that it was "great fun to do the modern stuff," but that the more traditional patterns offered "a unique satisfaction," he commented, "Of course this is a dreadful confession for the youthful harbinger of guts, ovaries, and death to make; but I'm sure you won't give me away to the Brothers, who would straightway cry, 'I told you so!'" [50]

Tate's editorial, entitled "Whose Ox?" chiefly concerned itself with the problem that Ransom had touched upon in his review of Graves's book in the preceding *Fugitive*: the relation of traditional form to modern poetry. In the following manner Tate explained to Stevenson his sending the piece, even though it was unsolicited:

[48] November 8, 1922.
[49] November 12, 1922.
[50] To Stevenson, November 14, 1922.

You may wonder at my presumption in contributing an editorial. It came about this way. While I was in Nashville last time, John and Don suggested that I write about the Procession, and I have done so, dealing with it in its two main aspects—radical and conservative. I believe that I have made a point not often emphasized, if indeed it has been given this particular application at all, and it may be worth printing. It seems to me that since we shall probably attract more notice through our visitors than we have got before it might be well to spread the news that we are at least aware of the large issues, and that if we ignore the more radical tendencies in the main it is because we have a defensible reason for doing so. My point is simply that the two main tendencies have each an equal claim to consideration; that the difficulty heretofore has lain in a confusion of issues; and that now, since Eliot has recently achieved the model of the extreme type, it is the office of criticism to maintain two standards so long as both genres produce notable things. . . .

Any changes you may suggest I shall be more than glad to know. I am rather keen to see how the thing strikes Stanley the incorrigible. I believe he has been converted to Modernism via Conrad Aiken and sich-like; and so I suppose I shall have to ask you to think of him when you come to my allusion to the "Side-Show." [51]

Stevenson wrote back his appreciation for the essay, and Tate replied, again referring to his presentiment that "Stanley and his analytical hounds, nose close to the scent . . ." would not like it, in spite of the fact that Tate was sure that he had struck "the beloved golden mean." [52]

Writing before the Fugitive meeting, Davidson called the editorial a "hum-dinger," and said that he, Ransom, and Stevenson were for it, although Ransom had suggested it might be made "a little less of a general pronunciamento . . . by a change in pronouns [from *we* to *I*]." [53]

Tate's editorial was an attempt to state more clearly the aesthetic position of *The Fugitive*. "We are told," he wrote, "that we evince a uniformity of outlook, of tone; that we have the earmarks of a

[51] Undated letter, sometime early in November, 1922.
[52] Tate to Stevenson, November 14, 1922.
[53] To Tate, November 16, 1922.

School." But he would qualify the unity of the Fugitives: theirs was a uniformity with interesting deviations, these divergencies lying within mechanical problems—versification, diction, composition. Heretofore, he maintained, it had been generally agreed that the poet's product must represent a comprehensible part of life; but the inadequacy of this premise was possible: ". . . perhaps the world as it is doesn't afford accurate correlatives of all the emotional complexes and attitudes; and so the artist, or poet, is justified in not only re-arranging (cf. entire English tradition) but remaking, remoulding, in a subjective order, the stuff he must necessarily work with—the material world."

This problem of representation, Tate wrote, was central to the poet, since it determined to a large degree his diction and his prosody. T. S. Eliot, for instance, had shown "for all time" in *The Waste Land* "the necessity, in special cases, of an aberrant versification." Most of the experimental verse then being written, Tate agreed, was mediocre; but mediocre poetry was hardly limited to either unconventional or traditional techniques. "It is a question, rather, of Whose Ox": "Perhaps T. S. Eliot has already pointed the way for this and the next generation. But there are and will be many still faithful to an older, if not more authentic, tradition; for the old modes are not yet sapped. However, the Moderns have arrived, and their claim is by no means specious. *The Fugitive* doesn't attempt arbitration; it is humble; besides, it has other fish to fry. But which tradition can the American honestly accept? A fair, if stale question." [54]

After the meeting, Davidson reported a favorable decision for the editorial but indecision over the poem,[55] most of the group having reservations about it because of its sordid subject. Hirsch had called it a "versification of a Ben Hecht novel." And, although the editorial was "well-received on the whole," Davidson enumerated a few points on which suggestions had been made for changes in it. Some thought Tate was perhaps too certain about the absolute value of Eliot's *Waste Land*; others thought he had in-

---

[54] "Whose Ox?" First draft, MS.
[55] To Tate, November 24, 1922.

correctly made a distinction between artist and poet, meaning perhaps painter and poet; and a few felt that his editorial *we* should be changed to *I*. But Davidson's comments ended on a tone of high praise: " I think everybody took it as a brilliant piece of work; none of us, except John, could write such an editorial." [56]

Tate reacted to this news with his customary impulsiveness, agitated particularly at separation from the group when the Big Issue was being produced. (He wrote in his November 27 letter to Stevenson: "And to think I'm away when the great show is going on!") Unable to argue his case at meetings, he felt sure his principles did not receive a fair treatment from some of the members. Sending a revised version of the editorial to Stevenson, he wrote: " I believe that the chief objections to the thing were based on the fear that the members en masse might be held responsible for my radical and perfectly terrible views, so I've changed a few pronouns and made other things clearer. . . . May I hazard the remark that if some of us weren't so lazy and would read a little to find out what is going on in the world which we contemn so lustily, perhaps there would be among us less prostration before the Idols of the Cave?" [57] But then he added, " Now please, Steve, laugh at this bile." Stevenson did better. He smiled sympathetically and undertook to explain.

. . . I wish gently but firmly to disabuse your mind of certain concepts now seeming lodged there. . . . I believe that you will remember, upon reflection, that the editorial policy of the group, so far as there has been one, is to make each person responsible for his editorial dictums, not with any inferiority or fear complexes in mind on the part of the rest of the editors, but owing simply to non-subscription to views expressed, or to that genial schismatism to which you allude. Really, you can hardly dye a man saffron for refusing to take responsibility for something he doesn't conscientiously agree with . . . .[58]

He made secure his argument by pointing out that Tate himself would not want to subscribe to an editorial written, say, by Hirsch.

[56] *Ibid.*
[57] November 27, 1922.
[58] To Tate, December 2, 1922.

Actually, the conservatism which so irked Tate at this time was one of the merits of the Fugitive association. Different from a narrow conventionalism, this reluctance to follow new theories held in check any programmatic approach to poetry, so that one persuasive person with insight was not allowed to pull the others over to his point of view. A willingness on the part of each of the poets to attack the work of others and to defend his own made not for unscrupulous egotism and backbiting, but for clarification of ideas and an enforced toleration of dissimilar views. Tate and Davidson, for instance, were convinced that Hirsch's " Nebrismus " was not of sufficient merit for publication in the magazine; nevertheless the committee voted it in. But most often, certainly, what was castigated within the group was the Eliot-Crane-Pound style.

At the next meeting, early in December, Johnson and Moore each read a poem; Davidson read two poems by Tate and one of his own; and one of the other members read two sent in by W. A. Percy. Then, after Stevenson had read his editorial, Ridley Wills, in the rôle of the evening's critic, assailed the group roundly. Davidson reported on the criticisms:

> He claims there is not enough modulation and shading in Fugitive poetry, says we all have " anthologies of perfect phrases." Charges also that we do not often enough conceive poems as wholes and don't write in a unity of mood . . . . Well, there was a warm debate, in which Sidney and I finally locked horns again on old lines, but without rancor, and in which everybody took interested parts. The evening wound up with an argument on sophistication conducted with Stanley as leader. In short we had a gay time,—quite in the old spirit. The Fugitive crowd are on their feet now, I believe.[59]

Immediately after the December issue was printed, before the magazines were delivered to the editors, Davidson sent Tate two advance copies with his comments. He still had doubts about " Nebrismus," felt that three of Moore's poems were perhaps too many, and was not sure the best choice of his own poems had been made. But, he wrote, " the committee did make some very pleasing

[59] To Tate, December 4, 1922.

variations,—as in their selection, for the most part, of shorter poems in varying moods, thus avoiding the turgidity of some earlier issues." [60] He considered "Nuptials," Stevenson's "He Who Loved Beauty," and Bynner's "Leave Some Apples" the best poems and was pleased with both Tate's and Stevenson's editorials.

Ransom wrote to thank Tate for his dedication of "Nuptials." "I like the compliment immensely," he commented. He did not, however, like Moore's poems in the magazine, nor Stevenson's "Rondeau for Autumn"; and he felt that Johnson's "A Certain Man" should not have been given the "place of honor." The "great poem of the number" he considered Percy's "Safe Secrets." Referring to Ridley Wills's criticism of the group, Ransom expressed his own idea of the Fugitives' limitations: "I think the most of us (not often you) are like jeweller's apprentices; we invent nothing, we hardly see the whole, but we are good at cutting the individual stones. Our patterns that we make out of all our treasures are either nil or they are perfectly standard: WHAT WE LACK IS ESSENTIALLY ARTISTIC TASTE. Would it be painter's parlance to say that we can paint but we can't compose?" [61]

Ransom's metaphor describing the group of poet-smiths seems applicable to their array of diverse gems presented in the December issue. The lack of artistic taste which he mentioned allowed the inclusion of a few poems dangerously below the Fugitive standard, ironically enough, one of them the piece Ransom had called the great poem of the issue. Of the four guests, one other besides Percy—Bynner—had contributed a poem of no artistic consequence. David Morton, the first Vanderbilt graduate to achieve literary recognition, was represented by a well-constructed sonnet of a quality roughly equivalent to the work of the less serious Fugitives. Robert Graves's two poems were something of an asset to the issue, chiefly because of their witty and flavorful language.

The members' contributions are, for the most part, below their usual standards. The three-page poem by Hirsch, "Nebrismus,"

[60] To Tate, December 17, 1922.
[61] To Tate, December 17, 1922.

two poems by Ridley Wills, one by Frierson, and two by Johnson fail to exhibit any artistic merit. One of the seldom-heard members, Frierson, who never seriously meant to be a poet, had sent in a dozen-lined tirade against Fugitive poetry; entitled "Reactions on the October Fugitive," it begins

> I am tired of being bitter.
> I am weary of the disillusionists,
> And of those who tell with uncommon zest
>   that corpses stink—
> As a joke on the Christians.

A comment on the "anti-poetic" trend of the group, this poem voices the attitude of Elliott and Johnson as well as of its author. Stevenson's two poems are, like all of his work, technically unimpeachable. They contain some lines of striking lyric beauty, such as

> When twigs, gray, black and brown through all the glade
> Loose their slow-sailing weight of sapless leaves,

and

> Dolorous, here he made his stand
> Like those who are beaten,
> Behind, the mountains, and in front, the sea,
> To the west a rock by the brown river eaten.

But Stevenson had not learned to avoid the tight, neat ending which drives home the "point"; as a result, these poems lack strength. Merrill Moore's work falls short on quite another count; his lines are always strong, but unkempt and neglected, the product of a somewhat scandalous liaison with the Muse.

Tate, Davidson, and Ransom, however, contributed work that would have been a credit to any poetry journal. Tate's much-discussed "Nuptials" appeared, a work of interest in his development even if its permanent value is doubtful. The impact of *The Waste Land* is strongly evident in both theme and method, but in "Nuptials" the intense particularization of object and idea

has not subsided into a completely embodied poem. It is most like
Eliot's "Preludes"— a sordid picture of soulless city life, but
without the redeeming beauty of language. And yet "Nuptials" is
not completely out of the line of Tate's work, for in it he makes
his first moral criticism of modern society. His other poem, "These
Deathy Leaves," in which he attempted the traditional mode, is
inconsequential, redeemed only by an occasional Tatian phrase:
"swift white mind's brain," "a quick sculpture of a fresh grace."

Davidson's three poems, like Tate's, show the effect of further
experimentation with the new poetry, but less in fundamental
elements than in texture. Like his verses in the October issue,
these evidence a general tightening of diction, a dropping of
romantic imagery, and a heightening of the sardonic tone:

> Thin lips can make a music,
>   Hateful eyes can see,
> Crooked limbs go dancing
>   To a strange melody.

His poems are, however, still lyrics; and unlike Tate's they retain
numerous traditional elements.

Whereas Tate and Davidson showed the greatest growth in
poetic conception and execution, it was Ransom who contributed
the one really good poem of the issue. "In Process of a Noble
Alliance" is, to make use of Ransom's figure, an exquisitely de-
signed piece of jewelry, far beyond the powers of an apprentice.
If it is form that Ransom conceived to be lacking in Fugitive verses,
this poem, by means of its intensely realized dramatic situation,
refutes its own author:

> Reduce this lady unto marble quickly,
>   Ray her beauty on a glassy plate,
> Rhyme her youth as fast as the granite:
>   Take her where she trembles, and do not wait,
> For now in funeral white they lead her
>   And crown her Queen of the House of No Love.
> A dirge then for her beauty, Musicians!
> Ye harping the springe that catches the dove.

Ransom's other poem of the issue is a not very successful investigation of the short-narrative allegory style which he later manipulated with great skill.

The prose contents of *The Fugitive* consisted of Tate's editorial, slightly amended as the other members had suggested, and short editorial comments by Stevenson: "THE YEARLING FUGITIVE LOOKS BACK with some pride and not a little amazement upon its initial twelve months. A genial critic noted our first adventuring, wandering in the Sahara of the Bozart, while we now with surprise and glee gloat over many a sudden oasis." Acknowledging response from Canada, California, London, and Berlin, "as well as from those who, from reasons of proximity or friendship" might be expected to lend support, *The Fugitive* announced its intention of publishing on a bimonthly schedule.

But the December number of the journal had provoked heated argument which had remained essentially unresolved, and so the Fugitives were left with an awareness of ineradicable differences among themselves concerning aesthetic theory and practice. Tate's poetry, since it represented the most daringly experimental attitude in their midst, became the locus around which each member graphed his own poetic beliefs. Describing a meeting on December 16, Ransom reported to Tate: "Your new poems offered last night under Don's sponsorship created a good deal of comment. The party lines were drawn about as usual, Whip Johnson and Whip Ransom polling their full party strengths."[62] But one "sinner" was saved, he said—Stevenson, who at this meeting stoutly defended the modern point of view. At the gathering, Hirsch recited four of his poems, and, according to Davidson's account, Mr. Frank "delivered a criticism which called Plato, Socrates, Cicero, Webster's Dictionary, and other learned authority to witness that lofty themes, not simply technique, is what we want to lay hold of."[63] Davidson read two of his own poems—"Twilight Excursion" and "Essene." Ransom read a poem called "Max."

[62] *Ibid.*
[63] *Ibid.*

But it was Tate's poems, read by Davidson, that became the *cause célèbre* of the evening.

All the members agreed in liking "Mary MacDonald," a smooth little lyric without much to distinguish it. But "Teeth," a more daring piece, provoked debate. Except for the first stanza, Tate later said, this poem was partly a parody of "modernism," written to pull the leg of the group.

> No music comes to sorrow like a thief,
>   No twitter of birds, as in Spring, for eucharist:
> Only the soft thrust of a falling leaf
>   And in the mind the bloodless lips of Christ.
>
> You cannot feel the teeth of this pain
>   Who gloat over the subtle movie queen,
> Howbeit your Lalage cut her throat in vain
>   When she comes home, seeing what might have been.
>
> (The composite image of spangled death and fear
>   Does not erase a chiselled arm—nor keep
> Alas, one's business friend from mixing beer
>   Inextricably with his concept of female sheep.)
>
> My sorrow is the passing of a look
>   From bending eyes that stiffened to a stare
> As I commented on some vellum book
>   Or lipped a silver phrase about her hair.

Davidson felt the first and fourth stanzas were "as good as anything . . . [Tate] had done"; the other stanzas seemed to him weaker. But to Johnson the poem appeared to be unnecessarily obscure; he considered it "too cryptic" and challenged Tate's trick of going "from the plane of artistic utterance into byplay and parentheses." Ransom defended the poem, chiefly on the basis of its "fine diction." The agreement of the group was finally, as Ransom wrote Tate: ". . . that while it is admitted that the artist is subject, during the act of creation, to marginal impressions of reality and incongruous (seemingly) divergencies, he should not jot these things down too, but should wait until he has made a synthesis of his ideas, and should express this synthesis, suppressing the extraneous and unaffecting grosser material." [64] If this process were not followed, the poem was likely to be too disjected and incoherent.

Ransom's December 17 letter to Tate marked the beginning of a correspondence which, in its exchange of aesthetic theory, was to be of far-reaching importance to both men. Continuing through the years with only slight interruptions, it was a less intimate correspondence than Davidson's and Tate's, less frequent, and less whole. Indeed, it was quite formal in its colloquial gentlemanliness. But it provided the two with their best opponents for philosophical argument, and, though they were to differ at times heatedly, their mutual respect never varied. In this first letter of the series, the chief topic that concerned Ransom was the "Waste Land question," which he had argued before with Tate. Ransom found it difficult, he said, to understand what he took to be a lack of agreement between Eliot's prose and his poetry. In his critical writing Eliot had lamented the absence of a form, a condition which was responsible for the vacuity of the human spirit, the desiccation of the land. Yet in his poetry, Ransom was convinced, Eliot was striving for this form but not attaining it: "The reason he hasn't got it I take to be chiefly because the form has got to be a philosophy and no less." Ransom went on to give what he called some "scattering generalities" about a work of art:

The art-thing sounds like the first immediate transcript of reality, but it isn't; it's a long way from the event. It isn't the raw stuff of experience . . . the core of experience in the record has been taken up into the sum total of things and its relations there discovered are given back in the work of art. That is why the marginal meanings, the associations, the interlinear element of a poem are all-important. The most delicate piece of work that a poet has to do is to avoid a misleading connection in his phrasing. There must not be a trace of the expository philosophical method, but nevertheless the substance of the philosophical conclusion must be there for the intelligent reader. The artist can't stay off this necessity—can't hold aloof, be the impartial spectator, the colorless medium of information, the carrier of a perfectly

[64] *Ibid.*

undirected passion, the Know-Nothing from Missouri. I can't help believing more and more (it must be the trace that the classical pedagogy has left on me) that the work of art must be perfectly serious, ripe, rational, mature—full of heart, but with enough head to govern heart.

At this point Ransom asked a question which Tate was to remember and to use against him: "Hasn't it struck you as amazing that he [T. S. Eliot] shows so much wisdom in his prose while he favors a poetic vernacular that is utterly irrationalized?"

Eliot's poem, which had appeared in the November *Dial*, provided a fresh fervor for Fugitive conversations. The group was meeting often now, and despite the magazine's precarious lack of finances, the gatherings were permeated with a sense of power. As Tate has since written, "All things were possible in that time to us all, the older and the younger men alike." [65] A gathering was planned for December 27, when Curry would be in Nashville on his way to the Modern Language meeting in Chicago. Although separated from the group and not contributing any poetry to it because of his intensive work in the British Museum and the Bodleian Library, Curry kept up his interest in the Fugitives and sent them words of encouragement from time to time. Davidson had mailed him copies of his "Corymba" and "Dryad," and had received in return a three-page letter of "excellent criticism." [66] At the coming reunion, Lockert and Mims were also to be present; and the group sent Tate a telegram urging him to come to Nashville for the occasion.

Thus, at the end of the year, the Fugitives could survey their accomplishments with justifiable pride. They had enlisted the support of such influential literary figures as Christopher Morley, Robert Graves, Louis Untermeyer, and Witter Bynner. They could look back on four issues of respectable, if not uniformly distinguished, poetry. The reward of seeing themselves in print was making most of them consider more seriously the problems of

[65] "*The Fugitive* 1922–1925," *loc. cit.*, 82.
[66] Davidson to Tate, October 11, 1922.

poetic art. None of them felt that he had mastered his materials; but the endurance of the magazine for this first risky period seemed to promise time in the next few years to experiment and to publish.

As unofficial dean of the group, Ransom had exerted seminal influence. But, although his own poetry was nearer its mature style than was that of the others, it was nevertheless many times inept and awkward. He was in a period of transition from his rough *Poems about God* to the classic and disciplined structures with which most of his present-day readers are familiar. Of the fourteen poems he contributed to the 1922 *Fugitive*, however, only three were not to be used in his next volume of verse, *Chills and Fever*: "The Hand-maidens," "Destitution Raiseth Her Voice," and "Poets Have Chanted Mortality."

Davidson had contributed sixteen poems to the first four issues, thirteen of which he was to collect later in his volume *An Outland Piper*. The three which have never been reprinted are "The Dragon Book," "The Valley of the Dragon," and "Teach Me." Of Tate's fourteen published poems in the first volume, his six in the first two issues are immature and completely unlike the later Tate.[67] The other eight poems look toward his seasoned poetry, but only two of them have been reprinted in his volumes. Tate was perhaps no further from his mature method than was Davidson; but the very nature of his talent caused him to sacrifice the completeness of a poem to experiments in technique, whereas Davidson's products possessed always a roundness that made them finished poems, even if not completely distinguished ones.

The group took pride in having earned the kind of respectful attention that Louis Untermeyer's letter to them represented: "Congratulations on your first year. Your magazine is alert, never without vitality, always provocative. I disagree with what I imagine are some fundamental tenets of some of your group, but that disagreement is founded on a respect for your tastes and a hearty sympathy with your aims."[68] But what gave the Fugitives pleasure

[67] Excepting again the translation from Sappho.
[68] December 8, 1922.

was more that Untermeyer's praise represented recognition from the current literary world than that it offered any basic corroboration of the quality of their poems. For this encouragement, the Nashville poets were dependent on no outside judgment. They had their own critical arena in which diverging viewpoints could be brought to bear upon their poems; and usually they more or less trusted the general judgment. But some of the individual members were becoming aware of an even more trustworthy critical standard —their own convictions, which relied, finally, on the praise and acceptance of no one.

CHAPTER FIVE

CONTROVERSY—

THE RESULTS OF

COMMITMENT:

1923

THE DISCREPANCY between artistic and finan-
cial success began to be apparent to the Fugitive poets by the time a
few weeks of 1923 had elapsed. Though the magazine had elicited
flattering praise and attention, only eighteen subscriptions and
twenty-seven renewals had come in by January 13—a pitiful $45
against the year's estimated expenses of $400. The strong local
support on which the group had counted was evidently not forthcoming.

Up to now these men had hoped that their obviously serious
poetry would be welcomed as a step in the direction pointed by the
section's intellectual leaders: toward cultural progress. If there
were a kind of renaissance in the South, as some authorities apparently believed, surely public support of the artist would not be
long in coming. As a matter of fact, however, the Fugitives had
not yet traced the widespread Southern optimism to a mere rise

of industrialism in a heretofore "backward" land; nor had they seen as inevitable the disparity between the kind of Southern literature welcomed by the promoters of culture and the kind that honest Southerners could produce. Finding no sponsorship in their section, their city, or their university, they were faced with the problem not only of financing the magazine but also of gaining their livelihoods. There was no profession of letters in the South. Once during this period when he sent in a check to *The New Republic* in response to a plea made by Babette Deutsch for a destitute German writer,[1] Tate made a corresponding plea for young American writers. They were in a situation quite as discouraging, he believed, if not so dramatic.[2] Their choice, too, was to desert letters or starve.

Among the Fugitives, two who from all appearances were inclined by nature to the literary profession—Alec Stevenson and Jesse Wills—had already turned their chief efforts to business careers, a decision that made them henceforward approach writing as an avocation. Curry, Ransom, and Davidson had accepted the university's shelter, one for which they were grateful but which nevertheless forced them to live on a pittance and to spend much of their lives overwhelmed by academic duties. Johnson, too, was for the present living by the grace of an academic rôle, but he was soon to be lured away from the pursuit of serious literature by the will o' the wisp of popular literary fame. Tate, more clearsighted about his aim in letters and less optimistic about the financial survival of the poet, was yet reluctant to accept the compromise of teaching, even though a clear-cut choice for literature did not seem available. For some of the Fugitives, of course, the choice was of no moment. Merrill Moore was dedicated primarily to medicine; James Frank, although a man of learning and sensitivity, could not have been a man of letters; and the elegant Hirsch, a dilettante not subject to middle-class morality, felt no economic pressure. But

[1] "Help for a Young German Author," *The New Republic*, XXXIII, No. 419 (December 13, 1922), 71.
[2] "Our Struggling Writers" [Letter], *The New Republic*, XXXIII, No. 423 (January 10, 1923), 177.

they were all concerned with the meager yield of poetry in the fertile land of their homes.

The financial situation of *The Fugitive* was the chief subject of discussion at the first meeting in January. Ransom argued strongly for a reduced size (twenty-four pages instead of the former thirty-two) against several other members who felt that the next issue must be an important one, "as much as anything else to make up for the lapse in the December number." [3] But the final agreement was to try the smaller magazine for one issue and to mail out an advertising circular to prospective subscribers.

If there was no support for *The Fugitive* from the general public, however, there were nods of recognition from other journals. *The Modern Review* and *The Nomad* traded half-page ads with the Nashville publication, and by January the well-established *Double Dealer* agreed to exchange advertising, but on a two-to-one basis.[4] And with growing frequency various periodicals were mentioning the Fugitive writers, both collectively and individually. The December issue, though not a source of pride to some of the members, nevertheless afforded the circle a bit of publicity. Percy's poem was reprinted several times [5] with a mention of *The Fugitive*: the *New York Times* reviewer commented on Percy's and Bynner's poems, treating them facetiously but at least giving evidence that the magazine was being read. The New York *Post* devoted a paragraph to the magazine:

> The *Fugitive* is edited at Vanderbilt University, Nashville, Tenn., by a group of young professors and students, of whom the best known are Allan Tate and John Crowe Ransom, who wrote " Poems about

[3] Davidson to Tate, January 13, 1923.

[4] The New Orleans magazine, with its circulation of about two thousand, reached approximately three or four thousand readers, its editor maintained, about three times as many people as *The Fugitive* reached. McClure politely explained the inequality in circulation by reference to *The Double Dealer's* year and a half headstart. His magazine exchanged with *The Dial* on a one-to-four basis, he pointed out (John McClure to Davidson, January 8, 1923 [misdated 1922]).

[5] The Kansas *Capital*, March 17, 1923; the Atlanta *Journal*, February 11, 1923; the Philadelphia *Public Ledger*, February 19, 1923; *Current Opinion*, LXXIV (March, 1923), 350.

God" (Holt), of which Mr. Morley and Mr. Benet have written in praise. This magazine is largely a venture of Vanderbilt University, but it receives good will contributions from outsiders . . . . The *Fugitive* is much more revolutionary than *Voices*, and tends toward the bizarre as the latter toward the beautiful.[6]

And in Tennessee at least one journalist gave the group serious attention. Writing for the Chattanooga *News*, Caroline Gordon, who at that time had never met any of the Fugitives, gave the group more praise than had any other reviewer. Under the heading " U. S. Best Poets Here in Tennessee," she surveyed the various little magazines then flourishing in the South, according *The Fugitive* by far the highest laurels.[7] She had written Ransom for the full history of *The Fugitive*, and Ransom mentioned her in a letter to Tate, in which he wrote that the group was " doing mighty well."

Have got as much attention in one month as we got all last year and ought to get it increasingly all this year. Having stuck it out a year they figure we are about as stable as the average of such sheets, I guess, and give us a perfunctory attention if nothing better. When I get copies tomorrow I'll send you one of the Saturday's Chattanooga *News* containing a Fugitive story in the magazine supplement. Written by one Miss Gordon, who has developed quite a fondness for us, and incidentally is kin to some of my kinfolks in Chattanooga.[8]

The indirect relationship with Ransom was not for long Miss Gordon's only claim to being part of the Fugitive family; she was to meet Allen Tate in Guthrie, Kentucky, during the summer of 1924 and to marry him in New York a short while later. At the present, however, her praise of the group was quite objective.

But neither praise nor the business of organizing and paying for a magazine could long divert the members from their business of poetry. At the first meeting in January, the troubled finances were forgotten as soon as Davidson, Frank, and the two Wills boys

[6] March 10, 1923.
[7] The Chattanooga *News*, February 10, 1923.
[8] February 11, 1923.

read poems. Frank's poem, "Pegasus," caused some consternation in the group, most of the men recognizing it as conventional and somewhat trite. It was a long allegory, depicting the winged horse's descent to earth, where, after being shown at a country fair and awarded all the prizes, he is mounted by a drunken fool and ridden off into the skies. Johnson, as might have been expected, liked the poem; Curry was noncommittal. But when Davidson, following the group's policy of open criticism, attacked the poem's inversions and hackneyed diction, John Ransom expressed his approval of "Pegasus" in forthright terms (to Davidson's amazement) and the group discussion was forced to rest.[9]

When Tate saw a copy of the poem, he was convinced, with Davidson, that the group could not afford to publish anything diverging so greatly from Fugitive principles. He wrote Ransom a vehement letter, and that, combined with Davidson's objection, persuaded Ransom to agree to the omission of Frank's poem. As he wrote ruefully to Tate, "You were so much more strenuous in opposition than we could possibly be in support."[10] Ransom explained his sponsorship of the poem as coming from the respect in which he held Frank; and, besides, he wrote, using it would have been an opportunity for a "friendly overture from Sinister to Dexter." As he admitted, "It was certainly about a couple of centuries late in coming, but was quaint rather than vicious, and consistent in its tone of pedantic, and not a bit pretentious . . . ."[11]

But, he promised Tate, the committee would henceforth be more rigorous in its selections. There had been an honest discussion at the meeting, and the matter of editorial choice was threshed out. It was decided that the committee must operate with a free rein, without attempting to heed any principle of representation. In a tone which he himself described as sounding a little like "an elder brother," Ransom went on to say that it behooved them (the more serious literary members) to be generous: "we are a group, and presumably committed to individual sacrifices. Least of all

[9] Davidson to Tate, January 13, 1923.
[10] Undated [early in February, 1923].
[11] *Ibid.*

would it become you or me, we two, to weep and rage. There is as you know a wide disapproval of our stuffs, and yet we have been most handsomely awarded with space." Tate answered " penitently sans asceticism," stating that he had " lost his balance " in the crisis,[12] a charge to which Ransom graciously pled guilty also.

For the next meeting Davidson had prepared—and the group approved—a schedule of publication for six issues during the year, the forthcoming one designated the February-March number. Stanley Johnson had been selected to perform the editorial tasks for the issue, and the members were submitting their poems to him. Merrill Moore, having been reprimanded rather severely by several of the group, submitted nothing; nor did Hirsch, who said he had been given so much space in the last issue that he would take none this time.[13] Stevenson turned in two poems he had written some time back, but they were not accepted. Tate, marooned in Ashland, Ohio, which he called " this abdominal little town," was discontented and working feverishly.[14] He sent in poems and versions of poems as quickly as he could compose them. On one occasion, he sat up until five o'clock in the morning composing a third version of a poem entitled " Yellow River," which he sent in to be read to the group, explaining to Davidson that in it the symbolism was " detached, and suggestive (I hope) rather than allusive. Of course that classes me with the 'moderns.'" And he continued:

If Dr. Mims should see the poem, I should like for him to know that it is a poem about the South first of all—her past and present, with no prophecy as to the future. I hope my personal failure to voice a song of hope will not be mistaken for a negation of the positive turn the Southern mind has been taking in the past few years. The pessimism is individual, not general . . . . Please write me a heartless criticism of this poem, and if you get a chance, ask Doc Curry to read, and tell me what he says. I am sending copies to John and to Jesse.[15]

[12] As quoted, Ransom to Tate, February 11 [1923].
[13] Davidson to Tate, January 23, 1923.
[14] To Davidson, January 14, 1923.
[15] *Ibid.*

Davidson praised the poem, and when he read it to the group at the next meeting, found his admiration shared, particularly by Curry.[16] Ransom, however, although he liked Tate's language, could not approve his method. He wrote:

> You are hitting a great stride these days. I return Yellow River with pensive annotations. Almost thou persuadest me to be a Christian—but I am a tough heathen. Still I am unable to see the art-thing in the heterogeny. I require for the satisfaction of my peculiar complex something more coherent than is offered in the mere cross-section of a brain at a given instant. You are attempting an art of the sub-rational. To me that seems as unnecessary and as limiting as is the American formula for the short-story. Everything in dramatic situation, no comments, no author's personality. We know what that produces. Or pure Imagism, in poetry. Isn't it an assumption that the poetic is antithetic to the rational?[17]

Tate was not convinced; but " Yellow River " was not published in its present version, at any rate.

All during this period Ransom and Tate exchanged poems for criticism; and, although their specific remarks about each other's work were somewhat invalidated by the fact that they held such widely diverging critical theories, nevertheless the two men were immensely useful to one another as keen and respected opponents. Between Davidson and Tate, on the other hand, there was a closer friendship and a curious bond of loyalty which predisposed them to look on each other's writing with sympathy, if not approval. But Davidson and Ransom united in protesting Tate's extreme experimentalism, just as Tate and Ransom joined in castigating Davidson's " romanticism." Each of these three was developing his own conviction almost as much in opposition to as in conjunction with his friends' attempts to persuade.

Concerning the romantic qualities of his poetry, Davidson replied once to Tate: " I agree with you and John in a general way as to my poems. Still I doubt the greatness of ironic lyricism, as you

[16] Davidson to Tate, February 1, 1923.
[17] To Tate, undated [early in February, 1923].

call it. . . . Poetry is surely something broader than a rather sardonic, half-beautiful laugh." [18] This was a view Davidson stubbornly refused to relinquish. He was to give up the supernatural and allegorical vehicles for his work, the last of his poems making use of these already turned in for the next *Fugitive*, and he was to experiment somewhat with the Ransomian irony, but always he would be more serious in his wryness, more biting in his satire than his friend who could balance with precision a dualistic world. In fact, Davidson was unable to consider himself a detached observer of society, isolated from it and in a sense alien to it; for this reason the devices of other modern poets were for him unusable.

The summer issue of *The Fugitive* would contain " The Swinging Bridge," the first appearance of Davidson's authentic style—a plain, essentially unwitty idiom, shorn of the conscious modernisms he had attempted in " Corymba," " Naiad," and the poems published in the early issues of the year.

> Not arching up, as some good bridges do,
> Nor glum and straight, like common iron things,
> But marvelously adroop between two trees,
> Trembling at slightest touch of foot, it swings,
> A span of sudden gloom and cool and a creek's vagaries.

One of Davidson's chief themes is the thinness of the present compared to the fullness of the past, and implicit in it is the cry to recapture not the past but its plenitude. Part of that plenitude was song, and in his own poetry Davidson attempted to recapture some of the union of words with music which occurred as simultaneous creations in folk poetry. His " Old Harp " in the October issue would sound that chord:

> Only the mute cool rust
> Fingers thee, loosely strung.
> And men read as read they must
> What once was sung.

It would be much later that Davidson would understand his

[18] February 9, 1923.

traditionalism; at the time he was not sufficiently sure of his argument, but only of his insight and conviction. And Tate and Ransom had always been better theorists and better talkers, able more readily to translate their intuitions into discursive reasoning. So there was nothing for Davidson to do but to continue attempting the kind of writing he felt he must, tempering it by the advice of his two respected friends. And friends these three remained, for all their differences and sometimes their sense of injury. It was to each other that they looked for support in the Fugitive circle, and the other members were never able to wedge between them.

On February 5 the printer delivered the fifth issue of *The Fugitive*, a thirty-two-page magazine. (After consultation with the printer, the group had found that the twenty-four-page size would be no less expensive.) A number of notable guests contributed to this issue. L. A. G. Strong and John Gould Fletcher had been approached by William Elliott at Oxford and both sent in poems in the spirit of helpfulness, Fletcher in particular feeling a sympathy for the group, made up as it was of fellow Southerners attempting serious verse. Witter Bynner was again represented in the magazine, this time with a translation of Charles Vildrac's "The Great White Bird"; and Louis Untermeyer contributed a poem dedicated to E. A. Robinson and written in the Robinson style. One other guest, Hermann Ford Martin, was a young doctor in Lexington, Tennessee, who had responded appreciatively to criticism Davidson and Tate had written to him on previous submissions. The Fugitives' own verse overshadowed their visitors, however, Ransom in particular publishing noticeably superior work, with Davidson, Tate, and Jesse Wills not far behind.

Johnson's editorial, which Davidson called "a regular solar plexus of one paragraph," [19] made clear its author's lack of sympathy with the growing tendency among modern poets to associate "Spinoza and the smell of cooking":

Now that modern poets have pointed out from time to time that there is no God, that pessimism is the end of knowledge, that the world is

[19] To Tate, January 23, 1923.

so hopelessly pluralistic that one is aware of itchings of the body and of alimentary sensations the while he endeavors to synthesize beauty, that sentiment is the naive reaction of morons to external stimulus, that truth in the relation of the sexes is lechery, that garbage heaps and dunghills are subject matter of poetry—and many other startling and, to them, seeming highly original discoveries—is it not time for one who is neither poet nor modern to suggest again that these young poets have prepared for themselves a freedom which looks tragically like slavery, a courage which smacks of cowardice, and in their creedless night have committed themselves to a creed of spiritual anarchy?

Johnson ended his comment with a poem stating his preference for the song of the bird rather than for the garbage-heap or the dunghill which might be in the same scene with the bird. As Davidson commented to Tate: "It's all very racy and rather violent,—perhaps partly intended to set forth the other side of what you propounded last time. It's cleverly written and will please many of our readers. Though I, of course, like you, will not consent to all or most of Stanley's remarks, I think this divergency of expression in the *Fugitive* is a healthy sign and one that will intrigue our readers, if not the critics, for whom you, my boy, have a keen ear." [20]

Johnson continued in his assumption of the part of minority opposition. Inherently more iconoclastic than either Ransom or Tate, he was certain nevertheless that negative elements had no place in poetry. This argument continued at the next meeting, on February 10, when Ransom's poem "Agitato ma non troppo" was the occasion of "bitter words." [21] Johnson attacked the poem, on the grounds of its insincerity, and Ransom's defenders embarrassed him by taking the poem—whose tenet is "I have a grief"—as literally true. To Tate Ransom confided, "Really it's a pretty barren thing of course; nothing at all by itself, and intended almost entirely to get its significance from its context when placed in a volume of dispassionate minors if I may so describe my volume— a statement of literary faith. The boys however agreed in taking it

[20] *Ibid.*
[21] Ransom to Tate, February 11, 1923.

John Crowe Ransom, about
the time of the expiration of
The Fugitive.

Allen Tate in the 1930's.

The five chief Fugitives at the time of the Fugitive Renuion, Nashville, May 4, 1956. From left to right are Tate, Moore, Warren, Ransom, and Davidson.

as the gospel truth story of a great sorrow about which I chose not to be communicative." [22]

Johnson's argument, which he had prepared beforehand and read, was an effort to prove that "a poem should be a story." Ransom's comment was that Johnson's thesis "was worked out damnably well and of course was absolute moonshine." The discussion which followed was heated and enjoyable, ending with Johnson retracting a great deal of his argument. But if Ransom was able to defeat Johnson on logical grounds, he was never able to convince him on aesthetic ones; and so Johnson remained in his relation to the Fugitives a dissenting voice—honest, blunt, and basically at odds with the dominant aims of the magazine.

By February of this second year, the editors of the magazine could maintain, in a letter soliciting the support of the Nashville Associated Retailers, that *The Fugitive* had attracted "more attention to Nashville than any other artistic undertaking, with the exception of the restoring of the Parthenon, in the past ten years." [23] The support asked for was the offering of a hundred-dollar prize for the best poem submitted to *The Fugitive* in 1923. The merchants granted the request—partly of course because their president was James Frank and their secretary Miss Sadie Hartman, a good friend of Davidson and other Fugitives. Emboldened by this success, the Fugitives convinced Dr. J. D. Blanton, the courtly president of Ward-Belmont College, that his school should contribute a second prize of fifty dollars.

Taking their idea from such magazines as *The Dial*, *The Lyric*, *The Nation*, *Contemporary Verse*, and *American Poetry*, which had all offered prizes during 1922, the Fugitives planned the contest as a way of opening the pages of the magazine to outside contributors. The editors were to select possible winning entries, these to be printed in the magazine and afterwards submitted for final decisions to a committee of poets and critics. The group chose as judges Louis Untermeyer, Witter Bynner, and Christopher

[22] *Ibid.*
[23] The Fugitives to Sadie Hartman, February 8, 1923.

Morley, but it developed that these three were unable to serve. They were replaced by Jessie B. Rittenhouse, William Alexander Percy, and Gorham B. Munson (this last, Allen Tate's selection). The Fugitives made plans to announce the contest in the April-May number and to publicize it in magazines and newspapers throughout the country.

When Tate returned to Vanderbilt in March to complete requirements for the degree his illness prevented him from receiving in 1922, it was not without some braggadoccio that he took his seat in the university classrooms. He has written of himself during this period:

> My conceit must have been intolerable. Had not the editors of *The Double Dealer* written me a letter saying that they saw in me the White Hope of the South? Add to that the easy lesson in shocking the bourgeoisie that I had learned from reading French poets, and was relearning for American use from Ezra Pound, and you have before you the figure of a twenty-two-year-old prig as disagreeable as you could possibly conjure up, until you see in him several varieties of snobbishness, when he becomes even more disagreeable. In that moral condition I returned to Vanderbilt to get my degree.[24]

Tate's "conceit" was never lacking in humor, however; his friends found him delightful company, and as for his enemies—the knife swing that severs the head cleanly from the body can hardly be called "disagreeable."

Soon after Tate came back to Vanderbilt he met sixteen-year-old "Red" Warren, a sophomore who was later to be one of the most famous members of the Fugitive group. Tate has recorded his first sight of Warren. It was in the spring of 1923. The young man wandered into Curry's room, where Tate was typing a poem. Since students were always coming to borrow Curry's books or his typewriter Tate at first took no notice. A glance, however, told him that this one was "the most remarkable looking boy" he had ever "laid eyes on."

He was tall and thin, and when he walked across the room he

---

[24] "*The Fugitive* 1922-1925," *loc. cit.*, 81.

made a sliding shuffle, as if his bones didn't belong to one another. He had a long quivering nose, large brown eyes, and a long chin—all topped by curly red hair. He spoke in a soft whisper, asking to see my poem; then he showed me one of his own—it was about Hell, and I remember this line:

> Where lightly bloom the purple lilies . . . .

He said that he was sixteen years old and a sophomore. This remarkable young man was " Red," Robert Penn Warren, the most gifted person I have ever known.[25]

Warren had come to Vanderbilt intending to major in chemistry,[26] but had found that subject so dull because of the way it was taught that he rapidly lost interest in it. The chief excitement on the campus was literary, and consequently he soon took up that enthusiasm. After his first term of Freshman English under Ransom, he was invited to come into the " English 9 " class in advanced composition, a course that Ransom had been teaching at Vanderbilt since his return from the war. Warren found Ransom a superb teacher, extremely stimulating in a quiet way.

In the fall of his sophomore year—1922—Warren was placed in Davidson's sophomore survey class. Davidson saw that the boy was unusual—not only brilliant but surprisingly well-read. He allowed him, consequently, to write poems instead of papers for the course—imitations of Chaucer and Beowulf, the first poems Warren had done in college. Once started, however, he kept writing, showing his work to Ransom and Davidson, as well as to Curry, under whose tutelage Warren studied English literature for the second and third quarters of his sophomore year. Curry criticized his work, lent him books, and discussed with him his literary heritage. On the epoch-making publication of *The Waste Land*, Warren had the advantage of being shown the poem immediately

[25] *Ibid.*
[26] Robert Penn Warren was born in Guthrie, Kentucky, April 24, 1905, the eldest child of a businessman and a schoolteacher. He had attended the Guthrie public school until he was fifteen and then had gone to the Clarksville High School in Tennessee for a year.

(Davidson brought him the issue of *The Dial* in which it appeared) and of discussing its revolutionary aspects with the three young professors of literature under whom he had studied. No less than other alert students all over the country, Warren picked up in it the indication of a new era of poetry.

It was later on in the same school year that this strangely gifted, nervous, shy young man encountered Tate in Curry's room and, soon after, showed Tate his poems. Delighted with Warren's work, Tate made sure that *The Fugitive* and *The Double Dealer* were acquainted with it, and before long Warren published a poem in each of these journals. Tate and Ridley Wills began taking Warren with them to Fugitive meetings, though not until a year later—in the spring of his junior year—was he made a member of the group.

Tate and Ridley Wills knew each other as Fugitives, but it was through Warren that they became close friends. Wills was, according to Tate's description of him, "small, graceful, ebullient, and arrogant, and one of the wittiest and most amusing companions" he ever had.[27] This unconventional trio decided to room together in Wesley Hall, a building for theological students, which, as Tate admits, was "no place for the heathen." It was a wild and boisterous time for all three, when they were intellectually snobbish, no doubt full of pretense and pose, yet withal intensely vulnerable to poetry and, for all their sophistication, innocent of the ways of the world. Their room was the scene for horseplay and for serious talk about art. Tate has described this exciting period in their lives:

In order to get into bed at night we had to shovel the books, trousers, shoes, hats, and fruit jars onto the floor, and in the morning, to make walking-space, we heaped it all back upon the beds. We stuck pins into Red while he slept to make him wake up and tell us his dreams. Red had made some good black-and-white drawings in the Beardsley style. One day he applied art gum to the dingy plaster and when we came back we saw four murals, all scenes from *The Waste Land*. I remember particularly the rat creeping softly through the vege-

[27] "*The Fugitive* 1922-1925," *loc. cit.,* 82.

tation, and the typist putting a record on the gramophone. Then one night in the spring Ridley and I went down to " the " dog-wagon and wrote by dawn the entire *Golden Mean*. When we showed the manuscript to Merrill Moore the next day, Merrill was pretty envious; so we told him that he could be in the book if he wrote eulogies of us; which he did. But his tongue was not where it should have been.[28]

The Golden Mean [29] (which was dedicated to *The Fugitive*) was a tour de force and a joke. It was a joke executed with a rather high level of artistic consciousness, however, for parody and burlesque, if they are to be effective, require talent, as well as some notion of the principal issues involved. This little prank done by two youths intending to shock their less daring acquaintances reveals lively intelligences, sharp wit, and a sense of verbal nuance.

The scheme of the venture was for the poems to achieve a balance between modernism and traditionalism and so to strike facetiously the " Golden Mean " (a favorite doctrine of Mims). Tate was to employ the experimental techniques in scansion, rhyme, and typographical devices, and Wills was to make use of the conventional methods. After an introduction by Moore and the three poems allotted to him (one to R. W., one to A. T., and the third, entitled " Panegyric to the Entity," to R. W. and A. T.), there follow eleven pairs of poems, each pair written on the same subject, usually with the same title, the first of the two written each time by Wills and dedicated to Tate, and the second written by Tate and dedicated to Wills. In one pair " The Waste Land " is burlesqued as " The Chaste Land," its two versions paralleling the original closely in the interlarding of quotations from other works, in erudite footnotes explaining several lines, and in actual imitations of passages from the Eliot poem. Tate's version ends, " Shanty, Shanty, Shanty," which he explains in a footnote: " Prakrit slang for the peace that surpasseth the pursuit of further ambition, i. e., the home."

[28] *Ibid.*
[29] *The Golden Mean and Other Poems,* Limited Edition, privately printed for the authors [1923].

The dedication of the volume to *The Fugitive* was not an idle gesture. Mimicked unmercifully in the frolicsome pamphlet are many Fugitive traits—most noticeably a penchant for long, pedantic, little-known words. The lines of both Tate and Wills are filled with such words as *uniquitous, nepenthal, coluthic, punctiform, myxomycetes, stramonium.* Further, the mystic tendencies of Hirsch are mocked in the two poems entitled "Oum," the footnote to Wills's poem reading as follows:

OUM (cf. OVM, OM), the sacred word of the Hindoos, is widely supposed to have originated in a combination of the initials of the three gods representing the Brahma Trinity. We hesitate to advance a new theory of the genesis of OM, but it does seem perfectly obvious that it is simply a mystical inversion of the word denoting the sound emitted by cows in moments of ecstacy, viz., MOO. This thesis may be supported by allusion to religious practice, immemorially antique, which attributed divine powers to the bull, an animal denominated in this age of decadence as the cow's husband. However, another theory may be sustained with equal cogency, that of a feline origin of the word (cf. Me-ow); and so the Authors, everywhere striving for the Golden Mean, propose this alternative view. The reader may take his choice.

After mutual tributes, *The Golden Mean* comes to an end, Wills having characterized Tate as "a bright and snickering figure on a fictitious horizon of bathetic intimacy with the rugged outline of Parnassus," and Tate having described Wills as "the most parabolic young man of the Younger Generation."

It was all great fun, and not much damage was done. But meanwhile, as Tate has recorded, this irrepressible trio was also attending the serious Fugitive meetings—"too serious we thought, hence the dedicatory pages of *The Golden Mean*—and we, the young ones, were trying all kinds of poetry, from Miss Millay to Eliot, from Robinson to Cummings who had just appeared." [30]

But the April-May issue of the magazine showed no very great imprint of the younger members' experimentation. Tate was the only one of them receiving space, and he was represented by poems

---

[30] "*The Fugitive* 1922–1925," *loc. cit.*, 82.

that unsuccessfully attempt to conform: "The Happy Poet Remembers Death" and "You Left." The latter nevertheless contains
a few lines of startling force: "Absence will cleave your portrait
in my mind" and "And yet perhaps the inner eye, unsplintered /
By a blast of beauty from a present ill"; but the whole poem is
inconclusive. The only other pieces of distinction in the issue are
Ransom's much-debated "Agitato ma non troppo," a neat and pungent declaration of his aesthetic attitude; Davidson's "The Man
Who Would Not Die," a long legend-like poem in blank verse;
and Jesse Wills's "To Jones," a sonnet which, like the one in the
preceding issue, views the present commercial age with blended
scorn and compassion. Frank, Hirsch, and Elliott, against whom
the other Fugitives were so frequently united, found a place in
the issue for their lines. None of the outsiders added any freshness
or individuality to the magazine, which must be rated as one of the
most conventional numbers of *The Fugitive.*

The editorial called attention to the forthcoming contest, to
the fact that *The Fugitive* was not connected with Vanderbilt
University, and to the group editorship of the magazine, this last
item emphasized conspicuously:

The Fugitives are a band of anointed spirits associated together on
principles not of race, color, conditions of servitude, nor academic
entitlements. It is constitutional in our plan that we are all equals.
We have no differentiation of ranks or titles, and even cling to an
old-fashioned, round-about method of group-action in doing the chores
of publication, with the very idea of securing the blessings of an
individual liberty against the possible suspicion of a tyranny.

The Fugitives had not yet recognized that actual equality among
poets, as among all men, is a goal impossible of achievement—that
charity, not equality, forms the only basis on which men can act.
Unconsciously, of course, the group functioned as a brotherhood,
with each man performing in the way he was most valuable; but
some of the members, holding in theory to the principle of absolute
equality, chafed at the unaccounted-for inequalities and, at times,
experienced a deepseated sense of injustice.

The summer Fugitive meetings took on a different character with two of the regular members besides Curry absent and the two peregrinating ones—Elliott and Frierson—back home. This year Davidson took his family to his wife's home in Oberlin, Ohio; Ransom made a trip West, to teach in Greeley, Colorado. Tate remained in Nashville, attending Peabody and trying to pass mathematics. Johnson, too, stayed in Nashville, studying and writing and sometimes going swimming with Tate, now living in Curry's room.

Tate took over the job of managing editor of *The Fugitive* and spent his afternoons answering the magazine's correspondence. "We are coming along nicely," he wrote Davidson; "the issue is now mailed out; and we are receiving almost every day a subscription or two which I enter apace with a great demonstration of efficiency." [31] Of his industry, Jesse Wills commented to Davidson, "I never saw anyone who enjoyed writing letters as he does. . . . He's carrying on a personal correspondence with several of our contestants of both genders." [32]

The issue that Tate and his helpers had mailed out contained the qualifying poems chosen by the editors for the first heat of the contest. Except for Warren's "Crusade," however, the entries lack energy and interest. Warren's poem possesses a degree of intellectual power and cogency not often encountered in a novice, even though it is flawed by an excessive obviousness. Of the members' poems in the issue, Ransom's are most interesting, exhibiting a growing pungency of intellect and diction. His concern for prosodical problems, however, gives his verse a peculiar though not unattractive awkwardness. One of the poems, "Spectral Lovers," makes use of Ransom's favorite theme—the danger of yielding to the allurements of the mind; like his later "The Equilibrists" this poem portrays two lovers who find themselves unable to allow physical expression of their love—they are "two immaculate angels fallen on earth."

Tate's contributions, "The Screen" and "Procession," both

[31] June 16, 1923.
[32] July 24, 1923.

possess imaginative power and suggestion. The first, a reworking of "Yellow River," is a poem of reflection which attempts, in the midst of the chaos of present experience, to assess the way in which the mind can know the past. "Procession," unlike most of Tate's poetry at this period, is a complete and integrated poem, without the structural incoherence produced by an imperfectly controlled metaphorical power. Beginning,

> Along the street with deliberate pomp
> March the stiff sutlers of an ancient Lord—
> And have marched since the falling of the first leaf
> That withered in the hand of Hildegarde,
> Crushing with iron the silly meadow-sweet
> After an old man's bones pass down the street,

the poem attains its full expression with a calm directness.

Of the other members, Moore contributed four sonnets that display indubitable poetic energy but an insufficient intellectual restraint; Ridley Wills supplied two poems that are his most serious ever to be printed in *The Fugitive*: "Once on a Grey Beach" and "Two Men." Both suffer, however, from a lack of rhythmic and verbal tension. The first begins:

> Once I lay on a grey, soft beach,
> And a diffident moon, pale in the fair, late-day sky,
> Saw me; and a mindful being of high, aged water
> Can swear that I lay on a grey, soft beach,
> Unclad, sprawled like a tired laborer rich
>   with a moment for drowsiness.

This passage and other lines in the two pieces contain some interesting phrasings, but the poems as a whole are facile and unconsidered.

Further, the magazine contained a good sonnet by Stevenson, two poems by Johnson in his blunt and vigorous fashion, and a brief but excellent little piece by Curry:

> He could not synchronize old shadowed pain,
> (Which moves detached along an under cave)
> With the present pulse, which sweeps in junketings
> To climaxes previsioning a grave.

But trefoils spring where fair Iseult
Once passed through love to martyrdom.
The flash of muscled arms in Babylon,
The porting ships of kings at Avalon,
Receding mountains of Icelandic gloom,
And dangered paths of queens in Ascalon,
Penumbral, tint the whitest flower
That tangles with the instant hour.

This is a verse much seasoned by a mature intellect and an austere but acute sensibility. It is not difficult to discern, from a reading of Curry's infrequent offerings in *The Fugitive*, why the serious poets in the group looked to him for comment and deplored his modest estimate of his own poetic abilities.

This summer issue was better than its predecessor. In its pages was no really bad poem by a member; however flawed and incomplete some of the individual pieces may have been, it was evident that the intellects informing the poetry were not inconsiderable. The issue should have brought the group serious critical attention. Ignominiously enough, however, the only evidence that it had attracted notice was a letter from an assistant editor of *Poetry*, protesting a comment in the *Fugitive* editorial. The comment in question had concerned Harriet Monroe, editor of *Poetry*, reproving her for a lack of critical judgment she had recently displayed. In a review of DuBose Heyward's and Hervey Allen's *Carolina Chansons*, Miss Monroe had spoken of the opportunity for poetry in the South, declaring that it was time for Southern poets to " accept the challenge of a region so specialized in beauty, so rich in racial tang and prejudice, so jewel-weighted with a heroic past." She had gone on to say that those who read *Carolina Chansons* would find that the " soft, silken reminiscent life of the Old South . . . [was] becoming articulate." [33]

Perhaps the Fugitives would have taken no exception to these rather saccharine lines had Miss Monroe not earlier expressed herself at greater length on the " local color " method. In April,

---

[33] " The Old South," *Poetry*, XXII, No. 2 (May, 1923), 91.

1922, the same month *The Fugitive* first appeared, the issue of *Poetry*, called a "Southern Number," had been turned over to the South Carolina Poetry Society, with Heyward and Allen (who was not a native Southerner, but living in Charleston and writing about it) singled out for especial commendation.

In the first place, the Fugitives resented the concept "Southern poetry." Poetry was poetry, south or north of the Mason-Dixon Line, and could not derive its *raison d'être* from any qualities not literary and universal. In the second place, if the South were to be depicted in literature, it must be by something more than super-ficialities, by the essences and not the accidents, as Tate later put it.[34] But Miss Monroe's editorial in the "Southern Number" was outspoken in favor of what she called a "strongly localized indige-nous art," [35] and her emphasis was placed on a mere awareness of locality, rather than upon any profound critical examination or creative interpretation of its values. The Fugitives could overlook her false emphasis in 1922; but by May, 1923, they were more secure in their standards and so were ready to disagree when she voiced the same theory in her review of *Carolina Chansons*. And though their relations with the South Carolina Poetry Society had been cordial (Ransom and Davidson had respected the group enough to submit poems for its yearly contest the preceding April), Tate, Davidson, and Johnson felt the time had come to protest that Southern poets need not write consciously Southern poetry. For Tate, to whom the literary man's task was partly polemical,[36] the necessity of an attack seemed self-evident; for the others, little argument was required to persuade them to take issue in print with a personage who, as one writer of this period commented, fancied herself the editor not only of *Poetry* but of poetry.[37]

[34] To Davidson, March 1, 1927.

[35] *Poetry*, XX, No. 1 (April, 1922), 31.

[36] In an unpublished letter to Hill Turner, Vanderbilt Alumni Secretary (March 3, 1941), Tate explained that as a "literary polemicist" he deliberately adopted a truculent manner in controversy.

[37] Theodore Maynard, "The Fallacy of Free Verse," *The Yale Review*, XI (January, 1922), 354.

Before he left for his summer in Ohio, therefore, Davidson penned the editorial protest against some of Miss Monroe's statements. Its last paragraph was purposely insulting:

All tribute to Mr. Heyward and Mr. Allen for their achievements! Undoubtedly the Old South is literary material to those who may care to write about it. But many may not. It is not the province of any critic to dictate the material these many shall choose. They will guffaw at the fiction that the Southern writer of today must embalm and serve up as an ancient dish. They will create from what is nearest and deepest in experience—whether it be old or new, North, South, East, or West—and what business is that of Aunt Harriet's?

The editorial office of *Poetry*, that had been myopic about *The Fugitive* for over a year, was keensighted enough to catch a bit of adverse criticism. In Miss Monroe's absence abroad, Marjorie Swett wrote a letter of rebuke, which Tate forwarded to Davidson. Realizing that they could carry the controversy no further without antagonizing " the South Carolina folks," [38] Davidson wrote a brief reply to Miss Swett, a copy of which he sent to Tate with the comment that he did not wish to argue much with a " subordinate." " If Miss M herself says anything further and gives us an opening, we can let go full blast," he wrote.[39] Tate wrote Miss Swett also, to make clear that the editors of *The Fugitive* had not misinterpreted Miss Monroe:

We do not disagree with Miss Monroe when she emphasizes the artistic possibilities latent in the traditions of the Old South; nor do we feel called upon to object if she feels—as she evidently does not—that this tradition is the only genuine source for Southern poets to draw upon . . . . But we fear very much to have the slightest stress laid upon Southern traditions in literature; we who are Southerners know the fatality of such an attitude—the old atavism and sentimentality are always imminent . . . .[40]

From Greeley, Ransom commented on the controversy, which, he

[38] Davidson to Tate, June 26, 1923.
[39] June 29, 1923.
[40] June 22, 1923 [carbon copy].

wrote, did the group "infinite credit." Nevertheless, he had a little rather "not altercate with them in print further"; in private, he said, the Fugitives should find it "amusing during the heat." [41] But Miss Swett said nothing more, and the small exchange was ended. In the August-September *Fugitive* the editors printed part of her letter, which protested that "Miss Monroe would be the last person in the world to wish to limit the poets of any section of the country." Commenting upon the disagreement, the *Fugitive* editorial maintained that the "jewel-weighted tradition" of which Miss Monroe spoke was inaccessible to "many of the present Southern poets" and concluded, "Whether the limitation be in the poets or whether there is something fatally oppressive about these materials most readily obtainable from the past, we do not know. At any rate, we fear to have too much stress laid on a tradition that may be called a tradition only when looked at through the haze of a generous imagination." This belligerent little episode, though perhaps a bit foolish, is quite characteristic of the Fugitives at this period, particularly Tate and Davidson, evidencing their excessive pride and touchiness mingled with their perspicuity and devotion to principle. It is interesting to note that after this time, for ten years or more, *Poetry* maintained a striking ignorance of the existence of the Nashville poets, despite the growing attention given them in other quarters.

There were other matters, closer home, even, than the local-color controversy, that were occupying the minds of the Fugitives during the summer. One was a financial arrangement with a local advertising agency managed by Mr. Jacques Back. It was always to be something of a mystery to most of the Fugitives that a businessman should have thought a poetry magazine potentially profitable; but the terms of his proposition were constructed so leniently and agreeably for the members that none of them could find any conceivable disadvantage in the liaison. Back proposed to undertake the publication of the magazine on a bimonthly basis, to pay for the printing and the mailing, and to furnish a minimum of a

[41] To Tate, July 14, 1923.

hundred free copies for exchange purposes.[42] The editorial committee was to continue furnishing without the slightest restriction
all reading matter and to supervise the proofreading and composition. Issues were to be published on or within one week of the
tenth of every second month. At the end of two years the advertising agency was to render an account and to receive twenty-five
per cent of the net profit, with the members keeping the rest. In
case of deficit, the agency was to bear any loss. The good offices of
such an "angel" were completely unexpected; it was only the
feeling that there must be some sort of catch in the proposal that
kept the group from signing immediately. And it was indeed
strange that here was a man totally removed from the group who
would make such a generous offer. In fact, Back never came to a
Fugitive meeting and remained all along unfamiliar with the poetry
he financed. Stevenson conducted all arrangements with him, and
toward the last part of July the contract was signed; on August 17
Back "took over the proposition."[43] Tate and Stevenson worried
about the outstanding debt owed to the printing firm, Cullom and
Ghertner, which they felt they could hardly ask Back to assume.
They finally decided to assess the brethren pro rata. But after
this time, Back was to handle all business matters: henceforth, it
seemed, the Fugitives could devote themselves solely to writing and
to editorial problems.

A letter from Ransom in July had brought up again the matter
of the editorial policy of the magazine. Christopher Morley, Ransom's old friend, who wrote in *The Literary Review* of the New
York *Evening Post* under the pen name of Kenelm Digby, had
commended *The Fugitive* in his column. But he had worded his
praise unfortunately. "John Crowe Ransom's 'Fugitive' especially
interests us," he wrote. "It is quite unexpected in quality."[44]
Ransom regretted Morley's error in ascribing the magazine to him
and in an attempt to prevent discord cut out the notice and sent it
to Tate with a few words of explanation and apology: "Friend

[42] Jacques Back to Editorial Committee, June 13, 1923.
[43] Tate to Davidson, August 18, 1923.
[44] July 7, 1923.

Digby has done it again, has put my foot in it, as you will remark from the enclosure. I send it in order to protest my innocence, and in the hope that Sidney will not compel me to sign another retraction. Also with my name left out, I should think these few words of his constitute about the best single exhibit from the press that we can boast of." [45]

But his precaution was not sufficient. The question of the equality of the editors had from the beginning set Ransom in a peculiar relation to the whole group. Aware of his more established reputation and his greater experience, the younger men stubbornly refused to be drawn into a coterie in which one man dominated. With his dry good sense, his cutting irony, Ransom was a difficult influence to resist, however; and during these years together all the Fugitives acquired something of his manner and a few of his turns of phrase as well as some of his keen and original ideas. He had been their teacher; they learned from but did not imitate him. But as time went on, Ransom was mentioned more and more prominently in connection with *The Fugitive*. In March, for instance, David Morton, reprinting Ransom's "In Process of a Noble Alliance," [46] had designated its author as the editor of *The Fugitive*; nothing had been done to correct the error, although some of the members felt that Ransom himself should have made a public disclaimer.

When Morley made his reference to the magazine, the misapprehension was not allowed to slide by. Tate had already seen the notice, and he and Johnson discussed the matter over lunch, agreeing that Ransom had consistently been given too much credit for the magazine.[47] The result of this conference was Tate's admonitory letter to *The Literary Review*, which Morley subsequently reported upon: "Allen Tate, acting managing editor of *The Fugitive*, informs us that the paper is *not* John Crowe Ransom's, 'nor mine even, nor truly anybody else's.' It seems that no one is ever likely to be the editor of it; it is handled by a board

[45] July 14, 1923.
[46] *The Bookman*, LVII, No. 1 (March 1923), 36.
[47] Tate to Davidson, July 14, 1923.

of some thirteen editors, each of whom has as much to say about it as any other." [48]

This incident added weight to some of the members' conviction that the editorial policy of the journal should be changed, since the work of getting out the publication had settled more and more on the same shoulders: Davidson's and—now that he was back in Nashville—Tate's.

Ransom had been the chief opponent of the proposal to elect one of the members editor; and since it seemed that the world at large regarded Ransom as the editor of the journal, those doing the work and receiving no credit chafed under what they felt to be an injustice. Consequently, while Ransom and Davidson were both away, Tate and Johnson took matters into their own hands by drawing up a plan for a yearly organization of the magazine. An editor-in-chief and an associate editor would be elected for each year, the other Fugitives delegating to these two the functions which had officially resided in the group but had actually been performed by a few overworked members.

Tate and Johnson wanted Davidson for editor. But Davidson felt some hesitancy about accepting the nomination, since he knew Ransom to be opposed to any change in editorial policy. In July, Johnson wrote explaining the proposed plan to Davidson in more detail; he went ahead to clarify the circumstances leading to its formulation. "All personal factors," he wrote, were omitted from consideration:

> Moreover, John has mentioned you for editor more than once as you probably remember, and his objection to the present plan as presented by Curry last Spring was probably more to table a plan in which some irritation was concerned than it was any opposition to you. Certainly it is true that for any one plan, as for any one editor, or other officers there will be some opposition from someone. That has been our trouble all along. We must come to that arrangement in which the majority, the largest majority, can concur. Now it is a foregone conclusion that the *Fugitive* is going under unless we have a per-

[48] *The Literary Review*, the New York *Evening Post*, August 11, 1923.

manent (i. e. definite and understandable and workable) organization—that is point number one.

Point number two is, that you are the only one upon whom we can agree whole-heartedly. If you bust up the plan, you bust up the Fugitives. The *Fugitive* may go to smash under your editorship—it will certainly go to smash without your editorship.[49]

A previous letter from Davidson had outlined several points which he thought had to be considered in the plan. Johnson assured him that each had been provided for: the Back arrangement had been completed, the duties of the editor and the curtailment of his power were outlined, and all plans after this time were to be written—in the form of minutes. "As for cooperation and suspicions and laziness and neglect," he continued, ". . . those things are scarcely predictable, certainly not reducible to writing."

Drawn up by Johnson and Jesse Wills, a resolution proposing adoption of the Tate-Johnson plan, with Davidson as editor-in-chief and Tate as assistant editor, had been submitted to all the members present in Nashville, seven of whom had already approved it before Johnson wrote his letter. Pointing out that Tate had voted for the resolution, Johnson urged Davidson's approval. "Personally," he wrote, " I wish and have wished for some time to release my interest and time from Fugitive policies and have not felt free to do so in the past. I can do so now—will be pleased, however, to do any work assigned me." Jesse Wills also wrote Davidson, emphasizing the necessity for the step taken: "You and Allen are the logical candidates for the positions named therein. Without honor or title you have done most of the work up to now. With or without, you will probably continue to do most of it." [50] Tate, too, felt that Davidson and he should vote for themselves, since they worked hardest and were "the only ones who took the trouble to keep up with ' the current pageant.' " [51]

But by the end of July the innovators were made acquainted with Ransom's sentiments concerning the change. In a letter to

[49] July 23, 1923.
[50] July 24, 1923.
[51] Tate to Davidson, July 24, 1923.

Tate dated July 30 Ransom stated that he was "dead against" the proposition: "Every member knows we have no editor in the dictionary sense of that term: then we have no business publishing on a false basis." Tate wrote Davidson bitterly resenting Ransom's action but stating that he was glad to have the affair out in the open.[52] Ransom wrote Jesse Wills in more detail, but Wills nevertheless renewed his pleas to Davidson to accept the position. The resolution had been approved by everyone except Ransom, Moore, and Ridley Wills. The last two had not replied to the communication, Moore because he was "lost in the wilds of Mittel Europa," (he and another student were in Germany for the summer) and Wills because he was "too uxorious" (he had just married) to answer.[53] Only Ransom, then, opposed the move; and his objection was not to the choice of persons but to the principle: he opposed having his name appear in a subordinate position. He had explained that his intention was not to be arrogant but to hold to what he understood were the sentiments of "every upstanding Fugitive."[54]

Davidson was in an awkward position. He, too, felt Ransom's attitude unfair, but he was anxious to restore peace, particularly since a small private feud on another subject between Ransom and Tate had been smoldering all during this exchange about Fugitive business, reaching its climax at almost the same time. The issue of *The Literary Review* that printed Tate's correction concerning the editorship of *The Fugitive* carried also a letter giving further evidence of dissension among the Fugitives: Ransom's reply to a letter of Tate's, which was itself written in protest to an article by Ransom. This minor literary controversy is insignificant in the light of the strong and lasting friendship between the two men; yet it is revealing of their fundamentally different casts of mind, as well as of their courage in a willingness to identify themselves wholly with the aspect of truth which they grasped. Tate was later to write of Ransom that he was "the last pure manifestation

[52] August 2, 1923.
[53] Jesse Wills to Davidson, August 5, 1923.
[54] As quoted in *ibid.*, August 5, 1923.

of the eighteenth-century South." [55] But, as a matter of fact, Tate and Ransom both bore a marked resemblance to the eighteenth-century men of letters; and nowhere is the similitude shown more clearly than in the "Waste Lands" controversy, in which each of the friends haughtily labelled the other "dunce."

Ransom had written an essay, "Waste Lands," for William Rose Benét to print in *The Literary Review*. In it he attacked T. S. Eliot's controversial new poem, using it as an immediate opportunity for expressing some of his objections to the subrational in poetry. Particularly disquieting to him in "The Waste Land" were the juxtaposition of incongruous attitudes ("We do not quote Greek tragedy and modern cockney with the same breath or with the same kinds of mind") and the use of "parody" by the weaving of quotations into inharmonious situations (the "When lovely lady stoops to folly" passage). According to Ransom, the new poem showed Eliot's earlier work to have been merely precocious. Concluding his essay with a characteristically easy, ironic paragraph, he doubted that Eliot's poetry would last: "The genius of our language is notoriously given to feats of hospitality; but it seems to me it will be hard pressed to find accommodations at the same time for two such incompatibles as Mr. Wordsworth and the present Mr. Eliot; and any realist must admit that what happens to be the prior tenure of the mansion in this case is likely to be stubbornly defended." [56]

Tate had long been the champion of Eliot to the Fugitives and could not let Ransom's essay go unrebuked. The long letter of reply he wrote to *The Literary Review* treated Ransom coolly, even somewhat disdainfully, and does seem, as Davidson put it in an admirable understatement, "a leetle bit pert." [57] It began: "Sir: John Crowe Ransom's article, "Waste Lands," in the *Literary Review* of July 14 violates so thoroughly the principle of free critical inquiry and at the same time does such scant justice to the

[55] "The Eighteenth-Century South," [a review of *Two Gentlemen in Bonds*] *The Nation*, CXXIV (March 30, 1927), 346.
[56] "Waste Lands," *The Literary Review*, July 14, 1923.
[57] To Tate, August 14, 1923.

school of so-called philosophic criticism, to which one supposes he belongs, that it may be of interest to your readers to consider the possible fallacy of his method and a few of the errors into which it leads him." [58]

Tate condemned the " theory of inspiration " that Ransom had built up and charged that he had offered " only an abstract restatement of superannuate theories of consciousness." After defending Eliot's right to change attitudes from one poem to another and ridiculing the idea that his first volume was invalidated by his second, Tate moved in for his concluding blow: " And if tradition means sameness, then Mr. Eliot cannot survive with Wordsworth. But Mr. Ransom doesn't say just where it is that poems survive. However, it is likely that the value of " The Waste Land " as art is historical rather than intrinsic; but the point of my objection to John Crowe Ransom's essay is that the method he employs is not likely to give T. S. Eliot much concern. And my excuse for this extended objection is that Mr. Ransom is not alone. He is a *genre*."

In the heat of attack Tate failed to recognize that a friend could be hurt by the thrusts a mere opponent might find stimulating. That he bore no malice is shown by his mailing Ransom a copy of the letter before it appeared in print. " It was a bolt from the blue," [59] Ransom answered, in a tone of reproof. He enclosed a counterreply which he said he might or might not send to *The Literary Review*. One week following the publication of Tate's letter, Ransom's reply appeared. In it his tone kept its customary urbanity, but his rebuke was unmistakable:

One might gather from this letter that it was written by an enemy bent on demolishing such scant reputation for scholarship as I might have laboriously accumulated, when as a matter of fact the author and I have enjoyed a long and peaceable acquaintance, and it is himself who sends me a copy of his letter with certain waggish additions for my private benefit. The truth is, Tate has for two years suffered the damning experience of being a pupil in my classes, and I take it his

[58] " Waste Lands," [letter] *The Literary Review*, August 4, 1923.
[59] To Tate, July 30, 1923.

letter is but a proper token of his final emancipation, composed upon the occasion of his accession to the ripe age of twenty-three.[60]

His "one serious" comment on Tate's argument would be, he wrote, that the quality which vitiated Eliot's writing was ". . . precisely the same quality that marks in a greater degree the prose of Mr. Tate's letter and the work of a whole sodality of younger critics—it abhors the academic (i. e., the honest and thoroughgoing) method, and is specious, after all, using its glittering scraps of comment and citation without any convincing assurance that the subject has been really studied."

Tate had considered his own letter objective, since it took no notice of personal acquaintance; hence by Ransom's reply he felt personally injured. He wrote a letter severing all connections with Ransom but was persuaded by Davidson not to send it. Nevertheless, the rift opened and it was to be more than a year before the persistent warmth of genuine affection would banish the coolness which followed the heat of argument. The dispute presented a real complication to Davidson in his attempt to make a decision about the editorial position. To refuse the office would seem an action motivated by pique and would add to the resentment of some of the others toward Ransom. To accept it would be to go against Ransom's clearly stated objections. But Ransom was a man without grudges, Davidson knew; so finally, to keep the Fugitives together, he decided to accept and sent his letter to the group in care of Tate, urging him to do all he could to promote peace. "You see it will be impossible or at least extremely embarrassing to operate the *Fugitive* under a cloud of controversial give and take." [61] The letter was, as Davidson himself had termed it, diplomatic, deferring "further debate" until fall and concluding: "It is unworthy of us, committed as we are to a worthy enterprise, to indulge in strife and recrimination. I wish to subscribe myself to the principle of conserving tomahawks and war-whoops for the enemy abroad, not squandering them among ourselves." [62]

[60] "Mr. Ransom Replies," [letter] *The Literary Review*, August 11, 1923.
[61] August 14, 1923.
[62] Davidson to the Fugitives, August 14, 1923.

Tate replied that Davidson's letter had struck " exactly the right note." [63] But the group balance was perilous. Of the three men chiefly involved, none was capable of assuming a mask of disinterested altruism. Since they were involved personally, their principles were also in question; they made no sharp division between self and ideals. It was this neoclassical quality in their gentlemanly fight that led Davidson to offer to try to obtain from Ransom whatever Tate would accept as a " reasonable satisfaction." [64] The spirit of the old code duello was not dead.

But it was difficult for anyone to remain angry with Ransom. In the middle of the controversy, for instance, while his relations with Tate were extremely strained, he wrote a genial letter forwarding praise which Untermeyer had given the group. The letter was addressed

Fugitive Editors,
    Whoever Ye May Be:

I have just received a jolly 3-page letter from friend Louis Untermeyer, mostly personal to myself, but containing matter of profit and interest to all Fugitives as follows: [He lists a change of address for Untermeyer and quotes the following passage from his letter:] " Here, far from the American scene, most of the sounds that issue from the U. S. poetry magazines come to me with a distressingly similar thinness. Which is why I write to tell you that the *Fugitive* has—at least for me—a continually increased volume and richness of tone. The June-July issue has a particularly strong gamut, and, although travel makes me shed magazines almost as fast as I receive them, I have torn out the pages devoted to Merrill Moore's four sonnets, your . . . ' First Travels of Max,' and the . . . ' Spectral Lovers.' " [The deletions are Ransom's.] [65]

When Ransom received Davidson's forwarded letter of acceptance, despite his staunch opposition to the change in policy, he immediately wrote a reply which Davidson considered " in excellent

[63] August 18, 1923.
[64] To Tate, August 22, 1923.
[65] August 18, 1923.

spirit." [66] After tendering Davidson felicitations—for a forthcoming volume of poetry and an academic promotion—Ransom went ahead to say: "At the same time I am not satisfied with our new masthead, and must declare my intention of agitation for a change as soon as I can attend a next meeting, but in doing so I cheerfully engage to abhor strife and recrimination and to conserve my weak arsenal of tomahawks and war-whoops against a more appropriate occasion and to approach the question with a feeling of good will." [67] His argument was, however, that *The Fugitive* was of direct professional importance to most of the members of the group; that it had been founded with the idea of a group policy, in which no one's part in the magazine was to seem of less importance than another's. He concluded: "In stating my personal and selfish attitude, I mean to pose only as an example of what I had heretofore conceived was the universal (or nearly so) Fugitive opinion." Davidson took the letter as conciliatory, but when he replied suggested that the group should realize that equality had been a "purely hypothetical thing" among the members and that actually they did not make "an equal contribution of time, interest, or poetry." [68] He was alarmed, however, at the possibility of a serious breach within the group. As he wrote Tate, "The status of a group such as ours is bound to be a shifting, bewildering thing at times. A faculty of operation can be preserved only by genially winking at each others' faults. We do so most of the time." [69]

And a "shifting, bewildering thing" the group appeared to Tate, who, in the midst of these two controversies, was trying to get out an issue of the magazine. To Davidson he wrote, ". . . the griefs and anxieties clustering about the birth of the dear *Fugitive* are almost enough to distract the devil from Hell." [70] Tate and Jesse Wills had been the only ones to read any poetry at the last meeting, and so the members' contributions were difficult to as-

[66] To Tate, August 24, 1923.
[67] As quoted, Davidson to Tate, August 30, 1923.
[68] To Tate, August 22, 1923.
[69] *Ibid.*
[70] July 31, 1923.

semble. Wills was to have written the editorial for the issue, but, according to Tate, he procrastinated, leaving Tate the task of writing it. "As usual," he wrote, "I had to get what you all call the Tatian taint in somewhere, but luckily I restricted it to the title, which I couldn't resist." The published issue lacks the taint, however, and, in fact, has no editorial. Tate must have decided to omit it at the last minute. But at any rate he finally got the whole thing to the press, and ended by feeling rather satisfied with its quality:

This issue of the *Fugitive* will not be so bad, I believe, as we at first expected. The outside stuff is pretty good, and helps out a lot. Warren's poem is a first-rate piece of work; that boy is a wonder, or I'm much mistaken, and deserves election to the Board; I might even go so far as to say that the Board deserves to have him. Potamkin's poems are very good, and Percy's is very decent (in the sense of *fitting*), and the Contest poems are better this time than before, due to Crane and, again, to Potamkin. Jesse's two sonnets are excellent, as we've come to expect; and your poems, while they aren't the best you've done, show no falling off and will grace the issue. My two poems for Oenia are trifles, but fairly well done—return to the Oenia poem of last summer, in a way.[71]

Tate's estimate of the magazine is a fairly just one. Except for his omission of any comment on Ransom's excellent "Blackberry Winter" and on Laura Riding Gottschalk's "Dimensions," one of the contest poems, his letter to Davidson mentioned most of the significant poems in the issue.

The contest was bringing in a considerable number of serious poems, along with many, of course, that were mediocre. Hart Crane's "Stark Major" was a real acquisition for the magazine, and Potamkin's "Malidon" was not greatly beneath the group's standards. As well as attracting contest entries, the publicity attendant upon the contest drew in from several young poets manuscripts intended for regular publication. Among these was the work of Laura Riding Gottschalk, then the wife of an instructor in history at the University of Louisville.[72] Early in the summer she had

---

[71] *Ibid.*
[72] She had been born Laura Riding of immigrant parents in New York City,

sent in poems which, despite their indubitable interest, did not seem to the editors quite suitable for *The Fugitive*. Davidson had written her a commendatory letter, but heard nothing more from her for a while; later she wrote a note apologizing for her sensitiveness to rejection.[73] Further, she promised to send a sizeable collection of her poems at a later date. In the latter part of the summer she sent in "Dimensions" for the contest, one of her best poems ever to appear in *The Fugitive*. Its beginning is sharp and direct:

> Measure me for a burial
> That my low stone may neatly say
> In a precise, Euclidean way
> How I am three-dimensional.

And it ends:

> Measure me by myself
> And not by time or love or space
> Or beauty. Give me this last grace:
> That I may be on my low stone
> A gage unto myself alone.
> I would not have these old faiths fall
> To prove that I was nothing at all.

But it would not be until early winter that the editors were to see a representative body of Mrs. Gottschalk's poems.

In spite of the summer's contention, it had been a profitable time for most of the Fugitives. Davidson's volume *An Outland Piper* had been accepted for publication, and Tate was not much behind Davidson in finding a publisher. Moreover, he had been

---

had lived at various places during her childhood, and had gone to Cornell on a scholarship. She wrote for the college literary paper and became interested in writing seriously during her three years there. After a brief stay at the University of Illinois, she gave up academic life to marry Louis Gottschalk and to write. By the time she encountered *The Fugitive*, she had had poems printed in *Poetry*, *Lyric West*, *Contemporary Verse*, *The Lyric*, *The Sewanee Review*, *Poet Lore*, *Nomad*, and *The Stepladder*, had written one novel and several chapters of a second. (These facts about Miss Riding are taken from an undated letter she wrote to Davidson sometime in 1924.)

[73] [Summer, 1923].

commended by no less a personage than T. S. Eliot and had placed a poem in *The Modern Review*.[74] Ransom had won the Southern Prize in the South Carolina Poetry Society Contest. Johnson, dissatisfied at Vanderbilt, was desperately seeking to get a start at supporting himself by writing. In July, when he had written Davidson concerning the editorial matter, he stated that he had completed five stories, " four of them pot-boilers that will sell," and the fifth " an art story which will not sell." [75] He had also completed two acts of a three-act play and about fifty pages of a textbook on the short story.

The Southern literary renaissance was being discerned even by academic observers such as Addison Hibbard, associate professor of English at the University of North Carolina, who in an article for *The Literary Review* mentioned Ransom and Davidson as two of the important new Southern poets.[76] To Tate and Davidson, the Fugitives who were most vigilant about modern poetry, the article seemed hopeful, although they both felt that Hibbard should have distinguished more carefully between groups in the South, and Tate thought one of his statements—that there was nothing like a school of poetry in the section—should be questioned. Tate revealed his essential generosity in rejoicing at the praise Hibbard had bestowed upon Ransom:

I am especially glad that John came in so prominently; it is the first time, so far as I know, that his *Poems about God* has received the praise it deserves, or even recognition; and if it weren't for the recent schism between us, which might lead him to misinterpret me, I should write him a note of congratulation. I think Hibbard could well afford to leave me out, but I can't deny that I should have liked being mentioned; it would have helped my volume along, besides the good it would naturally have done the Ego. But I am surely glad he mentioned you . . . .[77]

---

[74] William Elliott, who was in Nashville for the summer, had a letter from T. S. Eliot praising Tate's work, which he had seen in *The Fugitive*. " I feel like putting a record on the gramophone," Tate wrote Davidson in his jubilance (July 31, 1923).

[75] July 23, 1923.

[76] " The Lyric South," *The Literary Review*, September 1, 1923.

[77] To Davidson, September 7, 1923.

Earlier in the letter Tate had voiced his wish that Ransom and he might be reconciled. He would like, he said, to write Ransom that he "bore him no ill will and that the controversy was a closed incident." But he added rather wistfully, "I do believe that he should approach me first."

When the school year began, the regular meetings were resumed with little change in routine. Curry and Moore were back from Europe; Ransom and Davidson returned from their summer's location; Tate, who had just received his degree, decided to stay on a while in Nashville for the lack of anything better to do; Elliott and Frierson left for their winter posts. The only real change consisted of the loss of Ridley Wills, who after his marriage went to New York, where he took a position with *The Herald*. Most of the members, then, were present, and the habitual ease of intercourse among them, established by long practice, was not dimmed by the summer's tiff.

Actually, the relationship of the Fugitives was of a mysteriously binding nature. Not dependent on the members' personalities but on their character and intellect, the ties could not be severed by mere personal quarrel. William Elliott, writing from the University of California in Berkeley, where he had accepted a position in the Department of Political Science, discerned the essential indissolubility of the group of which he both was and was not a component. Aware of the almost belligerent individuality of the members and their sometimes passionate disagreements, he was puzzled at their solidarity. Certain that there was no such phenomenon as a Group Mind, he was yet forced to acknowledge its existence:

It seemed to me this summer there was some little rumor among you that *The Fugitive* was Fugitives.

And yet, God's truth, but you do mightily resemble one another. Who, that had known Steve these years, would think to find Philomela going flat on him, too? . . . Tate, that child of wrathful detachment, and Donald, the excellent Donald of a lyric Spring, now droop into the replete maturity of summer, and reflective autumn. It may be time, but

I should say it is a subtle tribute to the attraction of Johnny's bag of tricks. You all draw on it.

Perhaps this is no more than to say Johnny was the first modern among us. He it was who castigated sentimentality wherever it showed its simple head, and first set up the Baal of complexity for worship.[78]

But Elliott felt that the real music of poetry was lost in the members' efforts at intellectuality: "I derive considerable comfort from an occasional lapse from restraint among you, particularly on Donald's part or Tate's. Your poetry is too *social*. It is done for approval . . . ." And he added ruefully, "When a stranger comes among you, he is a marked man . . . ." Elliott realized that he was no longer in touch with the perplexing "Group Mind" which he denied; nevertheless, he was aware that he would never find elsewhere the kind of association that the Fugitives had provided:

I honestly miss the talks that Oxford can no longer make up for— the inspiration of Dr. Hirsch, the inevitable soundness of Johnny, the honest insight of Stanley, Donald's friendly warmth, and Steve's, Bill F's cynic search for motives and equally unmotivated good fellowship, the scintillant and errant Allen, and *l'enfant terrible*, our Merrill, never forgetting that Nestor, Dr. Frank. Looking back on our meetings together I seem to remember most clearly his Druid's brows and calm— never letting us forget the high regions even while we most mocked.

In the October *Fugitive*, the first to be published under the contract with Back, the thirteen poems by Fugitives were nearly all of a high order. Of Ransom's contributions, two—"Judith of Bethulia" and "Rapunzel"—are in one of his favorite genres: allegory in which persons existing already in myth or legend are made to bear directly the burden of reanimated and transformed meaning. Judith, the beautiful and sheltered, becomes in a time of invasion not only the protectress of herself but of her people. Yet the awful sight of the beauty with which she accomplishes the destruction of the enemy fevers the young men in her own camp; since the victory they have been wild and irrepressible: "Inflamed

[78] To Davidson, October 11, 1923.

by the thought of her naked beauty with desire? / Yes, and chilled with fear and despair." In the other, Rapunzel, modernized, has been shorn of her golden hair, and not without some responsibility for the deed herself, since the poet "accuses" her: "Was it well / How the old witch has enviously undone you?" She has deprived herself and her proper lover of consummation:

> Do you sit at the casement still,
> Braving the ruins of your smile but wanly?
> Prince there shall come not till
> He may climb to his kiss on a rippling ladder, only.

Another of Ransom's poems in the issue, "The Spiel of the Three Mountebanks," is written in a doggerel verse, a limping, Hudibrastic use of the rhymed couplet—almost a burlesque of poetry itself—to set forth Ransom's confirmed Pyrrhonism.

Davidson's three poems are different enough from Ransom's to make it evident that the resemblance Bill Elliott found among the Fugitives was one best seen by intimates. In Davidson's work the themes do not derive from an obliquely slanted insight but come from an almost Wordsworthian simplicity of poetic conception. And yet the poems are modern ones, proper products of their time. Two are wholly successful, evidencing Davidson's remarkable ability to absorb modernity into traditional forms rather than to submit to or compromise with it. In "Stone and Roses," the author draws a quiet and simple portrait with an easy flow of meter and language, and in "Old Harp" he strikes up an elegiac rhythm to sing a lament for lost songs.

One of Tate's two poems is a sonnet, tightly rhymed and linguistically condensed. In both poems the language is bright, put together with the impact of a fresh and startling mental context. Of the remaining members' poems, Stevenson's and Johnson's are most noteworthy. Soon to become a member, Warren contributed a poem, "Midnight," which is one of his most sustained pieces to appear in *The Fugitive*. Striking immediately through the carefully protected surface of events it moves to a world of psychological horror beneath:

> I cannot sleep at night for dread
> Of terrible green moons that haunted once
> The dark above our marriage-bed . . . .

The poem drives on through its murky images to a conclusion that, although not free of the Eliot influence, reveals an anguish far beyond the realm of any derivation:

> Your gaunt uncomprehending eyes
> Clutch at me as I start to rise,
> Rattling my newspaper, saying, " It is late."
> You draw the pins, release your flood of hair.
> Am I doomed to stand thus ever,
> Hesitating on the stair?

The other visitors present in the issue—Joseph T. Shipley, Harry Alan Potamkin, and Henri Faust—offered creditable if not entirely memorable pieces. The issue is marred somewhat by its female contestants, except for Laura Riding Gottschalk. But taken as a whole, it is a fine collection of poems with which the Fugitives greeted the oncoming winter of teaching and work.

The local public for the poets, however, was becoming less enthusiastic as time passed. Nashville citizens in general had begun to regard the young men as crazy or wild, or deliberately unintelligible. T. H. Alexander, a local newspaperman who had attended Vanderbilt back in the days when Davidson was a student, devoted two columns to good-humored sallies against Fugitive obscurity: "We generally read it [Fugitive poetry] frontward first, and then try reading it backward like a Chinese laundry ticket, but we never succeed in finding what it's all about." [79]

But if the Nashville reading public was finding the group bizarre, literary men elsewhere were taking increasing notice of the magazine. One of the most direct and enthusiastic bits of approbation came from William Stanley Braithwaite, American Negro poet and anthologist, who had been since 1913 publishing an anthology of "the best magazine verse" each year. In the

[79] The Nashville *Tennessean*, September 22, 1923.

October 6 Book Section of the Boston *Evening Transcript* he wrote a review of *The Fugitive* which was unqualified in its commendation. Announcing the contents of the 1923 edition of his annual anthology, in which were to be found seventeen poems by the Fugitive group, Braithwaite devoted a large portion of his article to the Nashville poets. After stating that the multiplicity of poetry journals in America was a hindrance to the development of the art, since most of them, dependent upon the financial support of their members, published chiefly their own work, Braithwaite continued:

There are exceptions here and there in which the group has been fortunate in the assembling and cohesion of its talents. An example I have in mind is *The Fugitive*, published at Nashville, Tenn. This poetry magazine displayed more character and originality during the last year than any magazine in the country. One found often in its pages themes, and the treatment of themes, that were often too strong with the tang of originality. There was, nevertheless, time and again, power of vision, and the very certain note of individuality.

He named the Fugitive members, praising them for their individual talents, and his final estimate of the group was strongly favorable: "This group seems wholly absorbed in functioning artistically and wasting no time on propaganda or self-advertising. These men are going to be heard from in no uncertain accents when the clamor of pride and authority has subsided in certain literary capitals."

The group was, of course, pleased at such detailed and approving criticism: writing to thank Braithwaite, Davidson expressed the genuine appreciation of all the Fugitives:

We want you to know that, whatever encouragement we have got from other people, your notice of us has been the clearest and most unqualified recognition we have received since we began publishing the *Fugitive*, a little over a year ago. And we should like for you to know also that your words represent our purposes and outlook—however short we may fall of recognizing them—only as we should have cared to represent them ourselves if avowals of attitude could ever be countenanced. To us this is the best phase of your remarks bearing on our work; it is no mean encouragement to a group of writers, isolated from the main stream of current letters in an environment none too friendly to the arts, to be able to feel that we are understood by a critic for whose work we have no inconsiderable respect.[80]

Braithwaite's perception in this instance should not be minimized; nevertheless, it is a peculiar and ironic phenomenon in the life of *The Fugitive* that most of its literary sponsorship came from such critics as Christopher Morley, Witter Bynner, Louis Untermeyer, and William Stanley Braithwaite, all well-known figures on the literary scene in the twenties. These seem now strange men to have appreciated a group of poets so metaphysical, so hard in their intellectuality, so counter to popular taste as Ransom, Davidson, Tate, and Warren.

One wonders at the lack of any alliance between the Fugitives and the most distinguished poets and critics in both England and America. It can be explained only by the admission that Fugitive poetry, during the time of the magazine, was "unstylish." It did not appeal to the young advance-guard experimentalists who were making their headquarters in New York and abroad and always, wherever they were, rebelling against the values of their society. For some of these dislocated persons, Marxism was the only refuge in a world that seemed to be falling into chaos; for others, salvation lay in an aestheticism in which art was superior to life and independent of it. Neither of these groups had anything but scorn for the writer who accepted the old forms and beliefs without first performing the "great labor of destruction and negation."[81] And the Fugitives were not social revolutionists nor, except for Tate, poetic experimentalists. They made use of traditional conventions in their poetry in a natural and unselfconscious manner that must have seemed, to the young litterateurs of New York, perfectly undistinguished and trite. Consequently they were not taken up into the sophisticated literary world of the day, and the men of real taste did not encounter them until later.

[80] October 18, 1923 [carbon copy].
[81] Dadaist Manifesto; quoted in Malcolm Cowley, *Exile's Return* (New York: W. W. Norton and Company, 1934), 159.

The Nashville *Tennessean* full-page spread featuring the Fugitive poets
a year after the founding of their magazine.

Kissam Hall, the men's dormitory at Vanderbilt. Here, as young professors, Ransom and Curry had their residence and several of the Fugitives occupied student quarters. The Calumet Club, a literary group to which most of the Fugitives belonged, met here in the 1910's and 1920's.

To men like Untermeyer and Braithwaite, who were not intense enough in their commitment to poetry to suffer the pangs of dissociation that other more serious literary men felt, the Fugitive poems offered lines that were neither shocking and unintelligible nor sentimental and ordinary. Such men were unable to discern that what they considered "flaws" in Ransom's and Davidson's poetry were integral; they failed to perceive the essential character of the poetry which they graciously sponsored.

Among Southern literary men, *The Fugitive* was warmly appreciated, although actually more for its function of promoting Southern literature than for its intrinsic merit. John McClure of *The Double Dealer* was an exception; he had made available the pages of his magazine to individual Fugitives from time to time, recognizing and applauding their ability. The Poetry Society of South Carolina, eager to sponsor poetry throughout the South, had established friendly relations with the Nashville group from the first. Hervey Allen, for instance, wrote to Davidson: "We all value 'The Fugitive' very much, and appreciate enormously the genuine work being done by your group. A little more fighting by the present generation and the old sentimental ghosts will be pretty well laid or confined to their natural habitat, the country churchyard." [82] Other members—Josephine Pinckney, Henry Bellamann, and DuBose Heyward—had written sending their good wishes. W. A. Percy, connected with no special group but possessed of his own following, contributed several poems to the magazine and had agreed to act as judge in the contest; and, although, as he admitted, he did not always like *The Fugitive*, he did like the spirit of it. [83]

The contest publicity had been gratifying; such periodicals as the New York *World*, the *New York Times*, the San Francisco *Chronicle*, the Cleveland *Times*, *Poetry*, *The Lyric*, and *All's Well* had carried notices of the prizes offered. As the Fugitives reported to the Associated Retailers, more than four hundred poets had sent

[82] November 8, 1923.
[83] To Davidson, July 23, 1923.

in verses, every state in the union being represented, as well as Mexico, the Philippines, Belgium, Canada, and Hawaii.[84] The three judges were instructed to rank the poems from one to twelve for the Nashville Prize and from one to six for the Ward-Belmont Prize and to return their decisions along with any comment by November 19 in order that the magazine might go to press by November 22.

The results of the contest were a little startling. With judges of so different bent, the club members no doubt expected fairly large divergencies of opinion; but they could not have expected each judge's choice for first prize to find no place at all in the listings of the other two. Munson selected Crane's " Stark Major," which he considered a genuinely distinguished poem, for first place, Auslander's " Berceuse for Birds " for second place, and Mrs. Gottschalk's " Daniel " for third. " Crusade " by Warren he placed fourth, " O Savage Love," by Miss Purnell fifth, and " Malidon," by Potamkin sixth. The remaining poems he rated in the seventh place, since he felt there was no real distinction among them; but on being requested by the editors to rank them, he rather half-heartedly decided on ratings for the other six. As for the Ward-Belmont prize, Munson was convinced that no prize should be awarded, since he found in none of the entries " any musical interest or any metaphorical ingenuity or any sense of an intelligence, however immature, dancing back of the words." [85]

Significantly enough, Percy's reaction to the contest was exactly the reverse of Munson's. Percy found judging difficult— because the Ward-Belmont poems were so good and the Nashville poems so mediocre! [86] In the Nashville contest, he ranked first Shipley's poem, which Munson had placed last; and in twelfth place he put Crane's poem, which Munson had rated as first.

Miss Rittenhouse, too, placed Crane's poem twelfth on the list; and altogether there was so little agreement among the judges

[84] Report of the Administration of the Nashville Prize, made to the Associated Retailers, October 20, 1923 [carbon copy].
[85] *The Fugitive*, II, No. 10 (December, 1923), 163.
[86] Percy to Davidson, November 6, 1923.

that the final decision was necessarily a mathematical one. Rose Henderson's " A Song of Death," with the ratings of tenth place (Munson), second (Rittenhouse), and third (Percy) tied with Auslander's " Berceuse for Birds," ranked as second (Munson), sixth (Rittenhouse), and seventh (Percy). The Ward-Belmont contest, based on the opinions of only two judges, was won by Louise Patterson Guyol, of Smith College, with her " Chart Showing Rain, Winds, Isothermal Lines and Ocean Currents." Roberta Teale Swartz of Mount Holyoke College and Margaret Skavlan of the University of Oregon tied for second place.

The contest results, revealing as they did the unresolved dichotomy in the consciously held aesthetic of the Fugitives (not greatly present in their actual practice), proved somewhat embarrassing. But out of the debris emerged, at any rate in the eyes of the group, two real winners who, through the medium of the contest, won their way into the pages of *The Fugitive* and finally into its membership roll: Robert Penn Warren and Laura Riding Gottschalk. Warren had appeared first in the magazine in the June-July issue, his poem " Crusade " being one of the three chosen by the editors for the first heat in the Nashville prize contest. Mrs. Gottschalk had appeared first in the succeeding issue, in which " Dimensions " had been selected by the editors.

Warren, of course, through his close association with the group had convinced the members of his genius. Mrs. Gottschalk, separated from the center of Fugitive activity, had made her conquest solely through her poetry. Sometime near the first of December she had sent a great packet of her verses to the editors, almost overwhelming Davidson and Tate, who both read them with great enthusiasm. Tate, recovering from a bout with influenza, took time to write her a letter of serious praise, which struck deep into this strange and turbulent girl. Starved for admiration and fellowship, she replied with a touching and sober letter which perhaps overstated the importance to her of the group's encouragement.[87] Tate, Davidson, and Warren were certain that they had discovered

[87] December 12, 1923.

a real poet; the verses she sent them were impressive—bold, direct, hard, thoughtful. In his letter reporting on the contest to Miss Rittenhouse, who had praised Mrs. Gottschalk's "Dimensions," Davidson expressed his confidence in the young poet's ability: "Before long we shall be publishing a group of her poems which we hope will further confirm good opinions. We consider her— particularly in view of her work that has recently come to us—our most interesting and promising 'discovery' of the year." [88]

The year was ending in a mood of heady power for the Fugitives, certain in their innocence that good poets could be discovered and developed by a disinterested though passionate concern for poetry alone. And though the December issue of the magazine was not so interesting as its predecessor, it was remarkable in its representation of more Fugitives than any of the preceding numbers during the year: only Frierson and Hirsch were absent. The more critical members recognized that all the poems in the issue were not exceptional; but they were firm in their conviction that the group publication was headed in the right direction—that without the sponsorship of commercial publishers, without the whole paraphernalia of literary connections, amateurs devoted to the art of poetry could write good poetry and find a hearing.

[88] December 15, 1923.

≈≈≈≈≈≈≈≈≈≈≈≈≈≈≈≈≈≈≈≈≈≈≈≈≈≈≈≈

CHAPTER SIX

THE BEGINNINGS OF

CRITICAL THEORY:

1924

THE YEAR 1924 marks the high point of *The Fugitive's* course. It was the last year in which editorial tasks were performed in an amateur fashion, with the whole group still taking an active part in the magazine's affairs. Hereafter, the group disintegration would begin, as more members found that the joint project could no longer occupy first place in their hearts and minds. It was during this year that the ones seriously dedicated to literature found themselves set apart within the group by their intensive study of the art of poetry; and, although afterward they were to recognize that they were bound as persons to discharge a responsibility to the body politic and economic, now they were content in the vocation of letters, cultivating their craft with single-minded attention. They published books, wrote reviews, and experimented in both poetry and criticism.

Indication of a growing concern for the profession of letters is to be found in the Editorial Comment of the February, 1924,

Fugitive: "Poetry is now having a hearing [in the South], where for a long time the audience has been negligible. The next need is critics. And may these not be long in coming." As token of its own interest in criticism, *The Fugitive* carried in the same issue the first of a series of brief critical essays, Ransom's "The Future of Poetry." A delineation of the dangers inherent to poetry in what he termed "Modernism," Ransom's essay continued his defense of traditional techniques for the poetic medium. Again he concerned himself primarily with the problem of prosody, this time openly deploring the modern abandonment of meter. As justification for this position he wrote:

> . . . it does not seem too hazardous to claim that poetry, as one of the formal arts, has for its specific problem to play a dual role with words: to conduct a logical sequence with their meanings on the one hand; and to realize an objective pattern with their sounds on the other. Now between the meanings of words and their sounds there is ordinarily no discoverable relation except one of accident; and it is therefore miraculous, to the mystic, when words which make sense can also make a uniform objective structure of accents and rhymes. It is a miracle of harmony, of the adaptation of the free inner life to the outward necessity of things.
>
> But we moderns are impatient and destructive. We forget entirely the enormous technical difficulty of the poetic art; and we examine the meanings of poems with a more and more microscopic analysis; we examine them in fact just as strictly as we examine the meanings of a prose which was composed without any handicap of metrical distractions; and we do not obtain so readily as our fathers the ecstasy which is the total effect of poetry, the sense of miracle before the union of inner meaning and objective form. Our souls are not, in fact, in the enjoyment of full good health. For no art and no religion is possible until we make allowances, until we manage to keep quiet the *enfant terrible* of logic that plays havoc with the other faculties.

In poetry specifically, Ransom continued, the modern mind scorned the admission into a poem of the "certain amount of nonsense" (archaisms, inversions, illegal accents) needed to provide the necessary latitude for the construction of form. The result of this enforced rigidity among poets was, he believed, a kind of paralysis; they were immobilized in the knowledge of their own inability to perform flawlessly. Under these circumstances, he feared, the future of poetry could not assuredly be considered immense.

Certainly in his own poetry Ransom was finding the problem of form pressing. He was constantly working toward perfection of the ritual with which he adapted the "inner meaning" to the "objective form." For him the very fear of the formal cliché led to its parody; and through ironic parody came freedom. Thus, in "Captain Carpenter," "Bells for John Whiteside's Daughter," and "Prometheus in Straits," all appearing in the same issue as the critical article, the "miracle of harmony" that Ransom described as the total effect of poetry has been accomplished, partly through the wry and tactful use of the cliché. "Captain Carpenter" is consciously archaic, beginning

> Captain Carpenter rose up in his prime
> Put on his pistols and went riding out
> But had got wellnigh nowhere at that time
> Till he fell in with ladies in a rout.
>
> It was a pretty lady and all her train
> That played with him so sweetly but before
> An hour she'd taken a sword with all her main
> And twined him of his nose for evermore.

And "Bells for John Whiteside's Daughter," too, is intentionally old-fashioned in its tone:

> There was such speed in her little body,
> And such lightness in her footfall,
> It is no wonder that her brown study
> Astonishes us all.
>
> Her wars were bruited in our high window.
> We looked among orchard trees and beyond,
> Where she took arms against her shadow,
> Or harried unto the pond
>
> The lazy geese, like a snow cloud
> Dripping their snow on the green grass,

> Tricking and stopping, sleepy and proud,
> Who cried in goose, Alas,
>
> For the tireless heart within the little
> Lady with rod that made them rise
> From their noon apple dreams, and scuttle
> Goose-fashion under the skies!
>
> But now go the bells, and we are ready;
> In one house we are sternly stopped
> To say we are vexed at her brown study,
> Lying so primly propped.

In these poems the quaintly pedantic language, the ballad meter, and the awkward rhyme are given grace by an ironic tone and a fairy-tale atmosphere—all providing aesthetic distance, so that technique functions not as a shackle but as a tool in the cohesive though multileveled meaning.

But his solution—the tenderly mocking use of conventional methods—was not the one for other Fugitives. Davidson's single piece in the issue, "The Old Man of Thorn," although superficially like Ransom's poems, since it uses the ballad stanza colored by a pervasive irony, is totally unlike them in spirit:

> Eph Dickon the old man
> The old man of Thorn,
> Plants thistles in cornfields
> As other men plant corn.

Davidson's irony is at once simpler and more mordant than Ransom's; in effect, it is a kind of lyricism in reverse. "The Old Man of Thorn" has a sureness of musical line that gives it none of the small ironic effects of the bumptious "Captain Carpenter."

Tate's single poem in the issue, "Touselled" (which the group did not like), indicates that its author was not concerned with the problem of form as Ransom described it. The difference between poetry and prose, for Tate, lay not in meter or rhyme, but in the exemplary nature of the poetic language itself, which, drawing upon both sense and intellect simultaneously, must present directly and not state. Tate was already committed to a carefully critical

attitude toward his poetic language: consequently a poem such as
"Touselled," though murky and disconnected in its rational framework, nevertheless shows a brilliant juxtaposition of vivid word-
groups:

> Unhappily fractured music in the scene
> Spills a hollow bird, perched
> On the bony Fall. Drip drip
> Sharply, vertically sharp the drops
> Plunged from the eaves . . . No wonder an interval
> Stalked by twin demons, Day and Night,
> Is defeated: it is a bastard hour, waiting
> While drops drop and wet warbles slight,
> Arise, hesitate on crooked legs of mist.
>
> No wonder, I say, dusk with her meek
> Redundancy of line, in one touselled color,
> Shrinks to a splotch of shaky black, albeit
> Inspiring with haste the bored philosopher.

To Merrill Moore poetic form presented no problem. He had
come upon his "sonnet" form a year before and after this year
would not desert it. Within its loosened limits he found the dura-
tion he required for his lively utterance, his poems from beginning
to end frequently being made up of a single sentence. In the
February issue, where he was represented by four pieces, his run-on
lines fit together with remarkable ease, particularly in the sonnet
"From a Conversation in the Chateau Garden":

> Those who could read erasures from a wall
> Of roses told me ivy had grown before
> Over the trellis and the iron door
> Now heavy with August, where leaves never fall
> But flutter as frantic as the roses laugh
> Over walls where ivy once grew in the time
> When the castle was more than forgettable rhyme
> And its walls not such a feudal cenotaph—
>
> They told me ivy had grown and added this
> That marble lends not so much to perpetuity
> Perhaps, as a rose seed, even, or a kiss,

> And that fugitive beauty finds a security
> Being caught and gathered away in some frail breast
> That dies and makes the earth a palimpsest.

The felicitous rhythm in these lines is all the more notable in being not perfectly regular, but full of the stress and pitch of actual speech. It is as though the artificial patterns of poetry were so familiar to Moore that he was able to think in them directly, without danger of falling into sing-song meter or false and imitative phrases.

Laura Riding Gottschalk illustrated, more than did Tate, the formlessness that Ransom feared. She was represented by four poems, her first "comprehensive group" to be published in the magazine. Her writing, though as immediate and unchecked as Moore's—and as full of the vitality of a fresh and original insight—found its natural expression in vers libre. At its worst, her poetic utterance was in the fragmentary and aphoristic vein toward which free verse tends. At its best, her style grew organically from a happy fusion of form and substance, as this passage from her poem "The Quids" illustrates:

> The little quids, the million quids,
> The everywhere, everything, always quids,
> The atoms of the Monoton—
> Each turned three essences where it stood
> And ground a gisty dust from its neighbors' edges
> Until a powdery thoughtfall stormed in and out.
> The cerebration of a slippery quid enterprise.
> Each quid stirred.
> The united quids
> Waved through a sinuous decision.
>
> The quids, that had never done anything before
> But be, be, be, be, be,
> The quids resolved to predicate
> And dissipate in a little grammar.

This is the poem that later so attracted Robert Graves that he was led to write to its author, offering her a position in the University of Cairo, where he was himself teaching. The Fugitives were no less impressed with it. On his way to Lumberport, West Virginia, to accept a high school teaching position, Allen Tate went by Louisville to get a sight of Mrs. Gottschalk. He found her a startling person: "Her intelligence is pervasive," he wrote Davidson; "It is in every inflexion of her voice, every gesture . . . . But always you get the conviction that the Devil and all Pandemonium couldn't dissuade her of her tendency." [1]

In this same month Davidson began a project that he and Tate had considered for two years or more—the editorship of a book page for the Nashville *Tennessean*, published by the colorful Luke Lea. For his reviewers Davidson made use of a large store of literary acquaintances and students, as well as his fellow Fugitives. Within the page, Davidson himself conducted a column—"The Spyglass"—wherein he commented on the weekly scene, emphasizing Southern literary affairs, with the aim of stimulating interest in the poetic movement stirring the section. Davidson's editorship of the page was to last until 1930, when Luke Lea's empire collapsed and the *Tennessean* began to feel the first severe effects of the depression. It was an excellent page during its whole career, but particularly in 1924 did it offer the Fugitives the chance to make public statements about current literature. For the four chief Fugitives—Ransom, Davidson, Tate, and Warren—it provided an outlet for honest critical writing, which at this stage of their development was extremely valuable. Tate in particular learned from the discipline of reviewing books assigned to him. His prose style had always puzzled the other members of the group, and he acknowledged in it himself an excessive turgidity. In his writing for the page Tate was willing to make changes whenever Davidson suggested: "I'm going to do my best to write the reviews as you require them," he wrote, "and if they don't suit you, send them back with the wicked parts of them marked; I'll revise and try them on you again." [2]

[1] February 21, 1924.
[2] To Davidson, March 8, 1924.

The outlook for *The Fugitive*, however, was not bright. The group was in debt, still owing the printers, Cullom and Ghertner, almost a hundred dollars on the "old account of *The Fugitive*," [3] and members were undecided about a policy for perpetuating the magazine. In West Virginia, Tate thought he should resign his editorial office: the only reason he saw for not doing so was the possibility of returning to Nashville for the summer, since "all things considered, it [was] still the most congenial place." [4] Reflecting on the lack of sympathy his views received from many of the other Fugitives, however, he was inclined to think he should resign. Davidson dissuaded him; yet he too felt that things were going badly with the group. He still believed, notwithstanding, that a large-scale resurgence was possible within the circle. "If there is any leadership in Southern literary affairs it ought to be here," he wrote, but the precarious financing of the journal made its prospects for continuance gloomy. [5]

Tate replied to Davidson's troubled report: "I balk at the prospect of our suspension . . . ." Money was not the chief trouble, he was certain. "Despite financial desperation," he wrote, "we could survive if we had enthusiasm (we ran a year before Back came; enthusiasm did it)." Tate was convinced that leadership for *The Fugitive* would have to come from Davidson and himself; the others were either committed elsewhere or limited by a lack of experience. Once Davidson had asked Tate if he took the magazine quite seriously, and Tate felt it necessary now to affirm his concern: "My recalcitrancy has been the measure of my enthusiasm," he stated. Justifying his attitude, he explained:

I think you were aware of my rather impatiently critical dissatisfaction with various compromises we were forced to make; I always accept compromises, but I can't conscientiously do it without asserting the principle of my objection. You may be sure that if I hadn't been deeply interested I wouldn't have ever asserted this principle, i. e., made

[3] Cullom and Ghertner to Davidson, June 25, 1924.
[4] Tate to Davidson, March 3, 1924.
[5] To Tate, March 15, 1924.

myself disagreeable. I was probably wrong a good deal of the time, but I felt like upholding what I thought was right.[6]

In a letter written a few days later, Tate outlined the three courses open to the group, as he saw them: first, to suspend the magazine—a policy which he feared would have to be adopted within the year; second, to unite with the Poetry Society of South Carolina—a step to which he would object, since it would discard the identity of *The Fugitive*; and third, to obtain a patron—but "alas, there are no more Medicis."[7]

Teaching in the Lumberport high school, with four classes in English and one in Latin, Tate was trying to save money for an escape to New York. With nothing much else to do in the small town, he spent about nine hours a day at his writing and study.[8] The projected volume of his poetry had not materialized, since his publishers, Lieber and Lewis, had gone into bankruptcy soon after accepting his manuscript. Tate had sent the returned poems to several other publishers without success and was now beginning to realize that he no longer cared greatly about seeing them in print: "As I look back on the past four years of my verse-writing, I recall that I was aware that I might have worked any two or three tendencies I experimented with and to as much success as attaches to the average volume of 'good verse' . . . but intellectual unrest over formal problems and an impatience with the meager statement imposed by the demand of intelligibility have about undone me."[9]

The ties between Davidson and Tate were the strongest within the group; hence their influence in each other's lives was not really weakened by distance. Warren more than Davidson felt Tate's absence, since Warren was as yet unformed in his convictions and badly in need of the daily companionship in serving the Muse that Tate's friendship had offered. "I value your criticism a good deal more than any other that I receive," he wrote, "for you know the sort that comes out in a Fugitive meeting."[10] Younger by

[6] To Davidson, March 24, 1924.
[7] To Davidson, March 27, 1924.
[8] Tate to Davidson, February 21, 1924.
[9] Tate to Davidson, March 3, 1924.
[10] To Tate, March 21, 1924.

several years than most of the other Fugitives, Warren felt that
he approached poetry with a different attitude from theirs, an
attitude which they did not sufficiently respect. Poetry to him was
a matter of life and death; it was not, as he sometimes thought it
to be with the others, a pleasant hobby or a means of exhibiting
erudition. He described his resentment in a letter to Tate:

> As I expected, my poem Romance Macaber was rather poorly
> received by the majority of the members. " Morbid, affected, uncon-
> vincing"—were among various criticisms applied. Hirsch with custo-
> mary pomp inquired if the thing was not extremely personal: " the
> expression of an extremely personal passion and emotion, etc." I was
> compelled to reply that had it been I would never have read it to the
> company there assembled . . . .[11]

This spring marked an emotional crisis for Warren; a sensitive
youth who had always been something of a prodigy in everything
he attempted, he came to literature with a brooding intensity. Tate
had greatly influenced his writing, and the group considered him
in a sense a follower of Tate's. " I am content for the moment at
least," Warren wrote, " and you should be happy for a bright
disciple." [12] Tate was a dedicated champion of Warren from both
personal affection and honest belief in the young man's genius.
Concerning poems that Warren had contributed to the *Tennessean*
book page, Tate wrote to Davidson: " That boy's a wonder—has
more sheer genius than any of us; watch him: his work from now
on will have what none of us can achieve—power." [13]

Wherever he felt praise due, Tate was always generous. Nine
days later, he was enthusiastic about another Fugitive's power as
poet. Davidson had sent to Lumberport a few manuscripts that
had been read at a Fugitive meeting. Tate was not impressed with
the poems, except for one—a long poem of Jesse Wills's, which he
considered the best poem yet produced by a Fugitive.[14]

[11] [Early spring, 1924].
[12] *Ibid.*
[13] April 17, 1924.
[14] Tate to Davidson, April 26, 1924. The poem was probably " Eden,"
published in the June, 1924, *Fugitive*.

Tate's critical opinions made up the content of the second essay published in *The Fugitive*. Appearing in the April number of the magazine, Tate's article was a reply to Ransom's predictions about the future of poetry, stated in the preceding issue. Under the heading, "One Escape from the Dilemma," Tate set out vigorously on his task of refutation. First of all, he would not admit that poetry is obligated to use words in a "dual role," to fit meaning into form. "If this were so," he wrote, "poetry would in no wise differ from prose except in the antic capacity of diverting us with a spectacle of virtuosity, of difficulty ingeniously overcome." In such an interpretation, Tate continued, poetry would possess the same content as prose; it would be concerned with "the rational exposition, rather than with the pure presentation, of intuitions or ideas." Wordsworth and Ransom saw no essential difference, Tate charged, between the diction of poetry and prose; hence Ransom could ascribe the failure of free verse to its lacking the "indispensable metrical scheme." Tate was willing to agree that free verse had failed; "but this does not mean," he wrote, "that a few writers who have written what we name free verse are negligible." In fact, Tate hesitated to divide the strains of modern poetry into "Old" and "New": "For the older song has assumed a variation —as I believe, a development, and is in a very real sense more traditional than any other mode practised by poets of the present time. Repetition, we seem to be saying, isn't tradition . . . ." Certainly the modern poet of whatever sort must modify the ordinary diction; he was forced

to a breaking up of a poetic idiom which, through the course of English poetry, has been rooted in the vitality of spontaneous expression . . . . But today the poet's vocabulary is prodigious, it embraces the entire range of consciousness . . . . Baudelaire's Theory of Correspondences— that an idea out of one class of experience may be dressed up in the vocabulary of another—is at once the backbone of Modern poetic diction and the character which distinguishes it from both the English Tradition and free verse (an escape from the dilemma of J. C. R.).

Actually, Tate held, none of the "radical" poets could be considered writers of vers libre, since all of them used traditional techniques, but with utter casualness. Their devices were set up in order to be destroyed and so to give a greater "illusion of freedom." The real poet of the age, aware that "Poetry the oracle" was gone, recognized that modern society had no myth other than machinery; "but at least our poet is aware of his own age, barren for any art though it may be, for he can't write like Homer or Milton now; from the data of his experience he infers only a distracting complexity."

Tate's contention that the modern poet, regardless of the form he used, was driven to modifications of the standard forms of diction is aptly illustrated in some of the best poetry of the April issue of the magazine—the three sonnets by Jesse Wills and the two sonnets and one three-quatrained piece by Robert Penn Warren, who had been added to the masthead in the previous issue. Wills's sonnets are grouped under the title "Snow Prayers," and the language is masculine and modern, as the following passages indicate:

> Dead years ring
> With blizzards, rivers frozen, wagging tongue,
> Beard like a city drift, and wheezy lung
> Mourn times corrupt, and change a bitter thing.
>
> When the lotus folk shall stir to a ghostly woe,
> Glimpsing across dim gardens and lagoons
> White-winged, their boreal heritage of snow.

The other poet whom Tate considered to have real power, Warren, exhibits also a diction distinctively modern in his first sonnet of the issue, an early version of his later "Iron Beach":

> Beyond this bitter shore there is no going,
> This iron beach, this tattered verge of land;
> Behind us now the tundra dims with snowing,
> In front the seas leap crashing on the strand.
> Faintly the sun wheels down its quickened arc
> While at our backs with inexorable motion
> Earth swings forgotten cities into dark
> And night sweeps up across the polar ocean.

> This place has its own peace, assuredly.
> Here we, once waked by tramcars in the street,
> Shall rest in unperturbed austerity,
> Hearing the surf interminably beat,
> Watching the pole star overhead until
> The arctic summer brings the carrion gull.

Ransom's contributions to the issue are " Ada Ruel " and " Old Mansion," one of his most mature and seasoned poems. Davidson was represented by " Fiddler Dow," a long ballad-like version of the *danse macabre*, and by " Prelude in a Garden," a sensitive portrayal of a moment between lovers when they are aware of their vulnerability. The setting is in a protected garden, where the two are about to come together in love and tenderness:

> But there, or ever love could take its captive,
> Before the lips could meet or arms entwine,
> They saw a face flashed up within the fountain,
> An old god entering at his favorite shrine.
>
> Invisibly revealed against their summer
> They marked a presence, beautiful, severe,
> And knew it well, that much too smiling phantom
> Nodding out doom where love was warm and near.
>
> Their bodies, that were sealed for dissolution,
> Chilled in the fragrant air. A somber breath
> Smote on their flesh with hindering strange assailment
> Reminding them that love begins with death.
>
> Or death begins with love. They named it not.
> After the magic pause were charmed no more.
> Too gallant to remember they were mortal,
> They kissed, as they had minded to before.

Of this poem, Tate wrote that he had been certain at first that it was Ransom's.[15] He began to recognize Davidson as he read on, but he still felt one line in particular was Ransomian. " I'm a jelly-

---

[15] To Davidson, April 14, 1924.

fish," he wrote, " if line four isn't John's! " [16] Tate considered the whole issue " mighty good "; one of Moore's sonnets was not quite worthy of print, he feared, but Curry's " neat quatrains " were " the best, by damn, he's done in a good while."

No poem by Tate was used in the issue, although he had submitted one (probably " Credo," which appeared in the subsequent issue). Ransom apologized to Tate for not using it: " As a substitute member of the Selection Committee (in Jesse's place) I might say it was declined for the April number on the ground that the prose piece of the same author's was already pretty esoteric, and more of the same might have tended to excess." [17] In the same letter Ransom took up the question of Tate's editorial, discussing what he called " some of the fine ideas . . . so precariously and prodigally therein hinted at." If, as he seemed to do, Tate defined poetry as having to do with " verse forms and kindred paraphernalia," Ransom wondered how a man could " ' casually ' use these paraphernalia when he knows he must." Furthermore, Ransom considered Tate too glib and saucy in his statement that poets " erect sound patterns only to break them down again for a greater illusion of freedom." And he wondered whether it was wise to assume that " pure presentation of ideas and sensations " was the business only of poetry. " But though I have trouble with your pp. ₂ and 3 [he wrote], your p. 2 seems to me as good a thing as you've ever done—or anybody else in that field. And I admire many other bits here and there. But honestly I question if the whole is worth the immense labor of working it out that falls upon the reader."

And, in a postscript, Ransom described as a " most nonsensical differentia " Tate's statement that the theory of correspondence was " at once the backbone of modern poetic diction and the character which distinguishes it from both the English tradition and free verse." It struck him, Ransom said, " as something fierce."

Ransom's concern, however, pleased Tate, for he wrote David-

---

[16] Lines three and four of the poem are: " Trembling was at her lips, and her petulant eyelids / Drooped, proclaiming him victor in that campaign."

[17] April 15, 1924.

son a few days later: "Received a fine letter from John, threshing me soundly for the late and lamented editorial." [18] To Ransom, however, Tate wrote challenging the statement that his article was not worth the difficulty it took to decipher it, and Ransom modified his charge in a letter written a week after the first one: "I particularly deplore my having raised the question whether it was worth the reader's time to work out your system: that, I suppose, was one of the overstatements which are pedagogically sound (receiving their justification from Plato himself) but damnable between friends. The difficulty of making you out was extreme: that was about all I had a right to say."

He modestly pleaded "plain ignorance" about the French poetic theory that Tate charged him with misrepresenting and ended: "I believe it is a fact that you are the only available victim for me, when it comes to giving my aesthetic theories an airing; and it is possible (though I do not wish to flatter myself) that I am one of the most accessible responses you yourself can find when you are similarly engaged." [19]

When it became evident to Tate that he had removed from Nashville permanently, he resigned from his position as associate editor of the magazine, to be replaced by Jesse Wills. Tate's policies had diverged so radically from those of the other members that he wondered if the Fugitives would not be better off without him even as a member; accordingly, he asked Davidson to "sound out" the sentiments of Ransom and Curry about his withdrawing. [20]

Davidson replied that Tate's leaving the group was not to be considered; no one was hostile to Tate, he insisted. [21] The constant disagreement and ill feelings among the Fugitives stemmed from the numerous small annoyances connected with the publication of the magazine, particularly now, with the question of the Back contract. This was not merely Davidson's private interpretation. At a meeting near the beginning of April, a resolution was pre-

[18] April 21, 1924.
[19] To Tate, April 22, [1924].
[20] April 16, 1924.
[21] To Tate, April 25, 1924.

sented which mentioned the waning Fugitive enthusiasm, Back's loss of about $450, and the paucity of current subscriptions (144). It was the opinion of the committee that " *The Fugitive*, founded as the poetry organ of a small group committed to a rigid application of an uncompromising poetic doctrine, has definitely alienated a large body of potential readers and subscribers . . . ." [22] Therefore, the committee recommended that, after two more numbers of the magazine, publication of *The Fugitive* be discontinued at the end of the calendar year.

But the controversy could not be resolved. Warren's letters to Tate at this period reveal the spirit of pessimism that had overtaken the Fugitive meetings, where evenings were " taken up by the usual fruitless discussion and wrangling as to how the magazine [was] to be continued and how this, that, and the other thing [were] to be done." [23] Warren reported that several of the members were in favor of abrogating the contract with Back at the end of its first year (in August) and continuing the magazine through the December issue on the group's own responsibility:

That would release Mr. Back from his somewhat unprofitable obligation during the summer and make the Fugitive members themselves underwriters for the next two issues which would complete the year. Mr. Frank opposes and is willing to make no change of contract if the magazine is to continue at all; he is, however, in favor of assisting Mr. Back financially without making any alteration of the legal terms. John and Jesse seem to hold with him after his presentation of the matter . . . .[24]

Frank was afraid that, inasmuch as the members were partners, not a corporation, Back would have a legal claim on each of them if the contract were broken. Hence, he felt that midsummer discontinuance of the contract was " an unsound business step." [25] As a result, the motion was passed that Frank inform Back of the impending

---

[22] " Report of Committee on Disposition of the Fugitive," April 7, 1924.
[23] [Early spring, 1924].
[24] [Early spring, 1924].
[25] As quoted by Davidson to Tate, April 25, 1924.

termination of the contract at the end of the year and of the intention of the group to help financially with the last two issues.

The next day Johnson (who had not been at the meeting) met Ransom and Davidson to discuss the future of the magazine. Ransom and Davidson saw the abandonment of *The Fugitive* at the end of the year as an almost certain event and were willing to pay with the other members whatever sums were necessary to maintain some self-respect in finishing the year. Johnson was full of new schemes, one of which concerned the formation of a stock company, with other literary men such as Harry Alan Potamkin and Joseph Shipley. He felt that the way *The Fugitive* had been run was the cause of the disruption: a minority view had no chance under the strong domination of Ransom, Davidson, Tate, and other partisans of modernism.

Wrangling was so chronic with the Fugitives at this stage that Davidson, sick at heart, himself considered resigning. He wrote Tate, " So long as high spirit was uniform, so long as the enterprise possessed nobility, it was truly a happy labor." [26] Their roles were reversed; and Tate was equal to the task of reassuring one who had often counselled him. He replied that he would never consent to Davidson's resigning: "You are the pivot of our activities; you mustn't unseat us suddenly. But I repeat that you have every justification for doing so." [27]

Meetings were being continued, in spite of the lack of an inner core of agreement between members. On the evening of April 21, Jesse Wills read what Ransom called "by long odds the best poem of considerable length (150 lines) that a Fugitive has yet perpetrated." Tate's sonnet "was read, admired, and condemned in the most standard manner." [28] The group had always charged Tate with affectation in his poetry; speculating on this criticism, Tate wrote ruefully to Davidson: "It is depressing to reflect that the only real piece of affectation I've committed, the only emotional *tour de force* is the very poem that was cherished best

[26] April 25, 1924.
[27] To Davidson, April 26, 1924.
[28] Ransom to Tate, April 22, 1924.

by the group—"A Scholar to his Lady." I am simply posing; but 'mob' sentiment, cliché emotion, never seems affected; it seems sincere because 'everybody' feels that way." [29] On the same day Tate sent Hirsch, as president of the Fugitives, an ironic letter which took the guise of a long personal complaint against the group, making satiric use of the various disgruntled attitudes of different members. He was well aware that several of the poets felt the managing of the magazine had been unfair; that its policies tended to support only a certain kind of poetry and so favored Ransom, Davidson, and Tate; and that this larger issue, masked by the financial problem, was the really troublous one confronting the Fugitives. Despite the group's apparent misinterpretation of the letter, the resulting controversy led to a clearing of the atmosphere. Ransom described to Tate the fruits of the discussion:

I wish you could have listened in on our meeting of last evening. In the first place, you would have been able to renew your slipping confidence that you had cast in your lot among friends. I believe a letter is in process of getting itself written to express to you more formally the sense of the group as deeply appreciative of your labors and loyalty on behalf of the common cause . . . which have never seemed to waver despite the fact that you so obviously were in the position of an extremely attenuated minority. We all, as a matter of fact, despite the naturally tyrannous tendencies of any overwhelming majority, feel thoroughly disposed to render you full credit for the value of your services and to give you the most ample representation in any exhibit of the work of the group. Of course in the long run, there is no estimating the value of any highly differentiated departure on the part of an individual—who knows which of the individual men may ultimately become the cornerstone of the edifice? Caution at least would prompt us against any exclusions.

Except in the case of the peculiar individualities of Messers Frank and Hirsch. And you would have been amused and edified to note how, in the course of a long and rather quiet discussion of the verities of group procedure, last night, we frankly took the position that the dear

[29] April 26, 1924.

magazine was open to any sort of performance that could style itself Modern . . . .

But best of all, Ransom continued, the boys were showing a reluctance to give up the magazine: "More and more, at each meeting, there develops a great disinclination to abandon The Fugitive. We are now committed to finishing the year on the present basis, with Back as goat; and with the expectation of going on ourselves indefinitely, the ways and means to be later determined. So I really believe there's life in the old carcass yet."

The argument with Tate over the idiom of poetry still plagued Ransom; he pointed out in this same letter that Tate had named three differentiae as defining the twentieth-century model which he advocated: the formal, the philosophical, and the rhetorical, whereas Ransom's own article had dealt almost wholly with the formal aspect of poetry:

Personally, my own disquietude is wholly over the formal difficulties; I would take it for granted that the other differentiae will attend any good performance, whatever the form may be; so it has been in the past. The traditional poets generally have defined themselves sharply but under a common conception of form; but it is this form that is broken down now . . . . An art defines itself as an adventure in a given form.

Lately, however, he felt that his own formal difficulty had "somewhat receded." His recent poems, in reverse order as nearly as he could remember, were "Miss Euphemia," "Tom, Tom, the Piper's Son," "Ada Ruel," "Bells for John Whiteside's Daughter," "Prometheus," and "Captain Carpenter." Tate had condemned two poems Ransom had sent him earlier for criticism: "Religio Medici Kentuckiensis," which Ransom agreed was worthless ("I have consigned it to oblivion," he wrote), and "Ada Ruel," (which had in the meantime appeared in the magazine) about which he replied: ". . . I don't believe I can agree with you entirely; I have kept it, with some change of title. I wonder if it can be that it offends you in some detail or other only? It seems to me quite tolerable stuff, but not calculated to make the great ones totter on their thrones."

But whatever compromises he might have to make with Tate's aesthetic theory, Ransom was certain that his objection to the younger man's prose style was valid:

I do feel entitled to impeach your treatment as exposition. I feel that you are in contact with red-hot truth, for you continually drop glowing and impressive sparks whenever you wax critical. But you tend to rely successively on the sparks, when we want a continuous blaze. In other words, you get hold of a beautiful intuition and immediately antagonize your followers by founding a Church thereon; when the probability is, you have stopped considerably short of the core of truth and are naming some accidental relation or other as THE FUNDA-MENTALS. I should think you ought to get your own consent to a little subordination among your (seemingly) perfectly insubordinate ideas. It is poetic, Modern, and pluralistic to exalt each in turn to the pinnacle; but the net result is confusion, which I feel is not really your purpose in prose, at any rate. Why are you not more provisional, tentative, qualified, disparaging, as you contemplate the Stream of your Ideas?

Before he could conclude his letter, however, Ransom felt it neces-sary, aware of his tendency to seeming coldness, to add a postscript which would make entirely clear the Fugitives' warmth of feeling toward Tate:

As to Monday's meeting: I find again that my tones seem rather cold. As a matter of fact, you are *persona gratissima* in our eyes—a priceless value to a dull and stodgy group. Even in absence you have inspired us to rededicate ourselves to *honest criticism* of our weekly stints: now each reading is followed by criticism from *each member in turn*, and the author is at last assured of having reactions to go by. But once more, we miss you sadly: parliaments are sleepy affairs when they are suddenly deprived of the obstructions, jibes, and provocations of their Left. We all hope you can be with us again this summer.[30]

This spring, proving so unpromising to several of the other Fugitives, brought to Davidson a tangible encouragement: his first volume of poetry, *An Outland Piper*,[31] which received quite favor-

[30] May 6, 1924.
[31] Boston and New York: Houghton Mifflin Company, 1924.

able reviews. *The Nation's* comment, written by Mark Van Doren, may be taken as representing the critical consensus:

. . . the first volume of verse by one of a group of young and original poets who have been making their magazine, *The Fugitive*, of Nashville, Tennessee, famous among Americans who look sharply for good verse. The prevailing tone is satiric—a reader thinks of T. S. Eliot, Maxwell Bodenheim, and occasionally E. A. Robinson—but there is evidence of a lively lyric gift, and on every page there is proof of a nimble, fearless mind. Mr. Davidson's next volume may well be a little more unified and much less obscure.[32]

Other reviewers emphasized the satiric vein in the poetry and remarked upon its lack of any distinctively Southern quality.[33] But no one label could cover the varied styles of the book's four sections. The first division is dominated by Davidson's tone of lyricism and made up of such poems as "An Outland Piper,"[34] "Old Harp," and "Following the Tiger." The second section of the volume is an ironic and in some instances heartless commentary on the tawdriness of the present. In this division is included the "Pan Series" that Tate had admired—"Corymba," "Dryad," "Twilight Excursion," and "Naiad." The third division, "Alla Stoccata," comprised of such poems as "Pot Macabre," "Iconoclast," "Ecclesiasticus I," and "Alla Stoccata," possesses an irreverent pertness of tone and an engaging liveliness of movement. The least successful piece in this group is "Ecclesiasticus II," a diatribe against the religion of Americanism. The volume ends with "The Man Who Would Not Die," a sharp, sardonic—yet not cynical—handling of blank verse which seems in Davidson's natural vein. It begins:

> The seasons had beleaguered Evan Thane
> With many a ravenous yearly trumpeting,

[32] CXVIII (April 2, 1924), 376.
[33] Later on in the year, Untermeyer, writing in *The Yale Review* (October, 1924, 160-61), did Davidson the justice of reviewing his book with the work of four other then important poets—Robert Frost, Wallace Stevens, Louise Bogan, and Edna St. Vincent Millay.
[34] A somewhat curtailed version of "A Demon Brother," published in the first issue of *The Fugitive*.

Pinched his defenses into crookedness,
And triumphed at the corners of his flesh,
And yet he would not tumble. Beards had wagged
Upon the lurking pestilence of humors
Pent in the damps to gnaw an old man's bones,
But no beards wagged for frosty Evan Thane.
He said he was no rotten Jericho
To shake for village prophets' reputations,
And scorned the bench where others whittled out
Their easy days with amiable discourse
Of usual death,—until at last they died.
Grimly he watched them coward it away;
Glowered contempt beneath the funeral cedars
Scarce long enough to hear the falling clods
Rattle the wood,—then lashed his horse and fled,
Like one who leaves a shameful battlefield.[35]

Twenty-four of the thirty-three poems in *An Outland Piper* had already been published in *The Fugitive*; it is interesting to observe that the unconvincing note of despair and cynicism in the volume derives chiefly from the nine added poems (some of them published in *The Double Dealer*, *Palms*, and *Folio*). The Fugitive group had not endorsed these other poems, and Davidson and Tate attributed such lack of approval to a blameworthy backwardness. Yet one of the benefits of a diverse and primarily conservative group can be seen here: less aware of dominant moods and fashions than were the two young experimenters, and possessed of an unspoken mistrust of aestheticism, the other members were able to discern the lack of genuineness which the disillusioned tone lent to Davidson's lyric and affirmative expression. Unfortunately, perhaps mistrusting this same lyricism, Davidson omitted from the volume three fine pieces—" Litany," " Swinging Bridge," and " To One Who Could Not Understand "—all published previously in the magazine.

As soon as Tate received a copy of Davidson's new volume, he wrote:

[35] *An Outland Piper*, 77.

It is the occasion for a renewed consciousness of the meaning of our compact, that covenant which was more significant than either of us could guess on the day of its almost casual making. For my part, its significance is quite separate from any idea of the greatness or immortality . . . [we may achieve].

As you say, it is the life of adventure, and I say that the reason of this is that it is the life of the soul; and it is the life of the soul despite the incidental frustrations we meet and the merely human foibles we display and the temporary misunderstandings of the flesh that we may suffer . . . .[36]

At the time, Davidson's volume received little notice in the South, where it might have been expected to arouse interest. Concerning this apathy on the part of his countrymen, Tate wrote: " It's just like the damn Southerners. No wonder we all get disgusted and want to leave. Some of us can't leave, though, which if it isn't a victory for them certainly is a kind of defeat for us . . . ." [37]

But Tate was on the verge of making his escape from a section which, as he later described it, " knew its own mind, knew what kind of society it wanted" and which would not support such " desperate men " as literary artists, " who mean business." [38] Hart Crane and Malcolm Cowley were urging Tate to come to New York, but he was afraid he lacked sufficient funds to embark yet upon a literary career. Another reason for not going to New York permanently just then was Warren's illness; aware of the younger man's spiritual isolation, of his need for affection and encouragement, Tate planned to spend the summer with him at Warren's home in Kentucky. Warren had arranged for a job for Tate in Guthrie, but since it would not be available until the end of June, Tate resolved to visit his mother in Washington, next make a brief trip to New York, and then come back through Nashville to Guthrie.

[36] To Davidson, March 24, 1924.
[37] To Davidson, May 7, 1924.
[38] " The Profession of Letters in the South," *The Virginia Quarterly Review*, XI, No. 2 (April, 1935), 164, 172.

As the Fugitives' vacation plans were being made, the early summer issue of the magazine went to press. It contained the third of the series of critical articles, "Certain Fallacies in Modern Poetry," which sets forth Davidson's convictions that reasoning about poetry does not necessarily produce it. "Systematic discussion of poetical theory, however stimulating it may be to the ego of the poets who engage in it," he wrote, "serves mainly to send thought rocketing and bounding down narrow channels from where there is little escape, and to which there is apparently no end. Poets need above all things to be perfectly unsystematic."

As a focus for his theory Davidson selected five "fallacies" which seemed to him connected with the false premise that a poet needs a program, the first fallacy being the idea that "a good poet must be possessed of an aesthetic." An aesthetic philosophy must of necessity be after the fact, Davidson pointed out; poetry must be produced first. Concerning the second fallacy, "that a good poet must perforce have 'local color,'" Davidson remarked, "Place is incidental; it may even form a definite limitation, and perhaps does in the case of much American poetry . . . . The poem, not the 'scene' or the business of interpreting the 'scene' must be uppermost in his consciousness." The whole group agreed with him on this point, as it did in proscribing the third fallacy, that poetry must possess a special vocabulary. But the fourth fallacy, "that the grand style is impossible to modern poetry," was an issue Davidson had frequently argued with Ransom and Tate. "The grand style is not, after all, a question of technique," he declared. "The grand style can be written only by grand men." The "apparent daring" of the proponents of modernism was not daring at all, he believed, but conformity to a set of inelastic dogma. The fifth fallacy Davidson listed encompasses the others: ". . . that any very specific limitations can be set for poetry." Throughout history, he maintained, poetry had accomplished the destruction of rules.

Davidson's pronouncements show him here, as always, striking out against the self-consciousness forced upon the poet in a world that increasingly analyzes and categorizes acts of the mind. Even though he was trying the experimental techniques in his own verse, he was protesting in his essay the strictures placed upon poetry by the modern experimentalists.

In the poetry of the same issue is to be found an expression of the aesthetic view opposed by Davidson in his article. Tate's "Credo," subtitled "An Aesthetic," depicts the plight of the modern poet who, faced with the "heterogeneities" of his age, cannot approach his subject with any degree of innocence or wholeheartedness:

> I can't revise my manners but I think
> If the decorative jet, which is your eye,
> And the restless pearl, which is your either breast,
> Would slough their antic imagery and shrink
> To impartial clay, like the dead fantasy
> Of tree tops, I could be shriven as the rest.
>
> Good manners, Madam, are had these days not
> For your asking nor mine, nor what-we-used-to-be's.
> The day is a loud grenade that bursts a smile
> Of comic weeds in my fragile lily plot;
> Comic or not, heterogeneities
> Divert my proud flesh to indecisive guile.
>
> Breast, eye: pearl, jet. Madam, have pity,
> Consider the precarious poetry of my Race—
> How, strictly, even Vittoria piqued the Angel
> By that much beauty he inserted in her face;
> (Wherefore synthetic wrath may breathe a city
> Upon any dim and doubtful perhaps Hell).
>
> My manner is the footnote to your immoral
> Beauty, that leads me with a magic hair
> Up the slick highway of a vanishing hill
> To Words—that palace of beryl and coral . . . .
> Often however I hear the music where
> Your sudden face rumors of twilight spill.

Here the Petrarchan imagery becomes in the protagonist's eyes the symbol for all inherited and meaningless conventions. If his lady's body could slough off its connotations of "antic imagery," connected as they are with the artificial attitudes of the past, if it could become natural in the way that "impartial clay" is natural, to be treated solely as part of the physical universe, then perhaps he could love her or write a poem with some sincerity. But since her body does have these associations, and since she herself has vague notions and expectations inherited automatically and unthinkingly from the conventions of courtly love, the young man is hard put to satisfy his mistress. For good manners are difficult these days, not to be had "for your asking, nor mine, nor what-we-used-to-be's"; they are impossible in a day where the awareness of the twitchings of one's own mental workings provide a sense of the comic. That "fragile lily plot," the delicate and retiring sensibility, cannot be maintained in the onslaught of "comic weeds."

The poet implores the woman he is addressing to "have pity"— to accept his manners both in love- and poetry-making, since the "precarious poetry" of his race must be considered. Even Michelangelo, he says, must have been made unquiet by whatever insincerity he used in his sonnets to Vittoria. And since, as he says, synthetic emotions can create a Hell even if we lack belief in one, the state of poetry is indeed precarious: if the conventional good manners are to be required of it, the price in falsehood is far too great. The young man makes no grandiose claims for himself: his style is merely the "footnote" to his lady's "immoral" beauty, which leads him "with a magic hair" (cf. Pope's "And beauty draws us with a single hair") "Up the slick highway of a vanishing hill / To Words—that palace of beryl and coral . . . ." The one realm of concern, then, for the modern poet is *words*, not beauty or love or his own emotions.

Warren's poetry in the issue, too, shows a complication in language as well as a change in direction: "Death Mask of a Young Man" is far less reminiscent of Eliot and the French Symbolists than his previous poetry has been:

Down the stair had creaked the doctor's feet
Shuffling. He heard them out thinking it queer

Tomorrow night at nine he would not hear
Feet shuffling out and down into the street
Past the one murky gas jet in the hall,
Past the discarded chair beside his door,
The Steinbachs' entrance on the lower floor,
And the cracked patch of plaster on the wall.

Just how that crack came he could never think
To save his life, though he remembered yet
How once a mouse ran in, quick as a wink.
It must have said, " Why here's a hole in the wall!
I'll just whisk in, into the dark, and let
Heavy and terrible feet tramp down the hall."

This piece makes use of a direct, natural idiom (some influence of
Merrill Moore is apparent) which seems as yet not quite sure of
its own intentions but which indicates, at any rate, a gain in
genuineness. Jesse Wills's long poem " Eden," too, has a colloquial-
ness of tone like Moore's. This is the piece that the group had
liked exceedingly (Ransom had called it the best poem of considerable length yet executed by a member); though it is impressive,
however, a sameness of pace throughout somewhat mars it.

Another poem in the issue, Ransom's " Blue Girls " is interesting as an early and less effective version of the later much-altered
poem:

If I were younger, travelling the bright sward
Under the towers of your seminary
I should get a look, and a thought, or even a word;
But I am old, and of aspect too contrary
For you who are less weary.

For why do you bind white fillets about your tresses
And weave such stately rhythms where you go?
Why do you whirl so lovingly your blue dresses,
Like haughty bluebirds chattering in the snow
Of what they cannot know?

Practice your beauty, blue girls, if you will;
The lean preceptress, she of history,
Showed you the manifold of good and ill,

> And all you saw was princes crooking the knee
> To beauteous majesty.
>
> Do you think there are thrones enough, one for each queen?
> Some thrones are chairs, some three-legged milking stools,
> Or you even sit in ashes where thrones should have been;
> And it is for this, God help us all for fools,
> You practice in the schools.
>
> Practice your beauty, blue girls, nevertheless;
> Once the preceptress, learned bitter one,
> Printed the sward in a flounce of purple dress
> And was a princess pacing as to her throne;
> But now you see she is none.

Though they are perhaps somewhat rough technically, these lines are written with an absolute certainty of poetic attitude. But Ransom was beginning to turn his mind more seriously to criticism: "for a while I don't expect to write further poetry very systematically, but to refine my critical views and work toward a prose volume," he wrote Mims.[39]

Despite the great strides being made by the four most serious Fugitives, William Elliott, at the University of California, had heard rumors of the lack of unity among his poet friends: "So the Fugitives are awearying. Well, that was to be expected, in due course, when some of the brethren got too good for the reward of seeing themselves in print. I haven't had a copy in some time. Are we defunct?" As far as he was concerned, Elliott admitted, they had been defunct for a good while. He had finally been made to realize that his poetry was worthless, he said, that the Fugitives might have meant "no more than a kindly sociability" in including him among them. But he still could not give up writing verse, and he wondered about his motives:

Is this business of versifying attributable in such as me to mere vainglory? Clearly the Fugitives have profited by their collective flight —but even for them, is there any possibility of cracking a chunk of marble large enough, of shaping a statue good enough, of leaving a

[39] July 6 [1924].

Typescript of Davidson's " Corymba," containing critical comments by Tate, with replies by Davidson. This interchange is indicative of the close attention each gave to the other's work.

Nuptials

When noon-time comes the whistle blows.
Down the crooked street in jagged rows
The multitudinous laborers shamble
Past Mike's saloon, through swarming flies,
To the vacant lot where they may gamble
With loaded dice, and gorge stale pies.
It is a time when stink and sweat
Subside and let the flesh forget
Contact with brick, mortar, lather,
The cold necessity to bathe —
And certain things one would forget.
The bones rattle, the nickels jingle,
Nuts and sevens alternate
While a pair of shoes balance fate
And Brady's tongue and fingers tingle:
Jit shots be lost or shots be won,
Tonight will be a night of fun,
Two dollars now prognosticate
An image supine and elate,
For she will keep the date early or late.

The clock has struck a dismal clack,
They tread the same well-trodden track,
A hunger flashing in the eye

Tate's manuscript of " Nuptials."

thing well enough done to make the leaving worthwhile? .... Even
Sidney has not been able to blow the fires of poetic madness into flame—
and you get more and more devilishly sane—till presently you will all be
writing sly commentaries on Reason—only slightly Impure. The times
are out of joint for such rationalists as me, alack! We are Fugitives to
Poetry to get into a realm where reason is not admitted to court—and
modern poetry says there is none. Needless to say, this is all very
unjust—to you, one and all—all the more unjust to you, D. Donald, who
boil and bubble and burn with the *ignis poeticus.*[40]

Elliott apologized for his bitterness, but even so, his objections
to the poetry written by his friends remained. If poetry partook
of the nature of a divine madness, why could not poets be content
with a wisdom so far superior to the intellect? To him, as to most
unpledged poets, the value of poetry lay not in its knowledge
through realized form but in its emotion. Elliott never quite saw
that perhaps the most important principle in the unstated aesthetic
theory of his compeers was the refusal to separate intellect and
feeling: to them, poetry had to attempt to say something not merely
inspiring but truthful.

Nevertheless, in spite of his perplexity at the brothers, he would
have liked to have been back with them, taking part in their
truculently frank argument:

How I'd like to be one of you again! Next summer I hope to be,
to hear Johnny's irresistible marshalling of argument, to see him grin—
to watch the fiery Tate and the smoothly-sailing Mr. Moore (Oh perfection of a young man—perfect, all too perfect), to row with my com-
peer in sentimentality Alec Brock (the Lord preserve him from ad-
mitting it), and to stand metaphysically dumfounded by the mysteries
of Mttron (Lord, but how I miss them in this land of outlines!). Enfin,
to Stanley, and to you, I should render special obeisance. You've got
the stuff—what more need I?

But the circle that Elliott visualized was an ideal one, with
all the members present at one time—an actuality that was becoming increasingly rare. Ridley Wills had left Nashville for New

[40] To Davidson, June 9, 1924.

York and the newspaper business after he received his B. A. degree
the previous June; and, although he was never a very serious par-
ticipant, the liveliness of the group had diminished somewhat with
his loss. Tate had been absent all spring, and henceforward, after
this summer, he would be separated from the Fugitives. During
the coming year Johnson was to withdraw from the group and
from Vanderbilt; Warren, too, was facing his final year of activity
with the Fugitive brotherhood. So this summer was to be the last
in which most of the members were fairly close together geo-
graphically. Ransom, teaching at Peabody College across the street,
was present for meetings, as were Davidson, Stevenson, Hirsch,
Frank, Curry, Moore, and Jesse Wills. And, for a few sessions,
Tate and Warren came to Nashville from Guthrie.

Earlier in the summer, Tate had gone on to New York for his
two weeks' visit without coming by Nashville, much to Davidson's
disappointment. "I'm turribly afraid you'll get to New York and
find it difficult to tear yourself away," [41] Davidson wrote prophetically. In his metropolitan surroundings, Tate was impressed with
Hart Crane, who treated him "royally." He was kept busy meeting
the city's literati (and found them much less "theory-ridden" than
the Fugitives). Gorham Munson spoke well of Davidson, Ransom,
and Tate and was extremely interested in Warren, according to
Tate's first enthusiastic letter back to Nashville.[42] In his next
report Tate elaborated on Davidson's reputation in the New York
literary world: nearly everyone he met knew and liked Davidson's
work, although they all maintained that he lacked "a structural
sense." Tate was constantly surprised in his dealings with these
people, however, to find them "far less conscious of being poets
than we are as a group." [43]

But by the end of June Tate was back in the South, spending
pleasant hours with Warren riding horseback, swimming, and
walking. They slept late in the mornings and basked in the afternoon sun, and Tate wrote Davidson that "Red" was looking

[41] To Tate, June 4, 1924.
[42] To Davidson [Early in June], 1924.
[43] To Davidson, June 15, 1924.

healthier than he had ever seen him.[44] Visiting Warren's family was the reviewer who had written the Chattanooga *News* article on the Fugitives, Caroline Gordon, whom Tate was to marry a few months later in New York. Warren invited Davidson to spend some time with him and Tate: ". . . we three might do nothing together with some degree of satisfaction," he wrote.[45]

But Davidson's duties in Nashville prohibited his getting away except for a brief weekend. The book-page was going well, though, like *The Fugitive*, it consumed a great deal of time. It was maintaining an unflagging high standard of literary criticism; Davidson, Ransom, and Tate (much of his work unsigned because of its frequency) contributed to nearly every issue, and Warren, Stevenson, Wills, and Frierson appeared often in its columns. Notice was being attracted by the page in other parts of the country. Among the comments about it were H. A. Potamkin's statement, "It sounds fresh, much more so than anything in this burg [Philadelphia]," and Joseph T. Shipley's avowal that its reviews equalled "those of any similar page in the great metropolis." [46] On seeing these compliments, Tate had written: "Begorra! If Shipley isn't right! It is a damn good page. I don't often speak of it, but I'm continually admiring this added fine feather in your cap." [47]

Davidson had sent Tate some of Laura Riding Gottschalk's poetry for comment, and Tate, although he admired her poetry immensely, felt that in it much brilliant satire was "embedded in a regrettable incoherency . . . ." He cautioned Davidson to send back her poetry with tact because of her "extreme sensitiveness to rejection." [48] And he thought perhaps the Fugitives had come to expect of her work such excellence that they often refused her poems when they would have taken them from anyone else. Mrs. Gottschalk had gone to New York for the summer, where she was attempting to find work; but she maintained a steady stream of

[44] [June, 1924].
[45] July 11, 1924.
[46] The Nashville *Tennessean Book Review and Literary Page*, May 25, 1924.
[47] To Davidson, June 2, 1924.
[48] To Davidson, August 6, 1924.

poems to the *Fugitive* offices. About this time she initiated another flow of contributions to the editors, of a different sort: the names and addresses of acquaintances that might be likely prospects as subscribers to the magazine. These were sent in with frank appraisals of financial statuses, habits, and idiosyncrasies. By fall, when she would return to Louisville, it would be with the decision to work perseveringly for the perpetuation of *The Fugitive*.

The summer's work meant much to Warren. For one thing, he was trying to catch up with back assignments, left over from the spring quarter's work. Of a thirty-page paper he wrote for Mims on the subject of his religious convictions, he commented to Davidson, "You ought to see my hair-splitting. I feel like a sort of Thomas Aquinas." [49] For Ransom's course he was working on a paper dealing with Conrad. But these troublesome academic tasks failed to keep him from the writing of poetry. In May he had had two poems accepted by *Voices*, and during the early part of the summer *The Double Dealer* accepted his trilogy "Portrait of Three Ladies." To Davidson he sent "Young Men in April Dusk" and "Admonition to the Dead," asking for "merciless criticism." [50] When Davidson returned them with comments, evidently finding some serious flaws in the first and praising the second, Warren promised to rework "Young Men in April Dusk." [51] He sent the *Fugitive* selection committee four poems, three of which were printed in the August issue.

This late summer number of the magazine omitted the critical essay that had been promised with each issue. "All theories perish when exposed to the torrid circumstances of mid-summer in a Southern city," the editorial apologized. "Cerebration ceases, or becomes agglutinated." But poetry somehow continued, and for evidence the editors pointed to the contents of the journal, though perhaps only one poem in it is up to the group's best standards:

[49] August 30, 1924.
[50] [June, 1924].
[51] [Later in June, 1924]. Both poems were published in the October issue of *The Double Dealer* (VI, No. 39, 2), the title of the first changed to "Autumn Twilight Piece."

Ransom's "Tom, Tom, the Piper's Son," an allegorization of a basic theme in Ransom's poetry—the discrepancy between man's and the universe's evaluation of himself. Yet if the other poems in the issue are not memorable, they are at any rate competent.

At the end of the summer, the "Committee on Ways and Means" met at Mr. Frank's house to draw up proposals (which the group adopted in the meeting of September 25) that the October issue of the magazine be consolidated with the December one; that the arrangement with Back be terminated at the end of the year; that an effort be made to secure funds for the following year from the Associated Retailers, Ward-Belmont College, individuals friendly to the magazine, and an increased subscription list; and, finally, that *The Fugitive* "for next year adopt a quarterly basis of publication, restrict itself as a policy to the publication of the work of Fugitives, and simplify its working administration as much as possible . . . [perhaps by] administration by a committee, possibly one of changing membership." [52] From Washington, Tate wrote that he was in hearty agreement with the plan.[53]

Thus the fall began with the members free of the responsibility of an immediate issue, the lull offering them a chance to prepare for the December issue and the contest awards. Their plans were to present three prizes for the most distinguished poetry contributed to the magazine by an outsider during the year, making the decisions themselves instead of referring them to judges unconnected with the magazine.

Davidson's volume was still receiving critical attention. In the current *Double Dealer*, John McClure, writing a long review of *An Outland Piper*, stated that he considered the Fugitive "school of poetry" the most interesting in the South: "They are perhaps closer to the genuine art of poetry—the beautiful music of speech—than any coterie in our [America's] literary history." The Nashville poets were not without their weakness, he admitted; they were too greatly influenced by Freudian theories and by the "sophisticated irony" of Eliot; they were concerned too much with being

[52] Report of the Committee of Ways and Means, Sept. 20, 1924.
[53] To Davidson, September 25, 1924.

brilliant and intellectual; but they were redeemed " by a genuine passion for the art of literature . . . ."

Davidson he considered "one of the best—at his peak probably the very best "—of the Fugitives. *An Outland Piper* did scant justice to its author, McClure felt, containing as it did a great deal of undistinguished poetry and some " positively bad "; nevertheless the good poems in the volume were remarkable: ". . . work so excellent that it gives ' An Outland Piper ' high importance in the year's output of books. Such poetry is not written by many men. Its author is one of a select few in the United States. Passages in these poems seem to me to be among the finest in American verse." [54] Tate was overjoyed at McClure's praise of Davidson: " I can't wait a moment [he wrote] to hail you with congratulations—and him, too, for that matter, for having sense enough to give you your due. It's by all odds the best you've received, I should think. See what he says about Ye Fugitives! You bring honor to us all." [55]

But another notice of Davidson's book drew Tate's ire. In an issue of *Poetry* [56] devoting seven pages to Carl Sandburg and three pages to Louis Golding, *An Outland Piper* was relegated to half of the last page in the magazine. The review, written by Harriet Monroe herself, ended with a quotation from " Requiescat," perhaps the weakest poem in the book. Tate was certain that the Fugitive quarrel of the previous summer with Miss Monroe had occasioned the summary dismissal of Davidson's poetry; indignant, he composed a letter of protest, sending a copy to Davidson along with an explanatory note. [57] The letter was printed in the December *Poetry* under the heading " A Polite Protest." [58] As was customary with him, Tate was in this instance direct and purposely bellicose. Stating that he had felt for some time a " growing inadequacy " in *Poetry*, both in its " outmoded editorial policy " and in the quality

[54] VI, No. 37-38 (August-September, 1924), 209-210.
[55] To Davidson, October 3, 1924.
[56] XXIV, No. VI (September, 1924), 344.
[57] October 5, 1924.
[58] XXV (December, 1924), 169-170.

of its verses, he accused Miss Monroe of one of three things: (1) personal prejudice, (2) "utter anesthesia in the field of aesthetic values," or (3) careless reading. Charging that she had quoted the worst lines from Davidson's volume as representative of him, Tate went on to say: "I do not maintain that Davidson's work is perfection. It is, however, more than often distinguished." He came to the point of his accusation when he expressed the opinion that Miss Monroe's slur upon Davidson was the result of Davidson's attack on her the year before in *The Fugitive*. Tate obviously expected an indignant reply; but "Aunt Harriet's" answer was calm and unargumentative: she merely stated that she had never seen the "attack" in *The Fugitive*, having been abroad in the summer of 1923; that she had not known or had forgotten that Davidson was editor of that journal; that her review was intended to be favorable. Not rating Davidson so high as Mr. Tate did, she had quoted from what she considered his best.

There was nothing for Tate to do but let her have the last word in public. But Davidson and Tate both resented her condescending attitude toward *The Fugitive*; and Tate, at least, felt reasonably certain still that her poor review of Davidson's poetry stemmed from her disapproval of the work of the Fugitives and her sponsorship of a Southern poetry in line with her own ideas of what Southern poetry should be.

Ransom's second volume of poetry, *Chills and Fever,* appeared late in August.[59] Davidson gave the book immediate attention in his book page, writing a long and carefully detailed essay which made clear that he considered Ransom the foremost poet in the South and one of the "very few really significant and altogether original literary figures in the entire country." The philosophy of the poems could be seen to be, Davidson wrote, ". . . not a growth of disillusionment or a maze of abstraction; it is the expression of a personal attitude toward the world, evident throughout his poetry—generous and inclusive acceptance of life for what it is, humility in the face of perplexing issues; a serious wish, essentially

[59] New York: Alfred A. Knopf, 1924.

religious, to find truth; the creed of a fine-spirited gentleman, sensitive to physical and spiritual wonders." [60]

A few months later Tate took up the volume in *The Guardian*, setting forth his thesis that Ransom's poems were essentially " in the Classical tradition." Like T. E. Hulme, Tate saw the chief characteristic of classical art as " the repudiation of a rhetorical Infinite in which the megalomania of man rhetorically participates." Ransom was actually more like H. D. or Catullus than like Donne, Tate maintained, in spite of superficial resemblances to the metaphysical poet. Yet " certain impurities " marred Ransom's otherwise distinguished work in the present volume: the encumbrance of " an outworn and, for his purposes, irrelevant Romantic tradition " had kept Ransom from achieving, according to Tate, " the precision that would make his classical spirit aesthetically significant." [61]

Other reviewers, writing over a period of more than a year, uniformly found *Chills and Fever* an important and flavorful volume, Louis Untermeyer and Christopher Morley in particular praising the book. To William Alexander Percy it was a surprise that a man brought up in the South could write such poems as " Agitato ma non troppo " or " Philomela "; forced to admire Ransom " unsympathetically, even grudgingly," he nevertheless expressed respect for the whole group of Fugitives.[62] John McClure, too, gave respectful notice to the whole group of Nashville poets as he reviewed *Chills and Fever*:

> The cynical and intellectual elements in the Fugitive school of poetry have come to flower in John Crowe Ransom's *Chills and Fever*, which is unquestionably (with H. D.'s *Heliodora*) one of the finest books of poetry published in America in the last year . . . . Mr. Ransom has developed the intellectually expressive cadence to a point probably not excelled by any American—not even by Eliot, Pound, or Stevens, and

[60] The Nashville *Tennessean*, August 31, 1924.

[61] " In the Classical Tradition," *The Guardian*, I, No. 1 (November, 1924), 25. In his next review of Ransom's poetry, three years later (" The Eighteenth-Century South," *loc. cit.*), which Ransom would call " the most inward examination " his poetry had ever received (Ransom to Tate, February 20, 1927), Tate was to perceive the necessary function of the two strains in Ransom's work.

[62] *The Double Dealer*, VII (January, 1925), 114.

certainly not by Frost—and he charges many of his cruel lines with an ideal and formal beauty of rhythm. It is possible that Donald Davidson if he fulfills his early promise, will do pure rhythms better than Mr. Ransom, and it is possible that Allen Tate will some day merge the cynical and formal elements of Fugitive verse as well. But in actual account, Mr. Ransom is the dean of the school which has made Nashville, Tenn., famous.[63]

Ransom took his place, McClure stated, with Eliot, Stevens, and Pound as a "distinctive and notable figure in contemporary literature."

Chills and Fever is a finished volume, expressing a clarified and consistent attitude. Thirty-six of the forty-nine poems making up its contents had first appeared in *The Fugitive*. That Ransom used *The Fugitive* as a medium for experimentation less than did the other members is evidenced by his inclusion in the volume of all but four of his poems published in the magazine up to this time. The thirteen others in *Chills and Fever* had appeared in *The Literary Review*, *The Bowling Green* of the New York *Evening Post*, *The Chaffing Dish* of the Philadelphia *Public Ledger*, *The Sewanee Review*, and *The Double Dealer*; one of them, "Armageddon," had appeared in a separate biblio published by the Poetry Society of South Carolina. Of these latter poems—not previously published in *The Fugitive*—only "Winter Remembered," "Here Lies a Lady," "Miriam Tazewell," and "Armageddon" are among Ransom's most distinguished work.

In a quite real sense, then, the volume may be taken as a summation of Ransom's early Fugitive career, representing the years in which he wrote his best poetry. He was turning now more to prose, almost as though he had learned everything he could through poetry. And indeed, although the poems are by no means repetitious, they do reveal that Ransom had by this time perfected the poetic form to express his fundamental theme. This theme is the result of his honest and inclusive view of human existence, an existence which, as he sees it, has posed the same problems to man

[63] The New Orleans *Times-Picayune*, February 22, 1925.

throughout all periods of time. Being irrevocably dualistic, man must live through these eternal problems without solving them, in the sense that a problem in logic may be solved. Unable to react simply either as body or spirit, he must attach his own evaluation to objects and events, but without losing sight of their cosmic insignificance. Three years later, in a letter to Tate, Ransom was to state his poetic intentions in a passage which applies equally well to *Chills and Fever* as to the later volume which he was discussing: "My objects as a poet might be something like the following, though I won't promise to stick by my analysis: (1) I want to find the experience that is in the common actuals; (2) I want this experience to carry (by association, of course) the dearest possible values to which we have attached ourselves; (3) I want to face the disintegration or nullification of these values as calmly and religiously as possible." [64]

In October, Tate had gone back to New York, where he found other writers friendly but jobs scarce. A position with the Climax Publishing Company (a pulp magazine firm) enabled him to earn a living without entirely preventing his serious literary activity. He found immediately that he could not endure most of the literary crowd of the metropolis, however, and decided to limit his reviewing to *The Nation* and the *Herald Tribune*, contemning *The Saturday Review, The Bookman,* the *Evening Post,* and *The American Mercury.*[65]

Tate did form friendships with people whom he valued, however, among them Malcolm Cowley, Kenneth Burke, Slater Brown, E. E. Cummings, and Edmund Wilson. He was able now to share ideas directly with Hart Crane, with whom he had corresponded for two years. Crane showed Tate some new poems which he called "Voyages," and Tate immediately discerned their importance. The new ideas and theories that Tate was encountering in his metropolitan surroundings gave him a skeptical attitude toward his own work in poetry; he lost interest in publishing a volume, gradually reaching the conviction that he should wait until

[64] March, 1927.
[65] Tate to Davidson, December 8, 1924.

his poems were mature. He was still placing poems occasionally with various periodicals, but he was "keeping others in the drawer because [he was] not sure of them." [66]

The other Fugitive in New York, Ridley Wills, was occupied with his own literary work. His novel *Harvey Landrum* [67] appeared in September with quite favorable notices. Davidson's review praised it for a sound achievement; it had local color, he felt, that was not obtrusive.[68] Wills had during the summer given up his work with the New York *Herald* to found a newspaper of his own in Rye, New York—the Rye *Courier*, which became a sprightly little periodical for sophisticated suburbanites. He wrote to Davidson:

Our aim is to make an international local sheet of it with literary qualities. Accordingly, I offer you a job, for the glory of it. Will you, from time to time, send us personal jots of what is going on in Nashville among worthwhile people. For an example, will you write under the head of Nashville Personals, that Knopf is bringing out *Chills and Fever* by John Crowe Ransom, on September 15, and that Mr. Ransom is working on another volume and has a new baby daughter. Or that Sidney Hirsch, author of The Rose of Washington Square has written a dithyrambic epithalamium to Om's third birthday and is considering having it published as a footnote to the Koran. You get the idea.[69]

Another letter from Wills a few months later is interesting for its comment on Mims:

I very much enjoyed Dr. Mims' visit here. Let young men with burdensome minds say what they care to—I'll stick up for Dr. Mims. He's fine and honest and zealous, and is justifying himself in more ways and to better effect than men less purposeful, less militant, and more organized. He's a Don Q and he finds many windmills. He knows they are windmills and wishes they weren't. And he tilts them at their own game, but he tilts them, and I am not one to say that they don't deserve tilting. He's my friend as you are.[70]

[66] Tate to Davidson, November 16, 1924.
[67] New York: Simon and Schuster, 1924.
[68] The Nashville *Tennessean*, November 23, 1924.
[69] August 8, 1924.
[70] To Davidson, November 16, 1924.

But Wills was permanently lost to the Fugitives. His fundamental lack of seriousness had always kept him from understanding the intentions and ideals of the group; and now, separated from it by so great a distance of space and of motive, whatever intimacy he had ever had with other members gradually dropped away.

One other publication by a Fugitive appeared in this fruitful autumn, an English edition of Ransom's poetry, *Grace after Meat*.[71] Robert Graves had come across a copy of *Poems about God* and, hearing that the book had received little attention in America, determined to sponsor an English publication by its author. At his solicitation and T. S. Eliot's, the Hogarth Press undertook the publication of twenty of Ransom's poems which Graves himself selected from Ransom's repertoire. Nine of the poems are from *Poems about God*; ten from the recently issued *Chills and Fever*; and one, " Ilex Priscus," is a hitherto unpublished piece. Graves contributed an introduction which was calculated to put the American literary public in its place, as the following passages show:

About two years ago I came across a copy of Ransom's " Poems About God " which had fallen completely flat in America, largely I believe because of its title. The literary editors had handed their review copies to the theological reviewers and the theological reviewers, perhaps slightly scandalized, at any rate found it a book impossible to praise in their columns.

Although Christopher Morley spoke a good word for Ransom in (I think) the New York *Evening Post* that was all the benediction " Poems About God " won. I became so interested in the book that I began to ask whatever authorities on modern American poetry I met— T. S. Eliot, J. Gould Fletcher, Edward O'Brien, Professor Kroll of Princeton, and others—about this most unusual writer. None of them knew anything about Ransom; Edward O'Brien wrote to his friend Braithwaite, an assiduous anthologist, but again no news. [Footnote: More lately I met Mr. Louis Untermeyer who knew about Ransom and seemed to rate his work as highly as I did.] It seemed then that the

[71] London: Printed and published by Leonard and Virginia Woolf at the Hogarth Press, 1924.

best thing to do was to publish a selection from " Poems About God " and from Ransom's later work, in England, hoping for the usual repercussion in America.[72]

In Graves's critical estimate of Ransom's work he remarked the similarity of the Southerner's poetry to Frost's. In both poets he found " an extremely fastidious art disguised by colloquialisms and a pretence of 'every-which-way' (to borrow Frost's own word)." Both men, he felt, acted as " spokesmen for those rebellious ' poor whites ' (in the political and plutocratic sense)" who revolted against the restricting puritanism of their fathers to adopt a " new religion of nature worship and toleration of their fellows."

Graves had another opportunity to praise Ransom at the expense of the South—in reviewing *Chills and Fever*. On this occasion he commented again about the backwardness of Ransom's environment, indicating that he had heard Nashville was " a byword in the States for comic provincialism: as here in England one need only say 'Wigan' and the gallery of any variety theatre will rock with sophisticated mirth." [73] Ransom's Nashville friends, who had taken some pains not to be " merely Southern " in their attitudes, found themselves nonetheless resenting Graves's derision. Davidson wrote a polite rebuke in his column, saying that he saw less resemblance to Frost in Ransom's work than to Edmund Spenser; [74] and Tate, objecting to the " poor-white " phrase, commented to Davidson, " I daresay John is quite as civilized as Graves." [75]

By now *The Fugitive* had made its way into the literary world; critics and reviewers frequently mentioned it with admiration. But in spite of its growing prestige, its subscription lists remained small, and its burden of debt from the preceding year (before Back took over) was still unpaid. At a meeting in Frank's home on November 5, at which all the Nashville members except Hirsch were present,

[72] *Ibid.*, 7-8.
[73] " Muscular Poetry," *The Saturday Review of Literature*, I, No. 22 (December 27, 1924), 412.
[74] " The Spyglass," the Nashville *Tennessean*, November 30, 1924.
[75] January 7, 1925.

the members discussed the plan for managing the magazine in 1925. They decided by a unanimous vote to require twenty-five dollars of each Fugitive, "contingent on the pledging of $250 through patrons or by other means"; to launch a subscription campaign; and to charge one dollar for four issues of the magazine.[76] For the administration of the magazine, they decided to elect two editors to serve for one year—Ransom and Warren for 1925—either of whom, together with a committee of two members, would select the poems to be used for each issue.

A short while later Ransom and Davidson sent out publicity material to potential and former subscribers, taking the pains to pen brief notes on the notices. But no doubt the most active efforts to publicize the magazine were made by Laura Gottschalk, who with apparently limitless vitality had adopted *The Fugitive* cause as her own. She had been sending in lists of possible prospects; and now she wrote Davidson asking if she might have the group's permission to speak of the Fugitives at women's clubs and to enlist whatever support she could. Davidson sent her a report about the organization so that she might be able to answer questions accurately; he described the foundation of the magazine, its personnel, the volumes published by its members and, attempting to define its literary policy, he wrote:

The Fugitives are not a unit in their literary beliefs and practice. I believe they represent all varieties of poetical creed and practice, from the wholly traditional to the more or less radical. Nevertheless we are prevailingly "modern" in tone, I am sure, occupying perhaps a middle position between the extreme conservatives and the extreme radicals. Some critics have professed to find a "Fugitive type," but this is a little surprising to us, as we differ widely to our own way of thinking. I believe the magazine will show that we look with a catholic eye on traditionalism when it is good, or on experimentalism when it is honest. We are foes to sentimentalism in all forms, whether it be the conventional sob-stuff that used to mark Southern literature, or the more pretentious kind that is peddled out in Harriet Monroe's magazine. Literature is a serious business to us. We are for no compromise in the arts,

---

[76] Resolution in *Fugitive* records.

and desire to publish in the magazine only what we consider the best poetry, without reference (or with as little reference as possible) to the demands of popular taste. We do not care to appeal to the many, and do not think we can, but we wish to reach, and are reaching, the intelligent few everywhere in whom lies the real hope of American literature.

He indicated the group's growing interest in the serious writers of its own locale, but stated its intention of publishing chiefly the work of Fugitives themselves. "Our distribution is remarkable," he wrote, "but the number is pitifully small. People don't subscribe to poetry magazines—we have found that out." He added, incidentally, that *The Fugitive* had few Southern subscribers outside of Nashville. As to whether the magazine would continue to be published, he commented: "Depends altogether on our ability to raise funds. Our personal resources are very low (too many profs! and students!). Therefore patrons seem to be the last resource. You can mention this if you wish." [77]

All during the fall Mrs. Gottschalk directed her zeal in the magazine's behalf; but in spite of her untiring efforts there is no evidence of any tangible support which she elicited. Meanwhile, the others, working again among relatives and friends, secured sufficient backing by the end of the year to enable publication to continue. When he heard the good news, Tate, always tremendously attached to *The Fugitive* even when he quarreled bitterly with the other Fugitives, wrote Davidson an enthusiastic letter: "Hurrah for the Fugitive in the past and emphatically for 1925. I can say, and with much sentiment of which I am so little ashamed that I am positively proud of it, that although I am swamped in the maelstrom of literary New York, I feel myself to be a Fugitive, in our special sense of the term, as I did in the spring of 1922. I hope, naturally, the emotion is reciprocated." [78]

Near the middle of November the group came to a decision about the contest winners. Laura Riding Gottschalk, the winner

[77] Davidson to Laura Gottschalk [undated].
[78] December 8, 1924.

of the Nashville Prize, was clearly "the discovery of the year" for the Fugitives. When on November 19 the members sent Mrs. Gottschalk a wire announcing her award, she wrote a letter of lavish thanks. Four days later she wired that she would be in Nashville the following week end.

The Fugitives were perhaps rather absurd in their reception of Mrs. Gottschalk at Nashville. Courteously, yet somewhat formally, they greeted her as a fellow poet rather than as a person. Most of the members had settled their personal connections on a satisfactory basis already and were not open to warm, enthusiastic friendships of the sort that their guest apparently expected. Not at all unsophisticated, they were nevertheless not bohemian in their private lives. They were accustomed to having their relationships with other people grow over a period of years and were totally unable to pledge a new personal allegiance immediately. But the Nashville visit was upsetting, for whatever cause. To these serious, rather courtly gentlemen, it must have seemed somewhat odd to admit a pert young woman on an equal basis; at any rate, the meeting took on a self-conscious atmosphere. Mrs. Gottschalk and Hirsch quarreled, and the whole event ended in confusion.

Nevertheless, in December she wrote Davidson again, sending more names and the poems she had read at the meeting, Ransom having asked for the poems to consider them at greater length. Ransom had also spoken of forwarding some of her work to Robert Graves, and Mrs. Gottschalk wanted advice about preparing it. But the young woman was to make only one other visit to Nashville, and, although at that time the members elected her to membership, hers was to be a very limited sort of association with the group. She was not really influenced by the Fugitive approach to poetry; indeed, some of the men were later to feel that, far from being a disciple, she would have liked to take the Fugitives over and influence *them.* Her representation in the December issue was generous, as it was to be in all the 1925 numbers. Nevertheless, in her connection with the magazine, she functioned only as contributor, not as a real member.

In the December issue, nineteen poems are by Fugitives, four by Mrs. Gottschalk, and only five by other outsiders. Tate contributed four poems, one a ballad, "Fair Lady and False Knight," another his translation of Baudelaire's "Correspondences," and the other two a pair of rhymed iambic-pentameter pieces entitled "Art." These last two poems are addressed to J. E. W. (Jesse Wills) in whom Tate believed strongly, insisting then and later that his was perhaps the most natural and powerful talent among the Fugitives. Wills had already indicated that he did not consider himself a real poet, but Tate was unable to accept this decision. Hence in these poems Tate makes a dire prophecy to his friend who has turned from "lonely beauty in the mind":

> When you are come by ways devoid of light,
> Cast to some nether hole of jagged gloom,
> Drinking the draught of your definite night,
> Thirsting therefrom—recall as an heirloom
> A dawn when stars dropped gold about your head
> And, so amazed, you knew not were you dead.

But aside from the occasion of its composition, it is powerful verse in mercilessly burnished language.

Jesse Wills's two sonnets in the issue reveal talent and sensitivity to language and to situation but still deny the commitment of self. In "Premonition" he makes an easy use of landscape to suggest inevitable disaster: "Could that bright, careless gold / Of dandelions, those grackles glittering . . . Portend a scoriac desert, chasms, and cold?" Then, "Earth shook as though it snored / Troubled by dreams of thunder . . . ." It is an accomplished and arresting piece. "He had an inexorable logic operating a keen analytical mind," one of the Fugitives later said of Wills; such a mind might find a commitment to poetry unseemly. But for whatever reason Wills remained, in the succeeding years, the most gifted of the Fugitives not to publish a volume of verse.*

* After this study was in galley proof, a book of Jesse Wills's verse (*Early and Late: Fugitive Poems and Others*) was issued by the Vanderbilt University Press.

Among the other Fugitives, none gave himself quite so lustily to poetry as Merrill Moore. It is tempting always to dismiss some of his verse, streaked as it is with cleverness, as the work of a superficial writer, but it is a poet of no mean ability who can begin a sonnet, "I know when no mice rustle in the sheaves / That Autumn is gone." The four pieces in the issue, although attesting his fecundity in the poetic image, exhibit some of his tricks as well, in particular a breathless rove-over from line to line along with an overuse of *and* to lend an anacrustic beat to his lines. Out of the fifty-one lines in the four poems, seventeen begin with *and*. Two of the poems are sonnets, the proposition, counter-proposition, and near-resolution of which Moore found particularly suitable to his genius; and the other two are isolated descriptive fragments which, in spite of a regular rhyme-scheme and a cadenced line, artfully suggest formlessness. These latter two poems, "Mrs. Claribel Diggs" and "Ephraim Diggs," concern "abnormal" personalities, giving evident example of what in general is true of Moore's work, that his aesthetic is grounded in psychology.

The most important poem of the issue is Davidson's long "Legend in Bronze," a symbolic account of the rape of beauty by mechanism. It makes use of what was to the Fugitives at the time a surprisingly even Spenserian stanza, without the discontinuities and esoteric vocabulary that, in the twenties, marked a work as modern. Like many other Fugitive poems, it is an allegory, in this instance constructed around the humanity of beauty. Steadily the poem advances from the opening suggestion of terror: "Closing the door, she first was softly ware / That a lone house at night is not the same." There are the simple fears: "So many a step to climb, so many a rail / Winding against her fingers up and on / Through circling dark that ever seemed to scale / The journey with her . . . ."; the simple bravery: "*Only the nameless stir of the nameless night!* / She said, and was ashamed of looking back"; the simple vanities: "Pausing, she must have known that she was fair, / The long glass caught the flicker of her smile, / A joyous thought made flesh, for a little while." Quietly she goes to bed as she hums an old song, reads an old book. But the monster is at hand, the metal beast whose loud clashings are not recognizable to the simple perceptions of beauty, wise only to human ways:

> She locked the door, for when was beauty proof
> Against live flesh when beauty's flesh is lone?
> Yet how should iron ever bolt aloof
> A brazen tread that she had never known?—
> The mirthless body creeping cold as stone
> With hard metallic pantings on the stair,
> Crashing at every move, though she might not hear?

Finally the invasion occurs while the fair victim sleeps, never knowing, never seeing the despoiler. Davidson has made traditional use of lyric details, pausing for the implications of horror to intrude as he advances the action toward its inevitable outcome. Both for its artistic merit and its thesis, the poem is significant in Davidson's poetic development.

Ransom contributed two poems, "Day of Judgment" and "Virga," that are interesting if not first-rate. Warren's two pieces, "Alf Burt, Tenant Farmer" and "Admonition to Those Who Mourn," are polished, somewhat formal exercises, not bursting with originality but nonetheless possessing serious intention. And Stanley Johnson's three poems, "The Grand Wolf," "Argument," and "Any Husband to Any Wife," are also well wrought, so that on the whole the December issue is one of the best numbers of the magazine. Commenting on it, Tate wrote, "Great stuff! Not so good an issue in a year." He considered the outsiders, excepting Laura Gottschalk, "mere fillers," as usual "much inferior to Fugitive material." [79]

A paragraph in the editorial announcements was devoted to Jacques Back. It noted the termination of the Fugitive contract and bestowed the gratitude of the group—the only coin the poets possessed:

> Without his service and generous interest, it is doubtful whether the magazine could have survived during the past eighteen months.

[79] To Davidson, December 11, 1924.

We wish to pay our public tribute to a rare spirit whose duties, in the present unremunerative condition of art in the South, often required as much philanthropy as business energy. When the annals of *The Fugitive* are written, let the chronicler pause here, and write Jacques Back into his record.

Back had never attended a Fugitive meeting; some of the members had never met him. But he was important to the Fugitives in the way Destiny is important. Unexpectedly he had offered them sustenance without patronage. But, just as they had suspected, poetry could not be made financially profitable. The experience with Back convinced the group that poetry is a product of personal sacrifice with a token of support from a few people.

CHAPTER SEVEN

ᔑᔑᔑᔑᔑᔑᔑᔑᔑᔑᔑᔑᔑᔑᔑᔑᔑᔑᔑᔑᔑᔑᔑᔑᔑᔑᔑᔑᔑᔑᔑ

THE END

OF

THE FUGITIVE:

1925

THE SOUTH was prospering: business every-
where was good; and at Vanderbilt, according to *The Alumnus*,
money had "flowed like a beneficent river" into the endowment
fund.[1] Most Southerners interested in the cultural development of
their section assumed that prosperity would bring with it an increased interest in the arts; and the various literary societies formed
throughout the Southern states were an apparent verification of
this innocent hypothesis. In spite of the preceding year's financial
near-disaster for *The Fugitive*, there still seemed to the Nashville
poets hope for poetry in the section. Near the beginning of 1925,
this last year of life for *The Fugitive*, Donald Davidson in his
weekly column spoke of the healthy creative spirit of the day:
"Pessimism is not the proper mood for a critic of this time," he
wrote, "which in the largeness and bouyancy of its spirit begins to

---

[1] The Vanderbilt *Alumnus*, X, No. 6 (May, 1925), 185.

take on some semblance to the Elizabethan Age. There is a kind of joy in the air, a zest in creation, an exuberance of production, a keenness in self-education that promises to make this the great age of American literature." [2]

At the beginning of the year Ransom assumed the position of editor of *The Fugitive*. Assisting him was Robert Penn Warren, who had so far exerted no strong influence on the group because of his youth and inexperience. Their task was made easier by the contributions of patrons, so that, before the orange ink struck the first of the new black covers, the financing for the year was secure. Thus the Fugitives could relax somewhat their concern for the management of the publication, to give their attention more completely to its contents.

The magazine began a series of book reviews in its first issue of the year, R. P. W. (Warren) reviewing Joseph Auslander's *Sunrise Trumpets*. His critical comments show him to be already distrustful of what he was later to call " pure poetry ":

Mr. Auslander is a poet who possesses great sensitivity to the minor strains of emotional experience, but this very preoccupation, if such it may be termed, seduces him into poetry that is scarcely important or memorable except for a certain neatness and glitter of phrase. His sensitivity often leads him to respond to a poetic stimulus so slender that when refracted through the medium of his verse it fails to evoke the appropriate reaction. And this overly facile emotional content lays him open to the charge of a feminine exaggeration or even insincerity on the part of readers who perhaps are not so delicately attuned to the frail modulations of which he treats.

In short, Warren felt, Auslander lacked " cerebration."

J. W. (Jesse Wills) reviewed Roy Campbell's *The Flaming Terrapin* in the same issue. But the important critical writing in the March number was tendered by Ransom in his generative essay "Mixed Modes." This piece is Ransom's first formal statement of his belief that poetry must ensue from the mature mind, since it deals with the various and disparate levels of experience

---

[2] " The Spyglass," the Nashville *Tennessean*, February 22, 1925.

which only a whole mind is capable of penetrating. Ransom made here his first public condemnation of Plato's sponsorship of the "pure and simple modes," a view which led, he feared, to the kind of juvenile poetry that the nineteenth century produced: Tennyson and Browning, for instance, had relatively simple minds; Swinburne wrote "nonsense melodies," and the Pre-Raphaelites possessed a "sinister naïveté." Earlier, Byron, Shelley, and Keats never "became quite sophisticated, or grown-up . . . ." In fact, "nobody in the whole century knew how to put his whole mind and experience to work in poetry as had Chaucer, Spenser, Shakespeare, and Milton." A few modern poets, however, Ransom found to be concerned with expressing their own mature minds and "not the mind of the hypothetical Wonder-Child"; these poets were doomed to be tagged "wilful and obscure by a trifling generation." But, if poetry has any value, Ransom concluded, it accrues from being the report which poets make of their own "mixed modes."

The poetry of the four chief Fugitives by this time was showing itself to be the work of mature minds expressing themselves in "mixed modes," though there was little similarity in the mixtures. To the March issue Tate contributed only one poem, "Homily," but—as he wrote to Davidson—it is in his "essential style."[3] Its tight, metaphorical lines exhibit a growing power in the difficult and oblique idiom Tate was striving to master:

> — And if your tired unutterable head
> Turn too neatly left and right,
> Crazed by the warlock of a curse
> Dreamed-up in some loquacious bed,
> And if this head of yours rehearse
> The energies spilled into the night
> When you fell down and bruised the stars
> With glitter of superior light,—
>
> Why, cut it off, stark piece by piece,
> And throw the proud cortex away
> And when you've marvelled on the wars

[3] October 3, 1924.

> That wove their smoke its intricate way,
> Tear out the tight, vermiculate crease
> Where death crawls wearily at bay!

This is the first of Tate's poems in the pages of *The Fugitive* that seems completely achieved; its fusion of violent, implicit metaphors and intricate rhythmic cadence excites an extension of consciousness to a state of spiritual illumination. Earlier in the year *The Nation* had printed a poem which was to become part of Tate's rigorously selected canon, "Advice to a Young Romanticist." [4] Tate felt that, at last, his poetic experiments were headed in the right direction. "In the end it will amount to a complete rehabilitation of technique," he wrote; "It will consist mostly in establishing a method of presentation of my own (in other words, a new form), within the traditional prosodical patterns."

Davidson's poems, "Boundary," "Fear in a Cubicle," and "Cross Section of a Landscape," represent a departure into a vein which is, on the one hand, plainer and less lyric and, on the other, less consciously "modern" and ironic than any he had previously employed. The last of these exhibits the protest against materialism which is one of Davidson's chief themes, but here the approach is philosophic and rational rather than lyric and emotional. The scientific attempt to explain the universe in terms of a substantial substratum is carried to an analogical conclusion:

> Here is the ice that girdles joyless ocean;
> Water girdling a sphere of quiet slime;
> Under it rock that has no life or motion
> Save from the twirl, the eternal pantomine.
>
> Under the rock is fire that dies by inches
> Over a slag and ash of old decay.
> Finally, what? The mathematician pinches
> Space to a point in his ponderable way.
>
> But when I was a boy I searched from pole to pole
> Of a gaudy globe, a rainbow-colored ball,
> Peeled the cover, unraveled the shiny whole,
> And was vexed to find at center nothing at all.

[4] CXX (January 14, 1925), 45.

Ransom published in the issue two of his most often anthologized poems, "Piazza Piece" and "Eclogue," both of which are
surely and elegantly handled. Warren's "Iron Beach," a revised
version of an earlier *Fugitive* poem, and "The Mirror" both deal
elegiacally with the theme of mortality. "Iron Beach" in particular the group had liked when it was first read at a meeting and,
later, when it was revised. Its fiercely ambivalent diction makes
it one of Warren's finest early poems.

Stanley Johnson was not represented in the issue; in fact, he
was never again to contribute to *The Fugitive.* Unable longer to
stand what he considered hypocrisy in university life, he had resigned at Vanderbilt late in December. His novel, *Professor,* was
due from the press in two months; and, like most books satirizing
the academic profession, it had made use of various traits of actual
people in its none-too-savory portraiture. The stir at Vanderbilt
heralding its appearance had led Johnson to take a long-contem-
plated action—to seek his fortune through writing. By the end of
January he had gone to New York and looked up Allen Tate. The
two decided to find quarters together and subsequently were established at 50 Morton Street, in Greenwich Village. Tate wrote that
he looked forward to "much work and many good times"[5] with
Johnson, and later, concerning the forthcoming novel, he commented to Davidson, "Your obvious excitement before the appearance of Stanley's book misses me to a great extent . . . ."[6] A Yale
professor could find himself in the book, Tate believed, as easily
as could a Vanderbilt faculty member. But when *Professor*[7] appeared in Nashville bookstores, townspeople looked for and were
certain they found satiric portraits of various Vanderbilt men.

Reviews of the book were brief. And, indeed, Johnson's novel
is a great deal less than a masterpiece, its chief flaw lying in an
excessive concern with superficialities. It fails to establish a compelling form capable of subordinating its personalities to the moral
urgency behind the theme. The novel is not poorly written so

[5] To Davidson, January 26, 1925.
[6] February 2, 1925.
[7] (New York: Harcourt, Brace and Company, 1925).

much as it is ineffectual; the author's lack of sufficient aesthetic distance, although understandable, is crippling. As a record of Vanderbilt life, of the English department, of the founding of *The Fugitive*, and of the lives of individual Fugitives, however, *Professor* is not wholly unreliable. Precisely because the subject matter has not been perfectly transformed into fiction, there exists in the novel much that may be taken straightforwardly as Johnson's actual views.

Professor centers around the activities of Dr. J. Tanksley Parkhurst, a Chaucerian scholar and head of the department of English at an imaginary Thurston College in a small New England town. Dr. Parkhurst is a man with an assumed façade of dignity through which may be glimpsed a naïve vanity and an ineptitude not wholly pleasant. In a word, Parkhurst is a hypocrite, mouthing phrases about literature that he does not feel, pretending to a rich amorous background that he does not possess, bullying men who are his inferiors in rank but by far his betters in character and comprehension. The section of the book most noteworthy is the part depicting the efforts of Dr. Parkhurst's downtrodden staff to establish a poetry journal. Elmo Davis—no doubt modelled on Ransom—is the oldest staff member, whose poetry, as the result of combining a "grim vocabulary with classic meters," has acquired a "satisfactory reputation." Davis broaches the matter of a magazine to Dr. Parkhurst: "A group of us . . . have been meeting together for some time to talk philosophy and read poetry and have a sort of literary improvement meeting. The other night it was suggested we publish a magazine like 'Voices' or 'The Fugitive' or perhaps like 'The Reviewer,' and we've been wondering what you would think of it." Dr. Parkhurst is dubious: "I wouldn't want my name attached to anything of a doubtful nature," he replies.

But the author's sympathies are not entirely with the young instructors struggling with their poetry journal. He constructs a telling parody of the general Fugitive style (or at least of Ransom's and Tate's). Dr. Parkhurst, in looking over the first issue of "The Little Magazine" with Davis, calls attention to a poem which he considers "about the worst modernistic drivel" he ever read:

EBULLIENT BEAN

A. Rauwolf, the cautery viands thought, no doubt—
Recalling dusky sisters' calorification in mere sunlight
And browned men in uniform needing a stomach clout—
Were vain, O Maracaibo, for his giant Cenobite.

Aurora on a gaunt shore wrought no more miracle;
Hunyadi Janos would have envied Boswell
The trachea's sylphic and modern caracole.
Indeed, thy aroma perfumed Europe's morsel.

In Minnesota, too, stimulation takes a rise
Where, clouting down, Gorsta Rudbak, the Finn,
Her fists clubbing at sleep-blistered eyes,
Puts the kettle on and learns to make it thin.

Embarrassingly enough, the poem turns out to be Davis's own, written under the pseudonym of " Oliver Twist." Parkhurst apologizes, explains that it is not like the poetry to which he is accustomed, and asks Davis to explicate the piece. The far-fetched interpretation is a burlesque of the methods of the Fugitives in analyzing poetry—the close textual reading that led into the " new " critical writing:

" Well, Doctor, you see, it's like this "—began Davis, " the other morning mother and I were having our coffee and the thought occurred to me that millions of people all over the world were having coffee at about the same time—a tremendous influence—coffee—and somehow the notion grew that it deserved a poem as a crystallization of the idea.

" Of course I wanted the reactions of a sophisticated person, a new, fresh, unusual approach to coffee—in modern poetry you have to avoid the obvious as you would the devil. So I decided to trace the psychology of a sophisticated mind, the thoughts any gentleman might have upon drinking a cup of coffee.

" A. Rauwolf, you will remember, was the man who introduced coffee into Europe " (Davis had discovered A. Rauwolf under " coffee " in Webster's Unabridged).

Parkhurst nodded. " Yes, I recall."

" Well, A. Rauwolf in eating his breakfast, or meat (the ' cautery viands ' of the poem), no doubt recalled the coffee beans he had seen in the hot tropical countries where he had traveled; the 'dusky sisters' are, of course, the beans heated ('calorification') in the sun. At the same time he would naturally think of the great need of coffee in Europe, as for example among the soldiers ('Browned men in uniform needing a stomach clout'). Now, let's go back. A. Rauwolf, then, thought breakfast were vain without coffee (the 'O Maracaibo' is a little conceit, I admit)—were vain for his own giant organism, or body— or, in a sense, Cenobite."

The rest of the poem is elucidated with the same dexterity, the subtleties of Davis's reasoning reducing Parkhurst to a state of confusion.

After Tate had read the book, he agreed with Davidson that the artistic worth of *Professor* was not great: "Stanley's book— though I can't agree with you fully—was rather a disappointment to me. I suspect Stanley's mind has yet to reach its maturity; its values are too much preoccupied with the incidentals in his subject matter; in short, it lacks the 'high seriousness' which, in various forms, exists in the writing of Sterne as well as in Wordsworth. But I think he will do better next time." [8]

Tate was still engaged in writing reviews and occasional articles and, at this particular time, in the publication of *Aesthete: 1925*, which was, as he explained, an attempt to continue the sort of experimental work that had been done in *Broom*.[9] Tate had been publishing his poems during the preceding year in several other magazines as well as in *The Fugitive: The Double Dealer, The Guardian, The Lyric, The Reviewer, S4N,* and *Voices;* and in 1925 his best poems were to go outside *The Fugitive*. Both "Mr. Pope" and "Death of Little Boys," for instance, were to appear elsewhere in print in 1925. For whatever reason, whether injury on Tate's part or lack of perception on the group's, when Tate's real mastery of poetry occurred, it was not in the pages of the magazine he had helped found. Yet all the while he had been sending poems to be read at Fugitive meetings and receiving them

[8] To Davidson, May 21, 1925.
[9] Tate to Davidson, January 21, 1925.

back with pencilled suggestions in the margins; and in return the group consistently forwarded for his criticism the poems read at the fortnightly gatherings.

But the constant friction over the small and niggling matters of policy was wearing to Tate, who, engaged in his own battle in the literary capital, was anxious not to give his sanction to methods and products of which he did not approve. His distance from the Nashville friends kept him nervous and touchy; and a sense of personal injustice at the hands of some members of the group led finally to his definite and sober resignation mailed to the Fugitives in February. "I feel I am doing myself an injustice by appearing nominally as a member of the group," he wrote. "It isn't that I wish to remove my name from an organization I simply disagree with; it is rather that I can't make my disagreement felt either to a successful or an unsuccessful issue at this distance." [10] Ransom replied to Tate, suggesting that he consider being inactive rather than disconnected and assuring him that his views were recognized and respected in the group. Tate agreed to the softening of the severance and described his feelings to Davidson: "I didn't expect anyone to submit to my views; I only wanted them recognized. They have been recognized in an excellent way." [11] In the June issue, accordingly, announcement was made of the inactive status of Tate and also of William Elliott, who likewise had asked to be removed from the masthead.

No doubt one reason for Tate's willingness to withdraw officially from the magazine was his growing conviction that, since *The Fugitive* had performed its function of allowing new creative talents to develop, it should consider its work accomplished:

I think the *Fugitive*, if the sentiment involved through several years of organized work be put aside, should have suspended a few months ago or should suspend pretty soon in the near future. The work of such a magazine must be limited in time; for it set out to introduce a group of new poets and, that done, it has no more to say. At the same

[10] To Davidson, February 9, 1925.
[11] May 21, 1925.

time, I can understand the natural emotions at the prospect of giving
it up; there may be a variety of motives, in the variety of persons in
the group, making for continuance, but I can't see how those motives
at this date can be strictly critical in their desires. The trouble with
Monroe's *Poetry*, and *Voices*, and *The Measure* is that their good work
originally is being discounted by the mistake of lifeless perpetuity.[12]

And, indeed, one is forced to admit that by now most of the
magazine's work was done: the individual Fugitives at this point
had not only decided upon the courses they must pursue, but had
become caught up and involved in responsibilities issuing from
their diverging commitments. Ransom, at thirty-seven, having
gained some recognition as an accomplished poet, was writing essays
for periodicals and planning a book of prose; Davidson, nearly
thirty-two, with one volume of poetry behind him, was engaged in
the critical activity required by his book page; Tate, twenty-five,
in his literary experimentation in New York, was extending and
deepening his artistic convictions; Warren, at twenty, had just
graduated from Vanderbilt, and, certain that his path led to writing
as a career, was contemplating graduate study for the forthcoming
year. These four, dedicated to the art of literature, had performed
an act of faith in adopting for their means of livelihood the profession of letters. Curry, engaged in completing his Chaucer
volume, was pledged to the scholarly profession; his research in
the esoteric aspects of great literature of the past would cause him
finally to view the writing of his own age with distrust. Jesse Wills
and Alec Stevenson, two whom the group considered poets of real
consequence, had by now decided against their own importance in
poetry. They would continue writing, but at their leisure and as
gentlemen amateurs. Stanley Johnson had gone the way of Ridley
Wills—into journalism, where cleverness and enterprise rather than
cerebration or sensibility are the necessary tools. James Frank and
Sidney Hirsch had been outwardly unaffected by *The Fugitive*'s
career. It had provided an engrossing activity around which to
center many profitable hours of conversation; but for both men the

---

[12] Tate to Davidson, May 5, 1925.

cultivated companionship of the group was more important than the solitary and earnest business of composition. Only Merrill Moore seemed able to pursue the double program of writing poetry assiduously and at the same time following another vocation. In his first year of training at the Vanderbilt Medical School, he was nonetheless able to write sheaves of poetry and to approach his writing as a real medium of expression.

Criticism was now the chief realm in which *The Fugitive* could offer a medium for experiment, and accordingly the June issue contained two reviews by Davidson and an editorial by Ransom. Davidson had ordered Eliot's *Homage to John Dryden* from England and devoted to it several seriously conceived paragraphs, in which he pointed out a basic agreement between Eliot and the Fugitives. Modern poets, Davidson stated, were discarding the nineteenth century, but they were not turning away entirely from the English tradition—the Elizabethans, John Dryden, and the eighteenth century, for instance. Consequently, Eliot's three essays discussing Dryden, the Metaphysical poets, and Andrew Marvell were doubly significant: they contained a new evaluation of poets with whom most readers were insufficiently acquainted, and they afforded an understanding of certain basic qualities in modern poetry. These now-familiar essays with their dicta concerning wit, the fusion of thought and feeling, and the modern necessity for difficult poetry, must have seemed to Davidson an uncanny coincidence with the major premises of Fugitive poetry. "A better apologia for a great part of modern poetry," he wrote, "especially a character of poetry in which *The Fugitive* has been interested, could hardly be devised. One might say that in this time it is more difficult to be simple than it is to be difficult: and that most kinds of simplicity are likely to fall under the accusation of dishonesty on the one hand and lack of a necessary diversity of equipment on the other."

Ransom's editorial, "Thoughts on the Poetic Discontent," enlarged upon the principle that he first set down in his "Mixed Modes." In this second essay—a revolutionary document which became the cornerstone for modern Southern literary criticism— Ransom delineated more clearly the character of the mixture:

" Irony may be regarded as the ultimate mode of the great minds—it presupposes the others." Ransom traced the course likely to be followed by a maturing mind in its attainment of the ultimate mode. In the first place, man is by nature dualistic, his very coming into the world creating an awareness of the chasm which separates himself from the universe—the spirit within from the material world without. He seeks to bridge the chasm, to " effect an escape from dualism," by erecting philosophical and metaphysical systems which encompass the observable world. In effect, he erects a " mystical community" so that he may " escape from an isolation which he cannot endure." He ascribes to the objects of experience the spiritual qualities which properly belong within himself. Thus, Ransom declared, the pathetic fallacies of the romantic poets stem from this desire to establish a mutuality of feeling between man and the cosmic order. In the light of man's scientific observations, however, this romantic construction cannot always stand; consequently, Ransom continued, the poet accepts a dualism again, but it is not like his original, naïve position. " For too much history has intervened, he is a dualist with a difference—reluctant, speculative, sophisticated rather than ingenuous, and richer by all the pathetic fallacies he has ever entertained."

That most of the nineteenth-century poetry was written in the second, or romantic stage Ransom made clear. But the " earlier and greater poets (Chaucer, Spenser, Shakespeare, Donne, Milton) along with or following their own share of lovely romantic adventures, turned back to the stubborn fact of dualism with a mellow wisdom which we may call irony." Irony, then, contains a rejection of the romantic solution; ". . . but this rejection is so unwilling, and in its statements there lingers so much of the music and color and romantic mystery . . . and this statement is attended by such a disarming rueful comic sense of the poet's own betrayal, that the fruit of it is wisdom and not bitterness, poetry and not prose, health and not suicide. Irony is the rarest of the states of mind, because it is the most inclusive; the whole mind has been active in arriving at it, both creation and criticism, both poetry and science." " The most inclusive "—this phrase was to influence strongly Ransom's

most able students and disciples: among them—besides Tate and
Warren—Cleanth Brooks, Andrew Lytle, and Randall Jarrell. In
fact, this phrase could be taken as a key to the attitude behind
the whole modern Southern school of writing. Among the Vanderbilt group Davidson alone was struggling to reclaim a poetic tradition less guarded than the seventeenth-century one from which this
style derives.

No poems better illustrate the "inclusive" attitude than Ransom's own in the same issue with his article: "The Miller's
Daughter," "Jack's Letter," and "Semi-Centennial," the first two
dealing with the ironic impossibility of romantic love; the third,
depicting the "intellectual condition." In this latter poem, an
old man, exiled from the physical world for fifty years, comes
out to view the spring, which turns out to be less exciting to him
than the "music and histories" which have made up his interior
life. He knows himself a god because of his ability to design large
schemes, though he recognizes his lack of power to execute them.
Nature will not obey him, in his "poverty and disrepute." Yet,
as he points out,

> "The better part of godhead is design.
> This is not theirs only, for I know mine,
> And I project such worlds as need not yield
> To this commanded April on the field.
>
> "And it is ample. For it satisfies
> My royal blood even thus to exercise
> The ancestral arts of my theogony.
> I am a god, though none attend to me."
>
> And he watched, with large head resting in the sun,
> The gods at play, and did not envy one.
> He had the magic too, and knew his power,
> But was too tired to work it at that hour.

Composed just before the Vanderbilt Semi-Centennial celebration,
the poem can be read as delineating the powerless yet withal
superior position of the university in relation to the actual world,
of the world of thought in relation to the world of action. The

old man's is the philosophical position Ransom condemned in his first volume, particularly in "The Swimmer," and it is the position shown throughout his poems to be fatally wrong, though eternally desirable.

Davidson's three poems in the issue mark a continuation of elements which were visible in his work in the preceding number. "Not Long Green" is constructed in a plain but heavily freighted idiom:

> For a heavy long time on the long green bough
> Hangs the apple of a summer that is shaken
> From its flat hot road to its apple-topped hill
> With the scraping of a mole that would awaken . . . .
> He is under the turf of the long green meadow,
> Snuffling under grass and lusty clover
> With a sure blunt snout and capable paws
> Up the long green slope past the beeches and the haws
> For the summer must be shaken and over.

Here Davidson's true poetic voice emerges, undistorted by attitudes foreign to his own talent. It is the essentially straightforward and impersonal nature of his lines that places them in sharp contrast to Ransom's sophisticated declamations, in which a speaker is always implicit if not openly portrayed. The grimness in the double meaning of such phrases as "long green" is a different quality from Ransom's irony or, for that matter, Tate's wit.

Six sonnets by Merrill Moore found room in the issue, all of about the same quality—provocative, enjoyable, impertinent—but lacking sufficient profundity to render them significant. Jesse Wills, too, contributed a sonnet, "Red Even," another of his disciplined pieces showing the ineffectuality of the modern panorama of gadgetry to avoid disaster and doom.

Laura Riding Gottschalk's two poems in the issue demonstrate her limits: "Druida," a piece of great imaginative powers fails because of formlessness: there is in it no formalizing principle preventing its incoherence. By contrast, her other poem, "The Circus," possesses a stark allegorical power which is almost sufficient to fuse the work into an organic entity:

The trained men tumble hereditarily.
The ringmaster has lost his way.
Back to the music, the band being
Not the same choir simple
Of primate tunes, as in the old days,
But a careful dissonance
Drowning elaborately the lost theme.

In this world of isolation, where "the universality is preserved / By the private ignorance of each ring in the tent," only two beings "disturb the gigantic self-possession." One is a tiger, beautiful, scornful, and hopeless;

The other, the poor poet and crier,
Renounces a prominent place in the accurate frenzy
And, perceiving a clenched philosophy
In the lean jaws,
Throws himself bit by bit
In rhythmic meat
To the starved yellow beast.

But the outstanding piece in the June *Fugitive* is Warren's "To a Face in the Crowd." This poem conveys the sharp awareness of the common loss suffered by men who must now view each other externally and momentarily as faces in a crowd:

My brother, brother, whither do you pass,
Unto what hill at dawn, unto what glen
Where among rocks the faint lascivious grass
Fingers in lust the arrogant bones of men?

Beside what bitter waters will you go
Where the lean gulls of your heart along the shore
Rehearse to the cliffs the rhetoric of their woe?
In dreams perhaps I have seen your face before.

A certain night has borne both you and me;
We are the children of an ancient band
Broken between the mountains and the sea.
A cromlech marks for you that ultimate strand

And dolorous you must find the place they stood.

Of old I know that shore, that dim terrain,
And know how black and turbulent the blood
Will beat through iron chambers of the brain

When at your back the taciturn tall stone,
Which is your fathers' monument and mark,
Repeats the waves' implacable monotone,
Ascends the night and propagates the dark.

Men there have lived who wrestled with the ocean;
I was afraid—the polyp was their shroud.
I was afraid. That shore of your decision
Awaits beyond this street where in the crowd

Your face is blown, an apparition, past.
Renounce the night as I and we must meet
As weary nomads in this desert at last,
Borne in the lost procession of these feet.

One of the most skilfully handled elements in the technical strategy
here is the juxtaposition of words with incongruous associations—
most often a latinate and affective adjective with a concrete, Anglo-
Saxon noun, as in "lascivious grass," "arrogant bones," and "taciturn tall stone." Sometimes the reverse is effected, the concretizing
of an abstraction, such as "ascends the night and propagates the
dark" and "shore of your decision." The associations set up by
such contrasts give an energy and a brilliance that would be lacking
in a more ordinary diction. This poem represents in quite tangible
form the fruit of the Fugitive movement. Something of Ransom,
Tate, and Davidson—and a little of Stevenson, Johnson, and Moore
—have gone into the making of this poem, though this is not in the
least to say that it is not in Warren's own voice.

Tate's respect for the work of his friends remained high. In
contrast to the leading literary men in New York, many of whom
were, he felt, petty and pretentious, his Nashville friends were
always serious and unfraudulent. The June issue Tate found particularly commendable; Ransom's and Davidson's critical ideas
expressed therein stirred him to an enunciation of his agreement.
Tate was aware that his two oldest and best friends were still the

men in contemporary American letters whom he most respected:
" It does seem after all in spite of dissension among ourselves that
you, John, and I have been looking toward the same conception
of modern poetry," he wrote Davidson; " and Eliot in England is
with us." [13]

The idea that emotion alone is the property of poetry had been
demonstrated as false, Tate continued, the ignoring of the intellectual, and therefore critical, side of the mind having permitted
the issuance into poetry of not only genuine emotions, but also
" faked " ones. In his opinion, the modern poet therefore had the
great difficulty of removing from himself all the spurious emotions
with which he had been surrounded; and, even greater, he must
". . . *in the lack of a criticism to prepare his audience* do his own
pioneering—he must not only make, he must sell his article, which
is nearly impossible. If Eliot had cared to explain the reason why
modern poetry is difficult (it *isn't* intrinsically) he would doubtless
have written something like the above: an audience with one set of
emotions, the poets, in advance, with another set, and this means
nothing else than a currency of two different languages. What do
you think of the idea? " The two *Fugitive* articles Tate considered
" the most important critical writing in months," and he was pleased
and excited to find in them corroboration of his own ideas. " I
believe you owe me a letter," he continued, " but I'm so full of this
idea this morning and so pleased to see other Fugitives in my way
of thinking, I couldn't resist writing."

The three friends were still exchanging poems in their letters
and, in spite of their differing aesthetic theories, were finding themselves in an ever growing closeness of accord. Of some of Davidson's critical remarks, Tate commented:

But besides your comment on my work, this letter contains some
of the most lucid and penetrating remarks on poetry in general I have
ever got from you. They easily go to show that we are rapidly approaching a common ground of principles, of which the fundamental one is
that poetry must be the expression of a whole mind—not gurgles and

[13] June 23, 1925.

spasms and ecstasies over every wayside hawthorne bush; in other words, it is not, as you say, a *report* of sensation, it is a resolution of sensation through all the faculties of the mind. Poetry to me is successive instances of the whole rhythm of thought, and that includes reason, emotion, extralogical experience, or as I put it a year or so ago, the entire phantasy of sensation.[14]

To Ransom Tate sent three of Crane's poems for *The Fugitive*, asking him to read them over several times before deciding about them. The poems were " Paraphrase," " Legend," and " Lachrymae Christi," all pieces which Tate admired greatly. Of " Paraphrase " he wrote, " This is one of the most intense poems on death I've ever seen. You'll notice there's no exposition of " sentiment "; the poem bursts right out of consciousness as a direct intuition of the imagined experience." [15]

Crane and the newly married Tates were in close conjunction during this period, working, reading, and talking together, their conversation dealing with, among other aesthetic matters, the problem of the poet's relationship to society, which in turn hinged on the problem of the structure of social values. The other Fugitive poets were also thrust into a consideration of traditional values by the loud and sensational publicity given to the Evolution Trial in Dayton. The Anti-Evolution Bill, or " Monkey Law," passed by the state legislature on March 13, 1925, and signed by Governor Austin Peay on March 18, prohibited the teaching of Darwin's Theory of Evolution in all state-supported universities, normals, and public schools in Tennessee. John T. Scopes, a high school science teacher, undertook to test the law by precipitating a trial. Vanderbilt was untouched by the statute; but its progressive and liberal leaders saw in the fight against Fundamentalism an opportunity to deal a sturdy blow against superstition and ignorance. " We shall build more laboratories," the Chancellor announced.

The Vanderbilt staff was in general unconcerned about the trial, deeming it not worth serious notice. A few men like Professor

[14] To Davidson, July 25, 1925.
[15] Quoted in *ibid.*

Sanborn realized that the issue was not so simple as it seemed, that, actually, the evolutionary theory was not taught in public schools or state universities by instructors sufficiently well educated to perceive its tentative hypothetical nature. Sanborn also recognized the growing disequilibrium in the modern educational curriculum: the student was not taught a coherent philosophical view of life; consequently he did not comprehend the relation of science to religion, of politics to ethics, of morals to metaphysics. He was increasingly under the tutelage of social scientists who interpreted man in terms of his physical nature. If moral values therefore were to be made subject to the evolutionary naturalism of Darwin, a loss of any traditional moral code would necessarily occur.

As the trial progressed, with its consequent world-wide publicity, private groups around the university engaged in serious colloquy. And soon those on the side of religion, even if it bore no relation to the fundamentalism that reigned over Dayton, found themselves uneasy in the face of an enlightenment which permitted so little of the supernatural to remain, so little even of the textural, the unique, the marvelous to stand. Obviously, those in favor of the New South movement saw the Scopes Trial as a backward step in a territory which had been making great strides forward. Mims, for instance, in an article in the September, 1925, *World's Work* lamented the fact that intellectual and cultural standards in the South had not kept pace with material development. Industrial progress would do slight good, he maintained, if it were to be used only to ballast a bigotry and prejudice that was growing worse instead of better. He listed the refusal of the Southern Methodist church to federate with the Northern church and the passage of the Anti-Evolution Bill as two incidents which militated against the good opinion of the South in the minds of educated observers. But Mims's contention was that the South was not so bad as it seemed; it was gradually developing an enlightened minority. "The chief trouble," he wrote, "is that the South still has a great mass of uneducated people—sensitive, passionate, prejudiced—and another mass of the half-educated, who have very little intellectual curiosity or independence of judgment." But, he continued, industrial progress had brought with it an increasing number of broad-minded men, and the young generation was "freer of traditions and prejudices." Another fifty years would see "great changes," he predicted.[16]

If the Fugitives were not precisely free of tradition, they certainly considered themselves free of prejudices. It would be at least a year after the Evolution Trial before they could affirm the worth not only of the tradition, but even of the "sensitive, passionate, prejudiced" Southerners. The savage and misinformed journalistic attacks upon the South were certainly one of the decisive elements in the later transformed and clarified thinking of Ransom, Davidson, Tate, and Warren. As in all cultural crises, the turmoil issuing from the trial brought into the foreground ideas and attitudes that, taken for granted in the past, were no longer generally accepted. It was with these basic tendencies in their society that the four chief Fugitives would be occupied during the coming year; but the greater part of the work had already been done—in the medium of poetry, which allows little importance to the superficial and accidental in a writer's surroundings.

Yet at this point both Tate and Davidson were still denying, in their published essays, any deep and pervasive connection between the poet and his native tradition. In a graceful essay, "Last Days of a Charming Lady," in the October 28 *Nation*, Tate set forth his ambivalent attitude toward the land of his birth. That the charming lady, Southern literature, was now to be found in Nashville or Charleston he did not deny; nevertheless, her existence was ephemeral: "Her conversation will be deft and serious but not too serious, because it will be cast in a whimsicality of fortitude before the intimate rumor of raped magnificence: It is certain to be an elegy on the perished amenities of the Old South, done much after the manner in which Mr. T. S. Eliot a few years ago lamented the decay of all modern culture. It is a scattering tradition, and its last living authority will scarcely survive the present decade." [17]

[16] "Why the South Is Anti-Evolution," L, No. 5, p. 548–52.
[17] CXXI, No. 3147, p. 485.

According to Tate, Southern culture had never been very hardy; the product of a "charmed idleness," it evinced "charm without energy," consisting basically "in a reflowering of eighteenth-century English manners and in the backwash, sterilized, of liberal thought from that century." For the South was committed to one idea— preserving its economic order—and so could not afford a critical look at itself. As a society, it was essentially irreligious, being "an aristocracy of social privilege founded in a rigid social order." Reft of that order, the Old South degenerated into "a sentiment susceptible of no precise definition."

Because the section had never viewed its limitations honestly, Tate continued, American literature had suffered. Yet, strangely enough, the lack of a real Southern literary tradition afforded the serious writer in the South more freedom than his other countrymen had:

His mind is open for experiment in form, for curiosity about world literature.

The modern Southerner does not inherit, nor is he likely to have, a native culture compounded of the strength and subtlety of his New England contemporary's. But he may be capable, through an empiricism which is his only alternative to intellectual suicide, of a cosmopolitan culture to which his contemporary in the East is emotionally barred.

Exile from the backward and narrow South, Tate concluded, was the only course open to the Southern artist.

Davidson made no such sweeping condemnation of the section. In a review of Ransom's *Grace after Meat* he was concerned only with refuting the false relation that Graves had established between Ransom's environment and his poetry:

The error Mr. Graves has made . . . is that he has sought to derive John Crowe Ransom from an environment without any accurate knowledge as to what that environment is. The volume P o e m s A b o u t G o d is a dramatic collation of the varieties of aspect in which the divinity makes his appearance to men; and though the book happens to be rich in "local color," Mr. Graves is not altogether right in identifying the poet's sentiments with those of his characters. Furthermore, to those who know Mr. Ransom, it is a bit absurd to think of him as "acting spokesman for rebellious 'poor whites'" in any sort of sense, or as doing the interpreter stunt for Tennessee as the other poets he names have done it for their sections.[18]

In fact, to Davidson, "local color" was so little present in the poetry of Mr. Ransom and his compeers, the Fugitives, as to seem hardly worth mentioning. No doubt Graves had been honestly attempting by his remarks to gain for Ransom the prestige he deserved, Davidson admitted, but neither Graves nor any other critic had come to terms with Ransom's work, which was "'pure poetry' in the sense that environment and immediate experience bear only the merest incidental relation to it. . . ."

Davidson perhaps overstated his case here, since for some time Ransom had been making use of specifically Southern subjects in his poetry—as allegorizations, it is true. But earlier than the other two, Ransom had in his poetry come to terms with his own relationship to the South. He had depicted it in parabolic form in "Old Mansion," published in April of the preceding year in *The Fugitive*. In this poem the old house by which the speaker passes, "exhaling his foreign weed," is one "whose annals in no wise could be brief / Nor ignoble . . . ." But the mansion is in a state of decay, and the "frightened heart" declares:

> "Your mansion, long and richly inhabited,
> Its exits and entrances suiting the children of men,
> Will not forever be thus, O man, exhibited,
> And one had best hurry to enter it, if one can."

The speaker raps at the door, but is rebuffed. "The old mistress is ill," comes the message; so the intruder must leave.

> But on retreating I saw myself in the token
> How lovingly from my foreign weed the feather curled
> On the languid air; and I went with courage shaken
> To dip, alas, into some unseemlier world.

[18] "An English Introduction," *The Guardian*, II, No. 3 (October, 1925), 456–57.

And a year earlier, in " Blackberry Winter," Ransom had displayed his tender awareness that the lady is ill, that her world must be allowed to perish: " If the lady hath any loveliness, let it die," the poem begins.

> But still would I sing to my maidenly apple-tree,
> Before she has borne me a single apple of red;
> The pictures of silver and apples of gold are dead;
> But one more apple ripeneth yet maybe.

Later, in an article on Southern literature, Ransom was to write of an old dying apple tree whose apples grew ever sweeter as the tree itself neared death. " Are the works of art like those apples, reaching their best when the society behind them is under sentence of death? " [19] he asked. Loving his society, then, not in rebellion against it, Ransom nevertheless seemed to have little hope for its survival.

In critical writing, too, it was Ransom who gave indication of the poet's reliance upon his historical tradition, and this in the fall issue of *The Fugitive,* in a review of Graves's new book, *Poetic Unreason.* Graves's contention was that the values of poetry are not absolute, but relative. With this sentiment Ransom found himself in agreement. Poetry intends to evoke a profound earlier experience, he pointed out; it has had this function for the poet and is intended to have it for the reader. The two evocations are necessarily different, however: " A poem records, for all its shining look of innocence, an intricate historical experience; but it can only hope to be intelligible to those minds whose history is tangled in just the same way as the poet's." Further, if a poet were writing for the widest possible audience, he would simplify and generalize his expression. How, then, would Ransom judge good poetry? To this question he gave what he denominated a " pragmatic " answer: " Good poetry is that which fits our own passionate history, and expresses that which needs expression from our private deeps." Bad poetry is the converse. In forming critical judgments, he reiterated,

[19] " Modern with the Southern Accent," *The Virginia Quarterly Review,* XI (April, 1935), 186.

these are the only "principles" which we may allow ourselves. "On this catholic platform honest poets should unite; but to dogmatize our own poetic likings into a standard for others is to subtract fatally from the conception of poetry as a spontaneous and expressive art." And yet what about a universal standard for poetry? Ransom's answer to this worrisome question seems admirably ambiguous: "Poetry is saved from being utterly licentious and chaotic by having a form and content based closely (as a general thing) upon the Tradition. It is a familiar art, and we all know what to look for and how to read it when we see a fresh specimen. Its privacy consists perfectly with its conventionality, its formality."

On the surface an espousal of the purely empirical basis of poetry, Ransom's article in actuality seems less concerned to advocate a doctrine of relativism than to establish the validity of a formal and traditional approach to the art. Implicit in his statements is the idea that whatever is universal in a poem must be arrived at through temporal and local rituals, by submission to the contingencies of history. If he is to be intelligible, the poet must speak in his own language to his own people, who have a common heritage.

The September *Fugitive* continued in its policy of giving space to serious reviews, containing, besides Ransom's essay, Davidson's critical estimate of two volumes: E. E. Cummings' *XLI Poems* and Hervey Allen's *Earth Moods*. To Davidson, despite the two poets' diverging attitudes toward the modern situation, both were faced with the same problem, which was for Davidson the chief question he continued to ask himself. "Given a rather chaotic modern world, disturbing in its complexity, and along with it the traditional instruments of the poet, how shall the poet orient himself, and what bearing will the bewildering condition of the cosmos have on his thought and on his form?"

Of the verse in the magazine, Ransom's dry and disciplined lines represent the most considerable contribution. In "The Two Worthies," a description of the dualism inherent in the Christian structure, as represented by Jesus the Paraclete and Paul the Exegete; and in "Husband Betrayed," a poem about a man who has married a pigeon-like girl only to find her pigeon-like, Ransom is meticulous and agreeable. "Janet Waking" and "History of Two Simple Lovers," the other two poems in the issue, are among Ransom's finest pieces. The second, a superbly rendered allegory, portrays man in his mortal "torture of equilibrium." Two lovers who desire each other are unable to consummate their love with honor: the woman's body invites the embrace, but the "officious tower" of her mind releases "grey doves" whose cry is "Honor, honor."

Since they are noble lovers, they are unable either to give each other up or to yield to their passion:

> At length I saw these lovers fully were come
> Into their torture of equilibrium:
> Dreadfully had forsworn each other, and yet
> They were bound each to each, and they did not forget.
>
> The beauty of their bodies was the bond
> Which these incarnate might not pass beyond;
> Invincible proud Honor was the bar
> Which made them not come closer but stay far.
>
> And rigid as two painful stars, and twirled
> About the clustered night their prison world,
> They burned with fierce love always to come near,
> But honor beat them back and kept them clear.

The narrator, angered at the lovers for ruining their beauty, comes "with puddled brow" to force them into a decision: "Man, what would you have?" And the dilemma he presents is the age-old one:

> Would you ascend to Heaven and bodiless dwell?
> Or take your bodies honorless to Hell?

The finite conception of a supersensible heaven is no more satisfying to lovers than is the idea of a spiritless hell; the pair have known they cannot choose, since choice would mean the renunciation of a part of experience in favor of simplicity. But now the spectator is convinced also, and his tone of raillery changes to admiration and tenderness:

But still I watched them spinning, orbited nice.
Their flames were no more radiant than their ice.
I dug in the quiet earth and wrought the tomb
And made these lines to memorize the doom:

Equilibrists lie here; stranger, tread light;
Close but untouching in each other's sight;
Mouldered the lips and ashy the tall skull,
Let them lie perilous and beautiful.

In a letter to Tate written a year and a half later, Ransom was to say: "Art is our refusal to yield to the blandishments of 'constructive' philosophy and permit the poignant and actual Dichotomy to be dissatisfied in a Trichotomy; our rejection of third Terms; our denial of Hegel's right to solve a pair of contradictions with a Triad. And here's a slogan: Give us Dualism, or we'll give you no Art." [20]

Even in death, then, the "poignant and actual dichotomy" cannot be simplified for the lovers: though their bodies are mouldered, their intellects ashy, the pair must lie "close but untouching" still. Because it is difficult to achieve, because a choice in either direction would be infinitely less heroic, the state of equilibrium is "perilous and beautiful." Man's conception of neither hell nor heaven is adequate for the lovers; and the speaker, a mortal himself, cannot inform us of their ultimate metaphysical disposition.

Like Ransom's other most successful poems, "History of Two Simple Lovers" achieves by the use of a dramatis persona a detachment which gives the poem an air of complete finality. The noble, statuesque beauty of the lovers is sustained throughout the work, the feudal imagery for the woman providing overtones of dignity and importance: "Body, it was a white field ready for love. / On her body's field, with the gaunt tower above, / The lilies grew . . . ." The device of the speaker (who represents—generically, one would think—the artist) gives form to the situation. At first angry, he becomes perplexed; then, in the act of clarifying the problem and placing before the lovers their two choices, he himself comes to an

[20] Wednesday [March, 1927].

understanding that there can be no resolution, that their precision of elegant and torturesome balance is admirable. It is the anonymous speaker who digs " in the quiet earth " to make the tomb, constructing his lines " to memorize the doom." The poem is Ransom's most completely successful dramatization of his major philosophical insight.

The other poems in the September issue are distinguished, though not uniformly so. After Ransom, Crane perhaps made the most valuable contribution to the issue, with his " Legend " and " Paraphrase." Davidson's three poems are of unequal merit. But in " Projection of a Body upon Space," in which, as in " Cross Section of a Landscape," Davidson makes use of mathematical constructions, the personal vision is transformed and reprojected, as in the following lines:

> What ribs of vacancy and shade are these
> Marked by the failing sun against the heaven?
> I am not wise in God's quaint pleasantries;
> A shadow it is, not a pillar of fire or a raven.

Tate's one poem, " To a Romantic Novelist," (a polemic directed against James Branch Cabell)[21] contains pointed phrases and a pleasingly malicious wit, but it lacks the integrating rhythmic form which Tate's best work shows, as well as the indirection of language. Warren's four sonnets and Moore's six, as well as Mrs. Gottschalk's three poems in the issue are all interesting and worthy of inclusion, if not memorable. William Yandell Elliott, inside *The Fugitive's* covers for the sixth time in the magazine's history, contributed two poems—one of which, " Before Dawn," is the best of his poems to appear in the journal, exhibiting a vigor of phrase and rhythm, as in the lines

> This is the thief's hour, wolf's, and the fly-by-night's:
> Now ghoul and goblin share the haunted dark
> With misshaped fear; a whippoorwill, from shadow
> In the churchyard yews, reviles the sleeping lark.

[21] Tate to Davidson, August 22, 1925.

To the list of members in the September issue was added Alfred Starr, a former Vanderbilt student in the class of Tate and Jesse Wills. Starr had graduated from Harvard, and on his return to Nashville he and his brother Milton, who were both good friends of several of the Fugitives, had come to meetings but contributed no poetry. In fact, Alfred Starr's relation to the group never became more than nominal. The truth of the matter is that by now the Fugitives realized that the next issue of the magazine would have to be the last. Despite the fact that group meetings had continued without abatement all during 1925 (and were to continue long after the suspension of the publication), the magazine itself had been managed during the year chiefly by Ransom, Warren, and Davidson. Warren had gone to the University of California at the beginning of the fall; this loss, combined with other circumstances—Tate's withdrawal from active membership, Johnson's break with the group, the failure of the minor members to supply poems in keeping with Fugitive standards, and a growing disinclination on the part of the group to continue a project that, however affectionately and proudly viewed, had consumed much time, energy, and spirit—made inevitable the necessity for discontinuance.

Ransom and Davidson were tired; the small details of keeping *The Fugitive* going in addition to their own writing and teaching had left them longing for time in which to write and study at some leisure. And like most professors, they were never free of financial worry. Ransom had offers from other universities; yet he preferred to remain at Vanderbilt, even though the Chancellor was not encouraging about his chances for advancement to the status of full professor. Davidson, discouraged, wondered if he had much future at Vanderbilt or, indeed, in the South.[22]

At the University of California, Warren was finding the literary men "fifty years behind the times." No stimulating literary discussion there gripped and enthralled him as the talk had in Nashville. Whereas the excitement on the Vanderbilt campus had

[22] Davidson to Tate, November 29, 1925.

concerned Pound and Eliot, the talk at Berkeley centered endlessly around Marx and Engels. During the summer, before leaving the South, Warren had collected a number of his poems at Tate's instigation and worked them over for publication. He wrote Tate that he had about thirty-eight in his manuscript and that he had edited them so carefully that he had " few illusions left about them." [23] But Warren was not to publish a volume of poetry until eleven years later, long after he had completed several years of the kind of scholarly study he was beginning at the University of California in the fall.

Laura Riding Gottschalk had gone to New York in the early fall, where she stayed near the Tates and made the acquaintance of Tate's literary friends. They were impressed with her brilliance and energy, and it was not long before she was involved in a number of projects. Tate commented, " Laura's successes drive on apace. That young lady has more energy than a phalanx of dynamos, with seven billy-goats thrown in." [24]

Tate's friendship with Edmund Wilson on the staff of *The New Republic* had led to his being a regular reviewer for that magazine. Other reviewing assignments likewise gave him the opportunity to express himself on serious topics, so that, though there was little money in this particularly gruelling activity, Tate recognized it as the path which an independent literary man such as himself must take. Consequently, in November, he resigned his position with the Climax Publishing Corporation, converting himself into a free-lance writer in earnest. He wrote that he was now " thoroughly a slave to reviews." [25]

In his poetry, Tate's upheaval was continuing. He felt that he was coming out of his stalemate and was striking out in the direction of more positive views, no longer content for poetry to express the negation of existence:

You remember [he wrote to Davidson] that certain " critics "

[23] July 11, 1925.
[24] To Davidson [Autumn, 1925].
[25] To Davidson, November 26, 1925.

thought our poetry in the first issues of *The Fugitive* was very much alike, perhaps written by one man? Well, it *was* much alike, in spite of the technical inequalities, for it was the expression of defeated men. Mine was a little more ragged and violent, being produced by a young man . . . .

I am not writing any poetry now; and the reason is obvious: I have no idiom for a Vita Nuova, for it will take a long time for me even to understand it. For poetry is the triumph of life, not a commentary on its impossibility.[26]

And concerning the social function of poetry, later in the same letter he remarked: "Society is pretty degraded just now, and we need poetry badly. But if poetry is *merely* a social defense it can hardly be serious . . . ."

In Nashville, however, with the demise of *The Fugitive* imminent, it was difficult not to feel somewhat cut off and defeated. Davidson wrote Tate:

I agree in the main with your estimate of poetry as a social defense, and with your determination of the elements of likeness in Fugitive poetry and the reason therefor. I would only supplement your remarks by saying that I do believe most of us really have approached poetry as a fine art and not in the spirit of dilettantes or moralists. That has been our great strength,—that and our seriousness. But I will acknowledge that the defeatism crept in, some strain of it at least, in the bulk of Fugitive poetry, and so our "pure art" has here and there been touched with indignation or with wistfulness depending on the reaction of the writer to his confinements. It is possible, though, that what you term defeatism isn't a permanent quality; I hope it isn't. And I think, in your case as in mine and others, the surest way to pass beyond and out of defeatism is to acknowledge the thing for what it is in the hope that some sort of purgation may finally be accomplished. Then may come the Vita Nuova and the triumphant idiom which you desire.[27]

In his fall summary of the year's poetry, Braithwaite had again singled out *The Fugitive* for special praise, designating it the "most distinctive poetry magazine in America . . . the best edited

[26] November 26, 1925.
[27] November 29, 1925.

of them all." [28] From New York Tate sent his hail and farewell to the journal: "I await the last *Fugitive* with much pleasure," he wrote; "not because it is the last—but because it's *The Fugitive!*" [29]

But the final issue of the magazine, though no disappointment in quality, indicates that the magazine would have had to change radically in character had it continued. Deprived of Warren's and Tate's poems (Tate contributed one piece to the issue, though he was no longer interested in publishing a quantity of poems nor in publishing often) the magazine had to rely for its bulk chiefly upon the six poems each of Moore and Laura Gottschalk, who had been represented at great length in its pages all year. Ransom and Davidson contributed generously to the issue, but Ransom was no longer concerned with using the journal as a means to print, and Davidson had reached a stage in his work where he needed to proceed with less haste and more privacy than the quarterly afforded. Stevenson was the only other Fugitive in the December pages, and three outsiders, Crane, Graves, and McClellan, took up the rest of the space.

In the back of the final issue a lengthy editorial by Ransom gave the reason for discontinuance: "The action is taken because there is no available Editor to take over the administrative duties incidental to the publication of a periodical of even such limited scope as the FUGITIVE. The Fugitives are busy people, for the most part enslaved to Mammon, their time used up in vulgar bread-and-butter occupations. Not one of them is in a position to offer himself on the altar of sacrifice." The announcement went on to make clear that a lack of neither financial backing nor poetry caused the suspension; and it assured the public that the group would still meet: "For that matter, the Fugitives will continue to hold their frequent meetings for the reading and discussion of poetry and philosophy; we were holding these meetings for years before the

[28] "Through the Year with the Poets," the Boston *Evening Transcript*, November 21, 1925.
[29] To Davidson, November 26, 1925.

thought of publication was entertained, and we shall go on holding them after publication, for the time being, has stopped."

And, although nothing definite could be promised concerning further publication from the Fugitives, Ransom expressed his hope that not a year might pass " without some kind of published exhibit to break the silence." The editorial assured its readers that the experience of publishing *The Fugitive* had been rewarding: " No Fugitive dreamed in the beginning that our magazine would meet with the success that it has. We have completed four years of honorable existence in the midst of the keenest competition for the ear of the lovers of poetry; we have supplied ourselves with rich experience, we have made many loyal friends, and we have, unless all signs fail, won a certain respect from the bigwigs which an unpretentious and provincial magazine had no reason to expect."

The final book review in the magazine, written by Davidson, is somewhat prophetically entitled " The Future of Poetry." A discussion of a book by R. C. Trevelyan, in which the author had found that the " primal song-function of poetry " had " atrophied and practically disappeared," Davidson's essay undertook to view the development of the art optimistically. Instead of lamenting the loss of its song-function, Davidson stated, we should perhaps be more concerned to appreciate the greater variety and subtlety offered in the " multiplication of species." The " distant and humble " ancestor of poetry is of as hypothetical nature, he suggested, as is the Missing Link in the story of the human genesis.

But, as though to refute their own author, three of Davidson's poems in the issue, " Pastorals Somewhat in the Modern Style," all sound the note of loss for the simple purity of the past:

> Oh, whom shall Echo love
> In a grey room where is
> No shepherd boy to claim her,
> Coming where Echo lies
> With no kiss to claim her?

Here certainly the poem predicts a theme that is to become an explicit tenet in Davidson's later criticism. Perhaps a poem represents a moment of actual grace, that intermittent light which clarifies and illuminates the occasion without enlightening the poet. To extend these separate moments of *claritas* into a coherent set of principles upon which to base one's life is a task requiring long work and self-integration.

So it was that, as the magazine expired, the four men to whom it had meant most were in stages of philosophic belief which they were soon to modify and enlarge; and *The Fugitive* must not be denied its share of credit in their development. It had provided the necessity and the opportunity for intelligent men to express themselves in poetry—to learn their art and to reach a public—without the restrictions of toadying to a sponsor or of conforming to a theory. Not only intrinsically, but also functionally, it had been the most valuable amateur magazine in literary history.

CHAPTER EIGHT

TOWARD UNDERSTANDING—
THE FUGITIVE ANTHOLOGY
AND THE BEGINNINGS
OF AGRARIANISM:
1926—1928

What shall we do who have knowledge
Carried to the heart?

THE END OF *The Fugitive* in no wise marked
the end of the Fugitives; on the contrary, relieved of the worrisome
details of editing and circulating the magazine, the group was able
to function again in the genial amateur spirit, with philosophic and
aesthetic discussion its chief aims. During the next few years meetings were untroubled by business matters, and such notable guests
as Louis Untermeyer, Æ, Robert Frost, and John Gould Fletcher
came to spend an evening in the Frank home and to share in the
group conversation, which in its character was gentlemanly, gracious, and astringent.

Of the members left in Nashville, Ransom and Davidson were
busiest at writing poetry and criticism: Ransom's third volume of
verse—*Two Gentlemen in Bonds*—was accepted by Knopf in the
spring of 1926, to issue from the press during 1927, and a projected
prose work had turned his mind to the consideration of aesthetic

principles; Davidson, having won the South Carolina Poetry Society's "Southern" Prize with his "Fire on Belmont Street," was occupied with a new idea in poetry which he called the "Long Street" series [1] and with his increasingly successful book page. Of the others, Moore was studying at Vanderbilt Medical School, producing new sonnets with unabated fecundity; Curry had recently completed the eight years of research required for his Chaucer volume; [2] Jesse Wills and Stevenson were prospering in their business careers, yet still writing verse that, if infrequent, was the product of fine craftsmanship and intelligent minds. Frank and Hirsch were back in their element now that the magazine was no longer the controlling interest in the meetings, for these two were second to none in the group in the pursuance of cultivated and widely ranging conversation.

For real literary exchange the most serious and mature writers in the group still turned to each other; and, though he was away, Tate was the common bond uniting Ransom, Davidson, and Warren, all from various points on a circumference that gradually assumed the fulness of a completed aesthetic and metaphysical circle. Ransom and Davidson, working together daily at Vanderbilt, were intimately connected with one another's thinking; but the Fugitive genius for thought required the additional stimulation of the written word. Thus, in these years immediately after the discontinuance of the magazine, the correspondence between Davidson and Tate, Ransom and Tate, and, to a smaller degree, Warren and Tate developed the mature view of each with a wholeness and clarity not available to the isolated thinker.

Tate was living in Patterson, New York, he and his wife sharing half a house with Hart Crane. Involved in publishing schemes and commissioned for reviews and articles, Tate was gaining in the literary world the foothold for which he had struggled. A venture he was planning with Edmund Wilson was a poetry series to be undertaken by the Adelphi Press, a presentation of new

[1] To be published as *The Tall Men* (Boston and New York: Houghton Mifflin Company, 1927).

[2] *Chaucer and the Medieval Sciences.*

poets in the following order—Laura Riding (the former Laura Riding Gottschalk),[3] Tate, Phelps Putnam, Malcolm Cowley, Crane, Wilson, and John Peale Bishop. Miss Riding had tried to assume the leadership in the project and ended by causing some little dissension; but, at the end of the year, she had sailed for England to join Robert Graves and his wife and children on a trip to Egypt. Soon after she left, the poetry series was abandoned, but her own book, *The Close Chaplet*, appeared early in 1926.

Tate's work had recently received from T. S. Eliot a minute criticism, the effect of which was both "flattering and discouraging." To Davidson, Tate commented, "Eliot is uncanny in tracing out my influences and defects."[4] But, though Tate was closely in touch with provocative and original writers in New York, he relied on sustenance from Davidson's criticism that he could not find elsewhere. "You are one of the few that can be depended on for a clean reaction," he wrote;

you have always given me your views forthright, from the time you didn't like my verse down to now, when you seem to be liking it better; and I must say I value the old unfavorable opinion as highly . . . .

It is the consistency of attitude—much more valuable than consistency of opinion—that I like. I can put it this way: you have not seen the necessity of fitting me or disposing of me in a fixed little cosmology of competitions and rivalries in which you make yourself safe for Donald Davidson.[5]

The letter which occasioned Tate's acknowledgment is brilliantly perceptive and—as Tate discerned—indicative of Davidson's ability to appreciate qualities quite alien to his own writing:

Heretofore [Davidson wrote], in your poetry there has been so often a lack of elasticity that you left your reader in a state of defeat, unable to bridge the ellipses which your close crowding of images and ideas produced; there was (as I saw it) not enough play in your lines;

[3] She began using her maiden name in 1927, according to a letter to Davidson, undated, written that year.
[4] June 26, 1926.
[5] To Davidson, April 2, 1926.

your association of ideas was very rich, but it produced that "tele-scoping of imagery" to which I recall Curry objected. In these three poems this defect does not appear, if defect it is . . . . You seem to me to be approaching or even attaining perfection in the only kind of poetry which your artistic conscience will permit you to write. I may regret that your conscience has driven you into a narrow lane from which I can see no emerging; but I accept, since it is your choice, both the lane and you, and I do not know of any other poetry in this field which has such a cast of the inevitable in phrasing or which represents more adequately the artistic reactions of a thoroughly twentieth century mind, encircled by a complex whirl of influences, yet so far abstracted from them as to be sensitive (if remotely) to tradition. Furthermore, though Dr. Mims and even Ransom would think of your poetry as poetry of the head, I do not see it that way; it is intellectual poetry, to be sure, but intellectual poetry pouring a definite light (as Donne's did) on physical and emotional experience.[6]

Reciprocally, Tate's opinion meant much to Davidson, for he acknowledged the other man's closer immersion in the real poetic experimentation of the day, as well as his critical acumen. David-son had sent Tate portions of his "Long Street" poems, and Tate replied with a lengthy and detailed criticism. Despite some rather serious reservations about the new work, he was certain that David-son could produce important poetry, totally different from his own or Ransom's:

First, let me say a word about the plan of a Tennessee Faust. It looks very impressive; and I think you can make it work. Just reading these selections, I am reminded of the true definition of poetry with respect to time and place—that it must be local to be universal; while on the other hand, much poetry that deliberately sets out to be universal merely exposes its provincialism . . . . As to the possible success, how-ever, of such a poem in the grand style, that of course I couldn't predict —any more than could you. But I'd like to see it tried out; and I can think of nobody else who could do it better than you. I couldn't even begin it; Ransom probably has too much of the same poison in his system as I have to do it.[7]

[6] To Tate, March 29, 1926.
[7] To Davidson, May 14, 1926.

But actually, Tate continued, he preferred Davidson's previous lyrics; Eliot was right, he felt, in pointing out the absence of important themes for modern poets. That the individual mind was less important in the production of literature than was the culture, Tate was certain; and the dissolution of our culture was a fact that could not be escaped even in Tennessee: "I think there is one fundamental law of poetry, and it is negative: you can't create a theme. Themes are or are not available. If you can name me a single great poem the theme of which the poet invented, I'll send you a case of beer for the Fourth of July. Remember—a great poem. You can't put your epic of Tennessee into the minds of Tennesseans; the precondition of your writing it is that it must (in an equivalent of spiritual intensity) be already there." [8]

In his reply, Davidson was concerned to set one matter straight: "But I must refute other implications by declaring that I am not writing an epic (Good Lord, surely not an *epic*) for Tennesseans. I will merely use your phrase and say that I'm writing the history of a mind—my mind, to an extent." [9]

By the end of the year, when the nine parts making up the "Long Street" series (which Davidson had now entitled *The Tall Men*) were completed and ready for publication, Tate was still dissatisfied with the work. He found in it many "fine lines and passages," but on the whole he considered that it represented a "failure to reduce the material at hand to order":

I think the best comment I can produce on the mixture of your performance is that I should expect you to keep on writing the poem indefinitely: the solution of your poetical problem is no clearer on page 84 than on page 1; so why should you stop there? Of course, you offer a solution of another sort; I may call it a doctrine of love. You didn't need to write a poem to expound the doctrine. On the other hand, there is no reason why the exposition of a doctrine shouldn't be poetry. I simply believe that on the whole yours isn't. [10]

Tate was so deeply convinced that the poem was not ready for

[8] To Davidson, May 14, 1926.
[9] To Tate, June 14, 1926.
[10] To Davidson, December 29, 1926.

publication that he wrote in great urgency: "For God's sake, Don, don't publish the poem in its present state. The material has great possibilities, but it is not yet mastered." [11]

A few days later, still concerned over the poem, Tate wrote again, recalling that he had once remarked to Davidson, "Our past is buried so deep that it is all but irrecoverable." He was convinced that, although Davidson thought his subject matter important to him, actually it was not, since it had not been converted into poetry. In this same letter Tate enclosed two "new ones" of his own, asking Davidson to "slaughter" them. [12]

One of these "new ones" was the "Ode to the Confederate Dead," Tate's now-famous poem dealing with modern man's inability to transcend the bonds of subjectivity and, hence, his failure to understand or accept the past. Davidson's dismay at his friend's direction in this work was as great as Tate's had been earlier at the method of *The Tall Men*. Charging that many of Tate's poems became "aesthetic dissertations" as much as poetry, Davidson indicated that he considered the method successful when Tate's writing was "out-and-out argumentative"; but, he wrote,

. . . when you deal with *things themselves*, the things become a ruin and crackle like broken strands under your feet. The Confederate dead become a peg on which you hang an argument whose lines, however sonorous and beautiful in a strict proud way, leave me wondering why you wrote a poem on the subject at all, since in effect you say (and I suspect you are speaking partly to me) that no poem can be written on such a subject. Your *Elegy* is not for the Confederate dead, but for your own dead emotion, or mine (*you* think).

The poem is beautifully executed. I do not quibble over a single word. Its economy is striking: its tone is sustained: it has very fine individual passages and is this much beyond anything of yours I have recently seen, that it is coherent, structurally unimpugnable. But its beauty is a cold beauty. And where, O Allen Tate, are the dead? You have buried them completely out of sight—with them yourself and me. God help us, I must say. You keep on whittling your art to a finer

[11] *Ibid.*
[12] January 5, 1927.

point, but are you also not whittling yourself? What is going to happen if the only poetry you can allow your conscience to approve is a poetry of argument and despair. Fine as such poetry may be, is it not a Pyrrhic victory?

Then later:

I do not see how you think the battle between poetry and science can be won in such ways as you use, for do you not strive for and attain a rigidity as inflexible as the rigidity of science?

Well, these are terrible questions. I assure you I tremble before them, and I do not feel at all satisfied over the statements I have put forward in this helter-skelter discourse.[13]

Tate's reply to Davidson made clear that there were no easy answers to the "terrible questions" Davidson raised. "If I were sure you had never fallen below the standard of this latest letter and never would again, I should greet thee, O Don, as peer of the greatest critics," he wrote. But, he was certain, Davidson was wrong. Just as Keats's "Ode to a Nightingale" was not *about* nightingales, so Tate's poem did not need to be about the Confederate dead. "As for your metaphor about whittling down my art," he continued, "I said all I had to say; you can take me to task in a moral sense for not having more to say but not for refusing to exceed my material. That was my quarrel with your new poem: you exceeded your material."[14]

As he explained to Davidson, it was in the epistemological rather than in the spatio-temporal sense that he considered the past irrecoverable. But Davidson, with his essentially historic rather than philosophic bias, felt that one comes to terms with the past through the will, by faith, rather than by means of the corroding and isolating intellect. The verities for which men have lived, suffered, and died are in some sense still existent and still, to the humble and perseverant, available. To Tate, on the contrary, the problem of transcending the enveloping framework of the critical mind was insoluble, complicated as it was for the Southerner by

[13] To Tate, February 15, 1927.
[14] February 20, 1927.

the vast cleavage between the modern world and the old one which his forebears had inhabited.

Tate's real objection to Davidson's poem, however, must have stemmed from a dissatisfaction with its language more than with its theme. For some time now Tate's energy had been brought to bear on the problem of the poetic idiom, which he was convinced must have the power to suggest the total texture of consciousness. Reality, to Tate, lay not in objects, since to him they existed in no purity, taking their shifting and varicolored being in the viewing mind's perceptions. It must be the poet's insight, then, that encompassed the chaotic and fragmentary within a rounded and completed experience. As Tate wrote in his Foreword to Hart Crane's *White Buildings*, "the poetical meaning [in Crane's poetry] is a direct intuition realized prior to an explicit knowledge of the subject matter of the poem." [15] Words, then, could not be used merely descriptively; they must be able to suggest—by dislocation if necessary and certainly obliquely by means of symbols—the intuitive form in the poet's mind. In the distilled lines of Tate's own "Ode," each word functions to suggest a network of incongruous and contradictory attitudes that make up the "feeling" of the situation, the reality lying in the consciousness of the protagonist and not in the exterior world. Davidson's language, on the contrary, is more one of reference than of suggestion, appealing to the conscious elements of memory and relying on a reservoir of genuine emotions which are associated with events. The directness of his simple language must have seemed to Tate an indication that the poetic process was not complete.

But later in the year, after *The Tall Men* appeared in print, Tate modified considerably his reservations about the poem: "the fine passages I missed in the ms. stand out, and I shall probably have to retract most of what I wrote to you," he stated in his congratulatory letter.[16] Likewise, in 1928, on re-reading Tate's "Ode" before him in the newly published Fugitive *Anthology*, Davidson was struck afresh by the poem's beauty and wished to withdraw

[15] (New York: Boni and Liveright, 1926), xv.
[16] To Davidson, October 8, 1927.

his earlier criticism of it: "My previous strictures on it were decidedly overdone and may, I suspect, have proceeded partly from unconscious wrath following your denunciatory remarks on my own book. I don't remember what unfavorable things I said, exactly, but let it be said here that I retract all the most considerable indictments." [17]

It seems profoundly ironic, on the surface, that these two friends who had participated in a program of mutual criticism and encouragement on their earliest efforts should find themselves forced to disapprove of each other's first really ambitious work. Yet from the beginning of their exchange of poems, Davidson and Tate had manifested a basic difference in poetic attitude. What they had shared was a common set of presuppositions about the sort of world the poet should inhabit. But they were different kinds of poets; and once they had reached maturity in their art, they could no longer follow each other's advice on matters of technique.

At the same time that the correspondence of Tate and Davidson was defining thematic attitude, the correspondence of Tate and Ransom [18] was making explicit a carefully thought out aesthetic. After his year's editorial work on *The Fugitive* was past, Ransom was looking forward to what he called a "delicious prospect" facing him in the fall—a four-month leave of absence to write and study.[19] Tate had for some time felt slightly injured by Ransom, and had not heard from him for several months; so, in May, 1926, he wrote Ransom expressing his feeling of being disesteemed. Ransom apologized in a letter that was open and honest:

I have great respect for your work; my personal feeling is warm and friendly; I greatly admire the uncompromising purity of your literary intention, and the quality of its recent output; I find a great deal of heroism in the course you have set yourself; and I share fully most of your philosophical ideas, as reflected in your current reviews and articles. The effect of these feelings on my part is vitiated, I know, by

[17] To Tate, January 27, 1928.
[18] Only one half of this correspondence has been preserved—Ransom's letters to Tate.
[19] Ransom to Tate, June 18, 1926.

my short-comings as a correspondent, for which I apologize unreservedly
. . . . Yet I have written you two or three letters which, upon re-reading,
I have consigned to the wastebasket. I always feel special reluctance,
here of late, to write to intelligent people, because in such exchanges
one is required to put his impressions of art and things to the last
analysis, and this is painful and laborious; I say to myself, we can get
together and talk it out . . . .[20]

Ransom's letter was more than sufficient to re-establish the warm
affection between the two; and beginning in the fall of 1926 there
was an exchange of letters between them that was immensely fruitful for both. Each man was laboring to develop his aesthetic
theory, and each wanted it founded on a firm ontological basis.
They approached their philosophy with diverging biases; yet since
they both assumed a common rational basis for argument they were
able to communicate and to affect each other's final formulation
of ideas.

Convinced that the important problem facing the literary
critic in the twentieth century was the maintenance of a firm
ontological position in the face of a dominant scientific knowledge,
Ransom had undertaken an ambitious project which he intended
to call The Third Moment.[21] Describing his volume to Tate, he
declared his plan of getting at an aesthetic kind of knowledge by
tracing the three moments " in the historical order of experience." [22]
Actually, as Ransom made clear later in the preface to *The World's
Body*, he was concerned in this first work " with urging that it is
not a pre-scientific poetry but a post-scientific one to which we
must now give our consent." [23] He refers to The Third Moment
as " a kind of Prolegomena to Any Future Poetic " and explains
that in it he may have been " rationalizing [his] own history ":
". . . for I came late into an interest in poetry, after I had been
stuffed with the law if not the letter of our modern sciences, and

[20] *Ibid.*
[21] This is the MS. which in the preface to *The World's Body*, p. vii, Ransom
said he consigned to flames.
[22] Ransom to Tate, September 5, 1926.
[23] *The World's Body*, viii.

quickly I had the difficulty of finding a poetry which would not deny what we in our strange generation actually are: men who have aged in these pure intellectual disciplines, and cannot play innocent without feeling very foolish. The expense of poetry is greater than we will pay if it is something to engage in without our faculties. I could not discover that this mortification was required." [24]

In the scheme of The Third Moment, as he explained it to Tate, the first moment of cognition is the original experience— "pure of all intellectual content, unreflective, concrete, and singular; there are no distinctions, and the subject is identical with the Whole." [25] The second moment is the one in which record is made of the first moment, a record which proceeds by the formation of concepts—abstractions which are actually "subtractions from the whole." In the third moment, ". . . we become aware of the deficiency of the record. Most of experience is quite missing from it. All our concepts and all our histories put together cannot add up into the wholeness with which we started out. Philosophical syntheses do no good—the Absolutists are quaint when they try to put Humpty-Dumpty together again by logic—they only give us a whole which, as Kant would say, is obtained by *comprehensio logica* and not by *comprehensio aesthetica* . . . ." [26]

The first moment can be recaptured by only one method, Ransom believed: images. "The Imagination [he continued] is the faculty of Pure Memory, or unconscious mind; it brings out the original experiences from the dark storeroom, where we dwell upon them with a joy proportionate to our previous despair . . . . What we really get . . . by this deliberate recourse to images, is a mixed world composed of both images and concepts; or a sort of practicable reconciliation of the two worlds." Dreams, fancies, religion, morals, art—these are the operations in which "we try to reconstitute the fugitive first moment." Ransom planned to deal exclusively with art—specifically with poetry: "Essentially, Poetry is always the exhibit of Opposition and at the same time Reconcili-

[24] *Ibid.*
[25] Ransom to Tate, September 5, 1926.
[26] *Ibid.*

ation between the Conceptual or Formal and the Individual or Concrete." This treatment of the subject, not conducted "in the constant company of the actual poems,"[27] Ransom was later to consider too theoretical. But an acquaintance with its chief principles does make explicit what is implicit in his poetry: the language of poetry must reconstitute experience by associating value with a concrete image upon which the poetic consciousness steadily gazes.

Tate had sent Ransom a number of poems, which Ransom read over many times, " each time seeing more fine turns in them "; but never, he confessed, " finding perfect satisfaction." The reason for this lack, he " cheerfully " acknowledged, was that he was not in sympathy with Tate's intention, which was, after all, " not a matter for debate."[28] He disagreed with Tate chiefly on two points: language and theme. One did not have to invent one's language, he felt sure; Tate's carefully constructed idiom he considered " Futurism." Constant preoccupation with the development of a "modern" language for poetry could be misleading, Ransom implied: " The course I have marked out for myself as the safest is simply that of not letting the question of the old and new get into my mind at all, of keeping up a certain heat of composition in the faith that the imagery will be sufficient unto the day and unto the nature of my subject." And about Tate's chief theme—" that we are fallen on evil days "—Ransom had doubts on two scores: first, he wondered if it were a good subject for poetry, since " the Ubi Sunt cry has traditionally been individual and personal "; and second, he was dubious of its truth as a thesis. Human lives at any period of history have been similar, he contended; it is only in the large cities that the individual feels dissociated, not in the provinces. But that his objections to Tate's poetry were given with some reservations he made clear: " These are cautions and fears—I don't put them very positively. I feel very reluctant to pass a judgment on your poetry at all; and admit that

[27] *The World's Body*, vii.
[28] To Tate, September 13, 1926.

your present work may be the necessary preparation for work which will transcend us all . . . . there is an almost unfailing brilliance in what you write." [29]

But if Ransom felt misgivings about the direction of Tate's work, Tate was moving toward a deeper understanding of Ransom's writing. In a review of *Two Gentlemen in Bonds*, he probed into the generating force behind the poetry: ". . . Mr. Ransom is the last pure manifestation of the culture of the eighteenth century South; the moral issues which emerge transfigured in his poetry are the moral issues of his section, class, culture, referred to their simple, fundamental properties. It is a great error to attribute the Southern quality to post-bellum sentimentalism alone, and to repudiate it at its best." [30]

As basic to Ransom's poetry, Tate isolated two attitudes which he designated "rationalism" and "*noblesse oblige*": "Rationalism, not in the sense popularized by the philosophers, but in the older and purer sense of the humane tradition, a tradition lying at the very core of the old Southern order, stiffens his poetry with an irony and lucidity, and a subtlety, which elevate it with a unique distinction in the present American scene . . . ." Ransom's "system of casuistry," Tate maintained, garbs itself in a "kind of solemn dandyism, . . . but back of the dandyism lurks a profound stoicism and an immovable detachment which feeds upon an intellect always sufficient unto itself." Tate's final sentence reveals an acute insight into the nature of the enveloping action behind Ransom's work: "Mr. Ransom can render a beautiful commentary upon his tragic personal vision because he accepts the code within which the characters struggle . . . ."

This review marks an important departure for Tate. More than a month before it appeared in print, Tate sent the manuscript to Ransom, who was "intensely pleased," wondering only if its fine praise had been dictated by Tate's usual honesty or by his friendly generosity. "In either case I find pleasure," Ransom wrote, "and

[29] *Ibid.*
[30] "The Eighteenth-Century South," *loc. cit.*, 346.

perhaps would as soon have it one way as the other . . . . You have done me the honor of more inward examination than I have yet secured from any source," he wrote; " I am obliged to see that in rationalism and Noblesse Oblige you have picked out two cues that penetrate very deep into my stuff—and I rather like, too, the more synthetic concept of the Old South under which you put them." But Ransom went on to testify, ". . . I don't write consciously as a Southerner or a non-Southerner." [31] And a few weeks later, he had more to say on the subject of his poetry's not being essentially Southern:

About Rationalism and Noblesse Oblige: You do me the honor to let me be a mouthpiece for a very noble historic culture. But this is the accidental and perhaps the questionable feature of your interpretation, and certainly the less important feature. What is important in your witness was that my stuff presents the dualistic philosophy of an assertive element *versus* an element of withdrawal and Respect. Your terms Rationalism and noblesse oblige are nearly as ultimate and pure as could be stated in discourse. If you are right, I am happy—I've put unconsciously into my creative work the philosophy which independently I have argued out discursively. [32]

What Ransom was saying here is that the inner content of his poetry derives not from any period of history but from the very core of human existence, which, as he made clear a few years later in his *God Without Thunder*, [33] is shaken by the two antithetical attitudes: the scientific and philosophic desire to possess and control and the religious and aesthetic urge to contemplate and love.

Various public statements by the two men also offered avenues of discussion between them. Tate's review of I. A. Richards' *Science and Poetry* elicited from Ransom a lengthy dissertation. In his article Tate had pointed out that the poet cannot, as Richards advised him to, renounce lines fortified by belief: ". . . as Mr. Richards very well knows, great poetry cannot be written without

[31] To Tate, February 20, 1927.
[32] To Tate, Wednesday [early in March, 1927].
[33] New York: Harcourt, Brace, 1930.

the background of a perfectly ordered world which men have assimilated to their attitudes and convictions." That the subjective world of the poet is too unfirm a structure for poetry Tate was certain. "The modern poet," he wrote, "has to construct besides his personal vision, the scheme itself." [34]

Ransom considered Tate's review "not only the best thing on the subject that [he] had encountered, but the best piece of exposition of a difficult thesis that [he] had found of [Tate's] anywhere." But he wondered if Tate did not, like Richards, "stake everything on the chance of recovering some cosmological values out of the debris." Ransom agreed that one had to reject Richards' device of "suspended belief" ("You can't tell truth by means of lies," he wrote); but he wondered if the poet could not simply renounce magical views and cosmologies. In the place of these "obsessions with pure magnitude," he should be using the "infinite of quality" that exists in every concrete event:

> The poet . . . will simply refer concept to image, with the intention and with the effect of showing how the concept, the poor thin thing, is drowned in the image, how the determinate is drowned in the contingent, and how, ultimately, this world can neither be understood nor possessed. In the poet's art we will have to see, if we are willing to look at all, the Objectivity of the World; this is a dreadful, an appalling, a religious, and a humble attitude to which we will come perforce after the conceited Subjectivism into which we have been persuaded by the practical and the scientific life alike.

The issue, in poetry, would occur "on its most emotional and poignant plane, of course, when the concepts referred back to reality are the dearest concepts." Serious poetry, then, must always approach tragedy, Ransom continued, a state in which we must "admit to the impertinence of the whole possessive attitude, to the failure of our effort to grasp and to dominate the world." Thus the critic must define not only the "fictions of science," but also the "fictions of philosophy":

[34] "The Revolt Against Literature," *The New Republic*, XLIX, No. 636 (February 9, 1927), 329–30.

Philosophy of the usual or "constructive" sort, and not of the Kantian or critical sort, is an attempt to formulate in a more sophisticated way, but still to formulate, the reality which science has quite obviously failed to grasp. So are religious systems . . . . They particularly are under illusions of grandeur and magnitudes. The State, the Soul, God, the World, the Cosmos . . . these are types of the scientific fiction put together by reason and quite exceeding the senses: Supersensibles. They have in this condition no aesthetic quality, no reality . . . . What we require always is to return simply to the sense; and this means, not that there is any superior *certainty* attaching to sensibles . . . but that every Sensible is a source of inexhaustible sensation, and carries its own infinity with it at every moment, in a way that Supersensibles cannot possibly do. Reality means simply inexhaustible quality.[35]

This letter to Tate was written while Ransom was preparing his own review of Richards' work for Davidson's book page.[36] The review, when it appeared, voiced the same objections to the volume that Ransom had already expressed to Tate, though in less detail and with less intimacy and warmth.

Tate's Foreword to Hart Crane's *White Buildings* interested Ransom, as did the article "Poetry and the Absolute," in *The Sewanee Review*.[37] This latter article had been written more than a year earlier; it took as a point of departure Ransom's essay "Thoughts on the Poetic Discontent," which had first appeared in *The Fugitive*[38] and was later reprinted in *The Calendar of Modern Letters in London*.[39] Contending that Ransom's proposed "warily sceptical dualism" described general knowledge rather than a specific poetic knowledge, Tate designated as the chief problem in an examination of poetic truth the understanding of the relation between poet (or reader) and poem, not the one between poet and the world. And since this relation is one of absolutism, the terms *monism* and *dualism* do not apply. The poet could be "at one" with things, Tate maintained, "in terms of form, in the absolute

[35] To Tate, February 20, 1927.
[36] The Nashville *Tennessean*, March 6, 1927.
[37] XXXV, 1 (January, 1927), 41-52.
[38] IV, No. 2 (June, 1925), 63.
[39] August, 1925.

into which he has created them." [40] It is the intensity and the order of poetry that give value to it, according to Tate; and this ordered intensity cannot be found in a metaphysics, but only in art: "This immediately explains the necessity for art [he wrote]. For if the irresistible need of the mind for absolute experience could be adequately satisfied in ordinary, cursory experience, this latter experience classified into moral states and defined intellectually in an absolute metaphysics would be sufficient." [41] But in poetic enjoyment, Tate concluded, the reader partakes of an absolute experience which he could not have assembled for himself.

Ransom praised Tate's article but felt that it gave more attention to his own "slight note" than was warranted.[42] He wrote that he admired Tate's style in this essay more than in anything else he had written in prose and that he thought Tate "emphasized exactly the right point for us." But he could recognize it to be "two years behind" Tate's present thinking: "You can't make your formula out of unqualified Absolute—your recent formulas have been dualistic," he continued.

Likewise, concerning the foreword to Crane's book, Ransom wondered if Tate would not have had more reservations about the poetry if the essay had been written near the time of publication: "Since [writing it] you have abandoned a position of All-Quality and no compromise with Quantity, and come to insist on (substantially) my own Dualism, and even gone me one or two better in requiring for a 'major poet' a grand quantitative system of fixed values in which to see the play of quality . . . ." Ransom's letter ends, "You are a damned good man and I respect you more and more."

This burst of aesthetic exchange came to an end in the spring of 1927; for a while thereafter the discussion between the two men took a different direction. But their sharing of philosophic speculation had been of inestimable value to both. At the very least, by providing a spur and an intelligent opposition, it had

[40] "Poetry and the Absolute," *loc. cit.*, 43.
[41] *Ibid.*, 49.
[42] Ransom to Tate, April 3 (and 13) [1927].

saved them a number of years in coming to terms with their own thinking; at the most, it had provided insights which neither would have achieved alone.

Shortly before this time, John Gould Fletcher, the Imagist poet and expatriate from Arkansas, spent an evening with the Fugitives. He came to Nashville to lecture for the Centennial Club and was excited about getting to know the Nashville poets. Interested in these men not only because they were good poets, but because they were *Southern* poets, he had followed their work from 1922, after William Elliott in Oxford had called his attention to them. To Fletcher, the group all seemed to be following T. S. Eliot, except that "where he was an uprooted expatriate, seeking for eternal and absolute values in a world that had gone back to chaos, they still kept a local point of reference for their art, in the shape of their feeling for the Old South and its tradition." [43]

Fletcher was a bit nervous before such formidably intellectual men to be emphasizing a tenet with which he knew they disagreed: that American poetry was likely to keep headed toward epic and dramatic forms, rather than toward the analytical and reflective. The Fugitives, however, did not challenge him during his lecture; nor did he find them disagreeably intellectual afterwards, when he was treated to their hospitality. Both Ransom and Davidson insisted that he look up Tate in New York; afterwards, Fletcher wrote back to Davidson, just before sailing again for Europe, saying that though he had lived for forty years before meeting another Southern poet whom he could respect, now he had met three. The circumstances, he concluded, would cause him to feel that at last he had comrades in America. [44]

Fletcher would not have observed quite so obvious a Southern bias had his visit occurred a year earlier. In the attitude which Ransom, Davidson, and Tate held toward the land of their birth, 1926 had been a year of transition. At the end of 1925, when the magazine was suspended, these three still considered themselves, as writers, disengaged from their society. But by the spring

[43] *Life Is My Song*, 341.
[44] March 25, 1927.

of 1927 they were to declare open war against the New South program of industrial progress and, even further, were to affirm a positive belief in the principles of the Old South. An immediate cause of this striking reversal was the Dayton Trial and the resulting misrepresentation of the South in Northern newspapers. Thus, an event that caused many intelligent Southerners to reject their native land propelled Ransom, Davidson, Tate, and Warren into a careful study of Southern history. For the sake of honesty, they found themselves forced to defend in their native section characteristics which they knew to be inoffensive and even valuable. And, finally, from an understanding of the deeply religious structure of life in the Tennessee hills, a structure which had its perhaps aberrant expression in Fundamentalism, grew the conviction that led these poets to their first overt defense of the South.

For Davidson, the connection between himself and his native land had always been close; his natural distrust of progress and of reform stemmed from a keen observation of the land and the people about him. Through his work on the *Tennessean* book page he had become well acquainted with the literary products of the rest of the nation and with the calibre of mind of its literary men; and nothing he found in the writings of Northern and Eastern authors seemed in any way superior to the kind of thinking that he had grown up with or that he had found himself surrounded by at Vanderbilt and in the Fugitive circle. His contention that the South was an accidental locale for his artistic expression began to lose force with him as he brought together his intellectual views and his own private beliefs; in the actual struggle to do so, his poem *The Tall Men* and an article which he wrote on the Southern artist functioned as media of clarification.

For some time Davidson had been thinking seriously of the problem facing the Southern poet. In an essay published in *The Saturday Review of Literature*, he asked the question, "What does it mean to be a Southerner and yet be a writer?" [45] The Southerner as a person was recognizable, Davidson felt; yet the serious

[45] "The Artist as Southerner," II, No. 42 (May 15, 1926), 781–83.

Southern author seemed undistinguishable from other writers. "It would be hard," he wrote, "to find a single Southern writer of merit who in his thinking and manner of expression is as clearly of the South as Robert Frost is of New England." This situation existed because the writer in the South was in a "forbidding situation," fitting in neither with the old nor the new:

> The gallantries of the Lost Cause, the legends of a gracious aristocracy, the stalwart traditions of Southern history,—these he may admire, but they come to him mouthed over and cheapened . . . .
> And in the new order his situation is equally baffling. He sees industrialism marching on, and can digest the victorious cries of civic boosters even less readily than the treacly lamentations of the old school.

The contrast between the figures of Lee and Lincoln in particular offered Davidson concrete example of the impossibility of using Southern themes and Southern subjects with the unselfconsciousness that poets require for their efforts. Lincoln had been the poetic subject for many fine works, but Lee had been extolled only in "the rhymes of the more puerile Confederate songsters." Yet, for the writer who could steer his course between the two extremes of provincialism and escape, the South would seem to offer material: "Exuberance, sensitiveness, liveliness of imagination, warmth and flexibility of temper,—these are Southern qualities in all lands, and we have a right to ask that the Southern writer give them full play. . . . In sum, the Southern character, properly realized, might display an affirmative zest and abandon now lacking in American art." Further, such aspects of the Southern character as Fundamentalism, although representing at its worst a "belligerent ignorance," also represented a "fierce clinging to poetic supernaturalism against the encroachments of cold logic"; it stood "for moral seriousness," a quality which the Southerner should be slow to scorn.

It is not surprising that Davidson's article set him thinking; he had made in it the first move toward affirmation, and he knew he was started on a new path. As a result, by the end of 1926, Davidson was ready to take his first public stand for the use of the local and indigenous in poetry. Surveying the literary scene in Tennessee and finding in it great creative activity, he wrote: " Let the Tennessee artist use, by all means, the new artistic methods which twentieth century experimentalism has put into his hands. But let him also not be afraid to be provincial, for though provincialism in the narrow sense is to be condemned, it is also a sin to lose all contact with one's own character and become a thing neither hot nor cold . . . . The very language of these hills, the gestures of Tennessee hands, the look of Tennessee fields were never anywhere else on earth and cry aloud to be spoken." [46]

Of all the Fugitive poets, Tate had been most uncomfortable in the land of his birth; he had found no niche for himself in a society which made no place for a man of letters or a nonconformist. But a slow recognition that the poet cannot evade seeking a close knowledge of the elements which have gone to shape his inner being set Tate to searching for his own past, in spite of his belief that it was " all but irrecoverable." Writing to Davidson two years later (1928) of the genesis of " Ode to the Confederate Dead," Tate admitted its origin in a longing to find his own relation to Southern history. Davidson had written a review of Tate's biography of Stonewall Jackson [47] and had conjectured that the book had its origin in Tate's lines " What shall we do who have knowledge carried to the heart? " [48] Tate replied:

The Confederate poem, specifically the passage you quote, is its germ. That passage came out of God-knows-where (as most poems do); and after it was on paper it served to bring up a whole stream of associations and memories, suppressed at least on the emotional plane, since my childhood. This quest of the past is something we all share, but it is most acute in me—more so than in you, I suspect. You, for example, have never changed your scene; your sense of temporal and

[46] " The Spyglass," the Nashville *Tennessean*, December 5, 1926.

[47] *Stonewall Jackson: The Good Soldier* (New York: Minton, Balch and Company, 1928).

[48] " The Critic's Almanac," the Nashville *Tennessean*, April 29, 1928. Davidson had changed the title of his column from " The Spyglass " a few weeks earlier.

spatial continuity is probably more regular than mine; for since the Civil War my family has scattered to the four winds, and no longer exists as a social unit. Such isolation is ordinarily a pitfall at the bottom of which lies eccentricity (some of which I probably have) and sentimental extravagance of the most appalling kind. In this situation I can only thank God for scepticism, which like formaldehyde, is a great preservative of all sorts of things—of a sense of how things really *were* and of a resistance against things as they are. To lack the one, I believe, is to lack the other.[49]

As early as March, 1926, Tate was headed in this direction. On pondering the implications of the Dayton Trial, he found that he was interested in collecting material for an essay on fundamentalism. To Davidson he wrote:

My purpose is to define the rights of both parties, science and religion, and I'm afraid I agree with Sanborn that science has very little to say for itself. I remember he used to emphasize that view, but I scoffed at it; I see he was right. The principle is, Science as we inherit it as mechanism from the 17th century has nothing whatever to say about reality: if the Church or a fishmonger asserts that reality is fundamentally cheese or gold dust or Bishop Berkeley's tar water, Science has no right to deny it. On the other hand, the Church has no right to forestall all criticism by simply saying science is wrong. The church these days is of course decayed, but the attack on it should be ethical, not scientific.[50]

It was in 1926, too, that, after the composition of the "Ode," Tate became interested in Southern history. He entered upon the course of reading in that subject which was to lead to his biographies of Jackson and Jefferson Davis.[51] Then, his review of Ransom's *Two Gentlemen in Bonds* brought his convictions to a focus. A letter

[49] Undated letter to Davidson [March, 1928].

[50] March 3, 1926. Tate never published an essay specifically on this subject, although his review of Oswald Spengler's *Decline of the West* in *The Nation*, CXXII (May 12, 1926), 532, entitled "Fundamentalism," deals with Spengler's re-enthronement of metaphysics. Tate speaks of this attitude as a "rational Fundamentalism."

[51] *Jefferson Davis: His Rise and Fall* (New York: Minton, Balch and Company, 1929).

written to Davidson soon after this review openly and boldly stated his new allegiance:

And, by the way, I've attacked the South for the last time, except in so far as it may be necessary to point out that the chief defect the Old South had was that in it which produced, through whatever cause, the New South. I think the test of the True Southern Spirit would be something like this: whenever the demagogue cries " nous allons! " if the reply is " non, nous retardons! " then you may be sure the reply indicates the right values. The symptom of advance must be seen as a symptom of decay . . . .[52]

This was a historic moment in American literature; for, by the time Tate could make his affirmation, Ransom and Davidson had reached the same position. As with the early Fugitives, there was to be here no leader imposing his ideas on a group of disciples. These were men united by principles held in common and arrived at simultaneously.

Davidson was quick to reply in kind to Tate:

As I believe John has written you, the Old Fugitives are far from dead; we still have ideas and vim; and somehow we hang together. I am delighted at your own new annunciation of the True Southern Spirit, and though I haven't yet read your review of John, I do most heartily agree with your line of thought as John relayed it to me.

You know that I'm with you on the anti-New South stuff . . . . I feel so strongly on these points that I can hardly trust myself to write . . . . But know this: though I trust my sense of humor and balance will save me from becoming a Bourbon in the extreme, I have fully decided that my America is here or nowhere. I am thinking that I may make that projected new book (for which I have been reading) not so much a " history " of Southern literature as a study of the Southern tradition— where it is, where it isn't, and what and how and so on. And I have been going through a spiritual " Secession," in fact, ever since that *Saturday Review* article which made me examine my own mind.[53]

Ransom's path to this momentous crossing place had been less

[52] March 1, 1927.
[53] March 4, 1927.

dramatic, less in the nature of a revelation than had his friends'. It involved no conversion in his life, since Ransom had known for some time pretty surely what he thought of the world, of life, and of poetry. He was less fundamentally attached to the South than was Davidson and less antagonistic to it than Tate had been, being essentially a detached thinker who concerned himself with the timeless and universal elements in man. Sentimentally he had always valued his native land, with its code of gentility and its fine manners; but the arrogant and ill-natured journalistic attacks on the South attendant upon the Dayton trial roused him to an examination of the philosophic bases of the dispute and placed him finally in the somewhat surprising position of defending Funda-mentalism. He recognized in the deification of science his old enemy abstractionism; and he knew himself obliged to think out his position justifying the aesthetic and religious attitude. His un-published manuscript *The Third Moment* had been the first fruit of that necessity; but with the gradual realization of the magnitude of the problem, he turned his thoughts more to the foundation of society itself, his work finally issuing in the remarkable volume *God Without Thunder*. By early spring, 1927, at the time of Tate's and Davidson's pledge, he had become convinced of the value of the Southern culture as an embodiment of the aesthetic and religious impulses; consequently he too was alerted to the necessity for preserving its tradition.

The Fugitives met last night [Ransom wrote Tate]. The more I think about it, the more I am convinced of the excellence and the enduring vitality of our common cause. Here at Vanderbilt, which draws a lot of Old South talent, we have a workable mine of young poets and fresh minds; always some one or two or more just clamor for the right food and drink and society. We've got to keep on working that field; we have some perpetuals for the carry-over, like Don and me; and our cause is, we all have sensed this at about the same moment, the Old South . . . . I like my own people, or rather I respect them intensely . . . . Our fight is for survival; and it's got to be waged not so much against the Yankees as against the exponents of the New South. I see clearly that you are as unreconstructed and unmodernized as any

of us, if not more so. We must think about this business and take some
very long calculations ahead . . . .[54]

Indeed, by now, each of these men was convinced that something must be done, some concerted action taken, to stem the tide
of the engulfment. Tate, as well as Ransom and Davidson, was
convinced that their function was not over:

> The remarkable thing about the Fugitives, as you say [he wrote
> Davidson] is their cohesive power. I have always thought of you John,
> and myself as the Final Causes, as distinguished from the merely Effi-
> cient Cause (Dr. Mttron-Hirsch), of the Fugitive. If there are any
> ideas to be formulated for the future, it lies with us to do it. What
> these ideas are, I have yet to see—as you already know if John has
> passed on my statement recently made to him. The situation implies
> more than the purely literary question.[55]

Near the end of March, Tate mentioned a project which was
later to become the controversial Agrarian volume *I'll Take My
Stand*.[56] He referred to it as a "Southern Symposium," saying
that it could be put off until the following fall: "It's not too early
to plan it. Fletcher wants to contribute; and Foster Damon, though
not of the South, would write beautifully of Chivers, a neglected
poet. Let's hear more from *you* about it."[57] The idea was taking
shape in the minds of all three men; the chief question, of course,
that needed settling concerned the nature of the book. Ransom
believed that it should concern the principle behind the Southern
tradition rather than exhibit the literary products of the Old South
themselves:

> I am delighted with your idea of a book on the Old South [he
> wrote], but have had little time to think closely upon it—. Our difficulty
> is just this: there's so little Southern literature to point the principle.
> I subordinate always Art to the aesthetic of life; its function is to initiate
> us into the aesthetic life, it is not for us the final end. In the Old

---

[54] Undated letter [early March, 1927].
[55] March 7, 1927.
[56] New York and London: Harper and Brothers, 1930.
[57] To Ransom, March 24, 1927.

South the life aesthetic was actually realized, and there are the fewer object-lessons in its specific art . . . . Our symposium of authors would be more concerned, seems to me, with making this principle clear than with exhibiting the Southern artists who were frequently quite inferior to their Southern public in real aesthetic capacity. But there are performances, surely, to which we can point with pride, if you believe the book should be one mainly of literary criticism.[58]

During these years Warren, the only other Fugitive who also became an Agrarian, was enduring the ordeal of graduate school, receiving his M. A. degree from the University of California in 1927. From there he went on to New York to spend a while with Tate, where the two talked over the new idea; and in 1928, when Warren was in Yale doing further graduate study, Tate helped him secure a commission to write a life of John Brown.[59] Warren's work on this book convinced him that the idealist is a dangerous man, since he serves a cause identifiable not with the common human lot, but with an abstract, pitiless " idea." Warren began to recognize this idealism as a tendency of modern secular man; this realization, combined with the naturally religious bent to his writings and his distrust of mechanization, spurred him into sharing in the defense of a traditional society now being worked out by his friends.

At the same time that these chief Fugitives were exploring the implications of their newly defined position, they were also occupied by a lengthy campaign to publish a Fugitive volume of poetry. It came to its completion in May, 1927, soon after Ransom, Davidson, and Tate had begun planning an actual strategy for the battle they would conduct under the banner " Agrarianism versus Industrialism."

After the suspension of the magazine at the end of 1925, a strong sentiment among the Fugitives had grown up in favor of maintaining some sort of joint publication, despite evidence that individual members could continue to publish their own work

[58] To Tate, April 3 (and 13) [1927].

[59] *John Brown: The Making of a Martyr* (New York: Payson and Clarke, Lt'd., 1929).

separately. The solidarity that had come into existence over the years had given a strength and completeness to their public utterances as a body that isolated appearances in print by single members did not entirely own. In his editorial for the final issue of the magazine Ransom had promised more group publication, a statement based on proposals that had been discussed at meetings all during the latter part of 1925. Then, some time before the appearance of the last *Fugitive*, Davidson began what was going to become a series of discouraging efforts to publish a collection of Fugitive poetry; his aims were to place in more permanent form some of the best work that had resulted from the group's four-year discipline and, even more important, to show in a body some of the new poems by Fugitives. He considered briefly a Fugitive press, but the difficulty of editing and of securing the proper backing was an obstacle that he and Tate decided must prohibit such an ambitious project.

At this point it seemed to Davidson that a yearbook would provide the best sort of vehicle for future group publication; consequently, at his urging, in June, 1926, the men meeting at James Frank's drew up a proposal to publish a yearbook of Fugitive verse. But in July, Tate suggested that an anthology would be more manageable than a yearbook, because it could use previously published material. Davidson approached Houghton Mifflin with the plan for an anthology, and Ferris Greenslet of that firm expressed great interest in seeing the manuscript.[60] Then Davidson began the labors of getting in touch with absent members and of selecting the pieces to be used.

Of the Fugitives who were away from Nashville, nearly all wrote their enthusiastic support of the undertaking. Tate sent eighteen poems for the editors to decide upon, with the request that he have their choice as soon as possible so that he could "argue" with them.[61] Elliott, now at Harvard, promised to send a "voluminous sheaf," though he doubted that any of it would

[60] Greenslet to Davidson, August 23, 1926.
[61] Tate to Davidson, September 11, 1926.

please the members.[62] Ransom was pleased at the idea of the anthology and sent a group of poems. Of his recent work which he included he commented to Davidson, "You've only seen the second part of 'Hilda' and none of 'Mr. Minnit' or 'The Unnatural Man' ['Man without Sense of Direction'], which are my last ones and which will strike you I wonder how." [63]

From California, Warren, beginning a term as a teaching fellow, found time between grading papers and course work to write Davidson about the proposed volume and to send some of his available work. The poems he had written recently were not, he felt, quite successful: "I am afraid they represent something that I am not quite able to do with any degree of conviction," he commented. His present poetry was "slipping into a vein of repetition," he feared, so he was trying "a little fiction." [64] He sent seven poems —more than his quota, he supposed—but, like the other contributors, he wished to give the editors some choice. Arranged in order of his preference, they were: "Letter of a Mother," "Kentucky Mountain Farm," "To a Face in the Crowd," "Images on the Tomb," "The Last Metaphor," "The Wrestling Match," "Admonition to the Dead." About them he wrote:

I feel that within the limits of its intention the *Letter of a Mother* is easily my most finished poem. *Kentucky Mountain Farm* is second because it presents a more specialized and perhaps more subtle if weaker treatment of the same attitude as that of the first poem named. The next four poems are about on the same level I suppose with little to choose among them, while *Admonition to the Dead* is technically well done, I feel, even if trivial and derivative to a certain degree.

The projected volume interests me tremendously, Don, and I devoutly hope that it materializes. I think the Fugitive group needs and is worthy of such a thing, which ought to be, as you say, important if the group fulfills its apparent promise. I can visualize a volume of

---

[62] To Davidson, August 12, 1926.
[63] September 30, 1926.
[64] September 14, 1926.

some dignity with Allen's, John's, and your work and Jesse's sonnets in it.[65]

Laura Riding, back from Egypt and now at Islip, Oxford, with Robert Graves, was rather cautious about an anthology, wondering if all Fugitives were to be included in a democratic organization of the book and pointing out that the position of editor-contributor to an anthology was rather different from that of mere contributor. She wondered also how far the authority of the editorial committee could extend in the selection of an author's work, feeling that she herself could not accept any limitations except space. But if these misgivings were allayed, she said, she would be glad to help get the book published, perhaps even to finding a British publisher for it.[66] Later, after she and Robert Graves had left London to go to Vienna, where they were collaborating on two books, Miss Riding sent Davidson some poems from her volume *The Close Chaplet* and a number written since, specifying that each group be represented about equally.[67]

In the meantime, Davidson and Tate agreed that the anthology should have an introduction by an outsider. Davidson wanted John McClure to write it, as did Ransom, who felt that McClure had "come nearer understanding our doctrine than anybody else in the universe of critics." [68] But Tate was certain that a New York critic would be the wiser choice, and for the position he suggested either Mark Van Doren or Edmund Wilson.[69] After the members decided to ask Van Doren, however, they found that he could not undertake the introduction without pay.[70] Anyhow, by this time Davidson and Tate were unsure of the wisdom of having a critical preface at all; so Davidson wrote a brief foreword for the book, which he forwarded to Tate for suggestions. Miss Riding had written in objecting to a preface, since she felt that so often its

---

[65] To Davidson, September 19, 1926.
[66] Undated letter to Davidson [sometime in 1926].
[67] Undated letter to Davidson [summer, 1926].
[68] Ransom to Davidson, September 30 [1926].
[69] Tate to Davidson, September 10, 1926.
[70] Tate to Davidson, October 22, 1926.

temptation was to show similarities and relationships where none actually existed. The title should be, she thought, *Fugitive* rather than *Fugitives*, since the volume would represent a period in the life of different poets, not a school of poets.[71]

But after the trouble of assembling the material, Houghton Mifflin decided that the volume would not be a sound risk because half of the material had already been in print elsewhere.[72] At the suggestion of Tate, the manuscript was sent in succession to Horace Liveright and to Harper and Brothers, both of whom rejected it because of its lack of commercial appeal. "Please give me advice about the Fugitive garland," Tate wrote Davidson in despair.[73] Davidson refused to give up hope and continued working toward publication, but Tate was beginning to feel that the project was impossible: "I'll try some of the publishers you suggest, but I fear nothing can be done unless we get somebody behind it. It is almost impossible to do this . . . . There can be no true provincial art (which is, of course, quite different from local color) until we can write directly for home consumption . . . ."[74] Tate was given full power to act as the group representative and tried earnestly to find a publisher. At last, when he submitted the manuscript to Harcourt, Brace and Company, it was finally accepted—in May, 1927.

Davidson and the other Nashville Fugitives were overjoyed at the good news: "I am sending out bulletins to Laura, Warren, and Elliott [Davidson wrote Tate]. The others are all around here. We had a great time the other night, reading the MS. aloud at meeting. We read something from everybody, we glowed and rhapsodized until a late hour."[75] The members officially gave a vote of thanks to Tate and Davidson for handling the project; in fact, Hirsch suggested that the group buy Tate a present as a token of gratitude, but Davidson felt the gesture unnecessary. As he wrote

[71] Riding to Davidson, November 5 [1926].
[72] Greenslet to Davidson, November 26, 1926.
[73] February 20, 1927.
[74] Tate to Davidson, March 7, 1927.
[75] June 7 [1927].

Tate, " I said I thought you felt thanked enough, very likely, in just having the job to do, for you still are, as ever, one of our ' prime movers.' " [76]

There followed some revision of the manuscript, which had been prepared a year earlier. For some of his previous choices Tate substituted " Ignis Fatuus," " Death of Little Boys," and his Confederate Ode, all written since the summer before. Ransom asked that three of the poems from *Chills and Fever* be omitted, and substituted for them " Equilibrists," " Our Two Worthies," and " What Ducks Require," writing of the last mentioned, " [This] represents me at this writing as a late piece and (as my poems go) a most adequate one." [77] Warren added two new poems, " Croesus in Autumn " and " Pro Sua Vita." Ridley Wills, who had never replied to communications about the project, belatedly sent some of his poems to Davidson in September, but by that time it was too late for them to be used.[78]

The proof was ready in early September, and Tate wrote that the title was to be *Fugitive: A Collection of Verse*—the one the publishers preferred of several submitted.[79] But by October the publishers changed the title to *Fugitives: An Anthology of Verse,* because they found *Collection* to be " an ambiguous word." [80] The Foreword that had been composed by Davidson was modified somewhat by Tate and " scrutinized by all the other members," who made a few changes in it.[81] As it was printed, however, it nevertheless contained a few inaccuracies, such as the statement that Tate was one of the original members meeting at Hirsch's home and that Curry had come into the group " within the first few months of publication." Primarily a brief history of the group, the Foreword in its concluding paragraph gives a few words in explanation of the anthology:

[76] June 22 [1927].
[77] To Tate, June 25, 1927.
[78] Davidson to Tate, September 23, 1927.
[79] To Davidson, September 5, 1927.
[80] Tate to Davidson, October 8, 1927.
[81] Davidson to Tate, June 22 [1927].

This volume is a survey of the past; it may also be taken as a prospectus. It looks back to some of the earliest work of the poets who ran *The Fugitive*, and it contains poetry that is now published for the first time. Each contributor is responsible for the selection of his own poems. There has been no editing, except in the mechanical sense of collecting manuscripts and fitting them to the limitations of space. Some of those who at one time or another were joined in the Fugitive enterprise have chosen not to be represented by poems. They have nevertheless contributed largely to the group activities, in ways poetical and otherwise, and the poets who appear in this collection wish to pay tribute to the energy and fine spirit of their absent friends.[82]

The book was released January 9, 1928. Tate wrote that he got a copy that morning.[83] "I suppose the local people will think at last that we are pretty good," he wrote, "because we bear the mark of a New York publisher." [84] All the members were greatly pleased with the appearance of the volume; the bird on the dust cover and the title page was a surprise, but one which they all liked, seeing in it the "Phoenix-Fugitive" arising, as Davidson put it, "out of the ashes of the old Regime." [85]

And well they might be proud. The volume is genuinely impressive, containing some of the finest poetry produced in America, some that was to be, after this time, frequently anthologized. Forty-nine of the ninety-four poems in the *Anthology* were reprinted from *The Fugitive*, and many of the others had come from the same period, having been published in various other magazines. As Davidson wrote in the Foreword, the volume was "a survey of the past." That it might also be regarded "as a prospectus" the new poems written since the suspension of the journal testified. When the Fugitives were thus spread out before the reader in one volume, what was apparent was that the group consisted of four poets of power and importance—Ransom, Tate, Davidson, and

[82] *Fugitives: An Anthology of Verse* (New York: Harcourt, Brace and Company, 1928), vi.
[83] To Davidson, January 9, 1928.
[84] To Davidson, January 19, 1928.
[85] To Tate, January 27, 1928.

Warren; two of agile mind and interesting technique—Moore and Riding; two others of serious intent and genuine though minor worth—Jesse Wills and Stevenson. The four whose poems showed the most sharply marked character were men who, in making literature their way of life, had approached poetry as a perilous and sober undertaking.

The poems which had not previously appeared in the magazine showed that in the intervening two years Ransom had experienced no lessening of skill and wisdom, Davidson had completed his transition to his grave though still lyric poetry of place and time, and Warren was continuing in his development of control over an anguished self-examination. The work of Tate, however, shows the one marked change which the three years had effected. Tate's poetry in the magazine had only very rarely exhibited the accomplishment it portended. In the last year of life for *The Fugitive*, however, and in the year immediately following its suspension, Tate had strengthened and made certain his technique, as well as his themes, at the same time that he was impelled to search for and understand his own heritage as a Southerner. The *Anthology*, appearing at the beginning of a year that was to see the publication of his first volume of poetry (*Mr. Pope and Other Poems* [86]), contains the best fruits of Tate's work in poetry from 1925 through 1927. Only one of his nine poems in the *Anthology* had previously been published in *The Fugitive*; the others were quite recent. In these eight new pieces is to be seen Tate's mature style—brilliant, sharp, and certain. In it Tate has been able to bind the various elements of his poetry into coherent form, with no loss of linguistic suggestiveness.

The volume excited a gratifying quantity of critical attention. In newspapers across the nation it was allotted extended space. A long, favorable syndicated review appeared March 18 in several cities. Writing in the Chicago *News*, Howard Mumford Jones commented, "The Sahara of the Bozart is a mirage." [87] In the

[86] (New York: Minton, Balch and Company, 1928.)
[87] June 13, 1928.

Greensboro, North Carolina, *Record*, Jay B. Hubbell stated, "We sometimes forget that the New South has passed into a Newer South which does not find its ideals expressed in the orations of Henry W. Grady . . . [or] the poetry of Sidney Lanier . . . ."[88] J. P. (probably Julia Peterkin) composed a careful review for the Charleston, South Carolina, *Post*,[89] as did Jack Bryan for the Knoxville *News Sentinel*.[90] William Knickerbocker reviewed the book for Davidson's book page, designating the group as the "most provocative and stimulating group of poets in contemporary American literature."[91] Actually, an unsigned review in John McClure's book page in New Orleans was the only uncomplimentary notice the volume received: "The Fugitive school, valuable as it was in the South, was by no means satisfactory. Speaking technically, it is a pity to see firm rhythms destroyed by conversationally sarcastic inflections. Speaking humanly, it is a shame to see a genuine emotion turned into a firecracker. The Fugitive school of poetry was in style and content too clever."[92]

In the journals, reviews dealt with the book as a considerable one. *The Bookman*, *The Dial*, and *The Saturday Review of Literature* treated the anthology with respect if not with very acute understanding.[93] Edmund Wilson in *The New Republic* discerned that the solidity of the association had enabled the members to "throw off the influence of T. S. Eliot," but he found Ransom's stigmata—"an accent of irony, a metaphysical turn, and a rich English vocabulary"—evident in the work of other Fugitives.[94] Mark Van Doren in *The Nation* wrote what should be considered the most penetrating and accurate evaluation of the volume:

[88] February 11, 1928.
[89] March 24, 1928.
[90] June 17, 1928.
[91] "Fugitive Anthology Exemplifies Nashville's Triumph in Poetry," the Nashville *Tennessean*, February 26, 1928.
[92] The New Orleans *Times-Picayune*, February 12, 1928.
[93] Babette Deutsch, "Poets and Some Others," LXVII, No. 4 (June, 1928), 442; "Briefer Mention," LXXXIV (June, 1928), 523; "The New Books," IV, No. 48 (June 23, 1928), 994.
[94] "The Tennessee Poets," LIV (March 7, 1928), 103.

That it is an important anthology no one abreast of the times will deny. But there is more to say about it than simply that. To me it is an intensely interesting document bearing upon the whole question of how vital poetry gets written . . . I am convinced . . . that the way taken by the Fugitives toward poetry is one of the best ways—it was the way, incidentally, of the thirteenth-century Italian poets, of the symbolists in France, and of certain late nineteenth-century English and Irish poets. It is the way of friendship and discussion; it is the way of the amateur society . . . . They [the Fugitives] were true amateurs, meeting for a purely practical purpose and giving one another purely practical help. It is not surprising, then, that they stumbled upon the real thing or that they made a permanent contribution to American poetry.[95]

Of this review, Tate wrote to Davidson that it contained a very good point: "I think, however, he really divined the spirit of our intentions several years ago, and it was important that they should be understood."[96] On the whole, Tate and Davidson considered the reviews of the book "most satisfactory."[97]

Appearing as it did after Davidson's second volume of verse, *The Tall Men*; Ransom's third volume, *Two Gentlemen in Bonds*; Tate's biography of Stonewall Jackson; and Laura Riding's *The Close Chaplet, Voltaire*,[98] and her study of "modernist" poetry written jointly with Robert Graves,[99] the anthology justifiably attracted a good bit of critical attention as a definitive representation of an important school of American poets. The literary world, aroused to real consideration of the group, no doubt expected future joint performances in the same vein. But the literary world was unaware of the strong body of convictions that had developed in the core of the Fugitive group since the suspension of the magazine, convictions that had been deepening and maturing concurrently with the efforts to find a publisher for work that had already served

[95] "First Glance," CXXVI (March 14, 1928), 295.
[96] March 14, 1928.
[97] Tate to Davidson, May 3, 1928.
[98] *Voltaire: A Biographical Fantasy* (London: The Hogarth Press, 1927).
[99] *A Survey of Modernist Poetry* (London: Heinemann, 1927; New York: E. P. Dutton, 1928).

its purpose for its creators. In a sense, then, it was fitting that the Fugitive *Anthology* should have been released from the press in January; it was itself a kind of *janua*, looking both ways: into the relatively uncomplicated past when Ransom, Davidson, Tate, and Warren could pursue their aims within the realm of pure aesthetic discipline; and into the future, where they must take the path that would prove far more thorny, into the ethical and religious (though still, for them, primarily literary) movement that was known as Agrarianism. In *I'll Take My Stand*, the symposium that was already taking shape in 1928, they were to make the transition from accomplished poets to men of letters and thinkers, almost the only concerted effort in that direction that America has known.

But it is the Fugitive poetry—the genesis of which has been here recounted—that led to the remarkable return to the mainstream of tradition which Agrarianism represents. The impact of this return was to be manifested later in literary criticism, in the editing of literary journals, in literary pedagogy, and in fiction. As poets, the Fugitives had held the simple aim of developing a craft; but their dedication to that purpose had led them ever farther into an exploration of their heritage. They had found that their true task was not the creation of an ideal world but the discovery of a real one, independent of their own thinking; they had learned that a genuine culture, whatever its moral flaws, is an analogue of something nobler toward which the human spirit aspires but which it can grasp only through submission to the actual. Hence, their poetry made available to themselves and to the writers following them a body of techniques, a language, and a core of belief drawn from a traditional society which, at its very moment of change, could by these means be transmuted into permanence.

APPENDIX

Contents of THE FUGITIVE

This table of contents has been annotated to indicate the poems by Ransom, Davidson, Tate, and Warren which, after their first printing in *The Fugitive*, were published in subsequent volumes of poetry. The titles of these volumes are indicated by the symbols below. Revisions in the first reprinting of the poems are indicated by an asterisk.

Fugitives: F—*Fugitives: An Anthology of Verse* (New York: Harcourt, Brace and Company, 1928).

Ransom: PG—*Poems about God* (New York: Henry Holt and Company, 1919); CF—*Chills and Fever* (New York: Alfred A. Knopf, 1924); GM—*Grace after Meat* (London: Hogarth Press, 1924); TGB—*Two Gentlemen in Bonds* (New York: Alfred A. Knopf, 1927); SP—*Selected Poems of John Crowe Ransom* (New York: Alfred A. Knopf, 1945); PE—*Poems and Essays of John Crowe Ransom* (New York: Vintage Books, 1955).

Davidson: OP—*An Outland Piper* (Boston and New York: Houghton Mifflin Company, 1924).

Tate: MP—*Mr. Pope and Other Poems* (New York: Minton, Balch and Company, 1928); SP—*Selected Poems* (New York and London: Charles Scribner's Sons, 1937); P—*Poems 1922-1947* (New York: Charles Scribner's Sons, 1948).

Warren: 36P—*Thirty-six Poems* (New York: The Alcestis Press, 1935); SP—*Selected Poems 1923-1943* (New York: Harcourt, Brace and Company, 1944).

258

Louis Gilmore
  Three Epigrams
Arthur H. Nethercot
  Mole
Isabel Fiske Conant
  Doors
  Chimes
  Half-Fairy
Henri Faust
  Conclusions of a Chinese Sage
Grace Hutchinson Ruthenburg
  Wharf

Volume III, Number 3 (June, 1924)
[Essay] Certain Fallacies in Modern
  Poetry, D. D. [Davidson]
Announcements
Ransom
  Blue Girls TGB*, SP, PE
  Adventure This Side of Pluralism
    CF*, GM
Davidson
  Swan and Exile
  Palingenesis
Tate
  Credo: An Aesthetic MP* (as
    Credo in Intellectum Videntum)
Warren
  Death Mask of a Young Man
    I. The Mouse
    II. The Moon
  Nocturne
Moore
  Lucia and Louis
J. Wills
  Primavera
  Eden
Johnson
  Story
  A Sonnet of the Yellow Leaf (The
    Awakening)
  To a Park Swan
Curry
  Will-o'-the-Wisp
John Homer Dye
  Mountain Love
Harold Vinal
  Scene
Louis Gilmore
  Greek Anthology
  Toward Utopia

Marie Emilie Gilchrist
  Gold in the Ottaqueechee
Witter Bynner
  Ascending the Pagoda
  Spring Thoughts
Idella Purnell
  Thunder

Volume III, Number 4 (August, 1924)
Announcements
Ransom
  Parting at Dawn   CF, GM (as At
    Dawn), SP, PE
  Tom, Tom the Piper's Son CF*, SP,
    PE
Davidson
  By Due Process
Tate
  Day
  Dusk
Warren
  Sonnets of Two Summers
    I. Sonnet of a Rainy Summer
    II. Sonnet of August Drouth
  Praises for Mrs. Dodd
Moore
  To a Memory
  Sonnet to Mr. Smith
  And to the Young Men
Johnson
  A Matter of Record
Elliott
  Black Man
J. Wills
  The Survivors
Riding
  For One Who Will Bless the Devil
Louis Untermeyer
  Schubert at Hoeldrichsmuehle
Ellen Glines
  Noli Me Tangere
Olive Tilford Dargan
  Far Bugles
Joseph T. Shipley
  Ruth
Idella Purnell
  The Gooseberry Bush

Volume III, Numbers 5 and 6 (December, 1924)

Announcements

Ransom
  The Last Judgment (A Fresco) TGB* (as Fresco: from The Last Judgment)
  Virga
Davidson
  Legend in Bronze
Tate
  Fair Lady and False Knight
  Correspondences (from the French of Baudelaire) MP*, P
  Art I and II MP* (Art II, only), P
Warren
  Alf Burt, Tenant Farmer
  Admonition to Those Who Mourn
Moore
  Sonnet
  The Cobbler's Confessions
  Mrs. Claribel Diggs
  Ephraim Diggs
Johnson
  The Grand Wolf
  Argument
  Any Husband to Any Wife
Riding
  Mortal
  Forms
  Saturday Night
  Lying Spying
J. Wills
  Premonition
  Dream
Olive Tilford Dargan
  In Doubt
Harry Alan Potamkin
  The Disintegration of Malidon
John Homer Dye
  Heritage
Virginia Lyne Tunstall
  Delilah
Marie Emilie Gilchrist
  A Horoscope Reading

Volume IV, Number 1 (March, 1925)
[Essay] Mixed Modes, J. C. R. [Ransom]

Sunrise Trumpets. By Joseph Auslander [review], R. P. W. [Warren]
The Flaming Terrapin. By Roy Campbell [review], J. W. [J. Wills]
Ransom
  Piazza Piece TGB, SP, PE
  Eclogue TGB*, SP, PE
Davidson
  Boundary
  Fear in a Cubicle
  Cross Section of a Landscape F*
Tate
  Homily MP*, P
Warren
  Iron Beach (revision of poem in April, 1924, *Fugitive*)
  The Mirror
Moore
  A Lady Is Buried Here
  Abschied
  Antwort
Riding
  Summary for Alastor
  The Sad Boy
  The Higher Order
Frank
  Mirrors
Katherine Estes Rice
  To the Unattainable
  I Have Played at Being Unfaithful
  Sonnet
Andrew Nelson Lytle
  Edward Graves
George H. Dillon
  To an Importunate Ghost
  Epigrams
Ellen Glines
  Pathetic Fallacist
  Amazon
  The Return

Volume IV, Number 2 (June, 1925)
Homage to John Dryden. By T. S. Eliot [review], D. D. [Davidson]
The Pot of Earth. By Archibald MacLeish [review], D. D. [Davidson]
[Essay] Thoughts on the Poetic Discontent, J. C. R. [Ransom]

Ransom
  The Miller's Daughter   TGB*
  Jack's Letter   TGB*
  Semi-Centennial   TGB*
Davidson
  Not Long Green   F (as Apple and
    Mole)
  For Example
  Portrait of a Wasp
Warren
  Easter Morning Crosby Junction
  Mr. Dodd's Son
  To a Face in the Crowd   F*, 36P,
    SP
  The Wrestling Match   F*
Moore
  Chronicle of an Acquaintance
  Autumn Dawn
  Scientia Vincit Omnia?
  You Can Never Tell
  Drowned in Dreams
  Revolution and the Sentries
Riding
  Druida
  The Circus
J. Wills
  Red Even
Walter McClellan
  For a Dying Child
George H. Dillon
  Unhappy Men
Richard S. West, Jr.
  Change of Weather

Volume IV, Number 3 (September,
  1925)
  A Doctrine of Relativity [Review of
    Robert Graves, *Poetic Unreason*],
    J. C. R. [Ransom]
Two Ways of Poetry [Review of E. E.
  Cummings, *XLI Poems*; and Her-
  vey Allen, *Earth Moods*], D. D.
  [Davidson]
Ransom
  The Two Worthies   TGB* (as Our
    Two Worthies), F, SP, PE
  Husband Betrayed   TGB*
  Janet Waking   TGB*, SP, PE
  History of Two Simple Lovers
    TGB* (as The Equilibrists), F,
    SP, PE

Davidson
  Sudden Meeting
  Lines for a Tomb
  Projection of a Body Upon Space
Tate
  To a Romantic Novelist
Warren
  Images on the Tomb
    I. Dawn: The Gorgon's Head
      F*
    II. Day: Lazarus   F*
    III. Evening: The Motors   F
    IV. Night: But a Sultry Wind
      F*
Moore
  Why He Stroked the Cats
  The Flies
  John's Threat
  Conte Erotique
  Green Trousdale and Sam Sevier
  Detour
Riding
  Mary Carey
  The Only Daughter
  Virgin of the Hills
Elliott
  Before Dawn
  The Lie Called Royal
Hart Crane
  Legend
  Paraphrase

Volume IV, Number 4 (December,
  1925)
Announcement
The Future of Poetry [Review of R. C.
  Trevelyan, *Thamyris*], D. D.
  [Davidson]
Ransom
  Lady Lost   TGB*, SP, PE
  Moments of Minnie   TGB
  Amphibious Crocodile   TGB*
Davidson
  Pastorals Somewhat in the Modern
    Style
    I. Echo
    II. Advice to Shepherds
    III. A Dirge
Tate
  Prayer to the Woman Mountain
    MP*

INDEX